D1289044

FIRST TO LEAVE
THE PARTY

First to Leave the Party

MY LIFE WITH ORDINARY PEOPLE . . .
WHO HAPPEN TO BE FAMOUS

SALAH BACHIR
(HE/HIM)

with

JAMI BERNARD
(SHE/HER)

SIGNAL
McCLELLAND
& STEWART

Signal and colophon are registered trademarks of
Penguin Random House Canada Limited.

Library and Archives Canada Cataloguing in Publication
Title: First to leave the party : my life with ordinary people . . . who
happen to be famous / Salah Bachir with Jami Bernard.
Names: Bachir, Salah J., author. | Bernard, Jami, author.
Identifiers: Canadiana 20230165605 |
ISBN 9780771006111 (hardcover) | ISBN 9780771006128 (EPUB)
Subjects: LCSH: Bachir, Salah J. | LCSH: Philanthropists—Canada—
Biography. | LCSH: Art—Collectors and collecting—Canada—Biography. | LCSH:
Businesspeople—Canada—Biography. | CSH: Lebanese Canadians—Biography. |
LCGFT: Autobiographies.
Classification: LCC HV28.B33 A3 2023 | DDC 361.7/4092—dc23

Jacket design by Jennifer Griffiths
Jacket art: Guntar Kravis
Typeset in Heldane Text by M&S, Toronto
Printed in Canada

Published by Signal,
an imprint of McClelland & Stewart,
a division of Penguin Random House Canada Limited,
a Penguin Random House Company
www.penguinrandomhouse.ca

1 2 3 4 5   27 26 25 24 23

Penguin
Random House
Canada

TO MY JACOB

Contents

FIRST TO LEAVE
THE PARTY

A WORD FROM
Alan Cumming

Often, I find myself plonked down into a strange city for sustained periods of time. It's both an occupational hazard and a cornucopia of magical possibilities, the best and most lasting of which is meeting new people.

Having been around the block a few times, I have become skilled in homing in on those with whom I truly connect and who do not enjoy the glare or wake of celebrity more than the actual person who, by dint of happenstance, just happens to be a celebrity themselves.

This enchanting collection of stories about Salah Bachir's encounters with stars who have passed through his beloved Toronto over the years opens on a backyard garden barbecue with Marlon Brando, and bread continues to be broken with icons as fascinating and seemingly disparate as Muhammad Ali and Liberace, Margaret Atwood and Cesar Chavez, and Andy Warhol and Princess Margaret, to name but a few. But the true literary coup is that the biggest, brightest star we encounter is the author himself.

I know his adopted homeland's inherent characteristics of modesty, bashfulness, and just being sorry will make him refute this, but the proof is in the pudding—and in this case the pudding is Lebanese and fabulous and accompanied by fruit jams made by Salah's mum.

It is most telling, perhaps, that this memoir revolves around other people, just as Salah's life has been one long exercise in helping others in need. But the very fact that he has so many great friendships and rendezvous to share also shines a light on Salah himself. We see his vast kindness and passion, his struggles with health and body image, and, most of all, his utter authenticity and joie de vivre.

You are about to sit down at Salah's feast. Bon appétit!

ALAN CUMMING

A WORD FROM
Atom Egoyan

Anyone reading this marvelous book will wonder how Salah Bachir was able to strike such intimate and immediate trust with all these fabulous people. As someone who has fallen under the spell of his unique presence, let me explain.

I was in the early days of my career, long before Academy Award nominations and prizes at Cannes. Somehow, Salah had heard of my first features and ventured to meet me in my funky studio space in downtown Toronto. This was the first time I had ever had an interview with someone from my neck of the woods (I was born in Egypt; Salah in Lebanon), and it was also the first time I had ever met a journalist with such a sense of style.

Salah was one of the most immediately intriguing people I'd ever met. On this day, he was devoid of any big jewelry or lavish headgear. There was something disarming about his intoxicating mix of mysterious shyness and furtive self-confidence. Despite the absence of all the external markers that would later become his "Salah Style," he was still wearing one of the most beautiful suits I'd ever seen—a black, imaginatively distressed Comme des Garçons two-piece with delicate white detailing from the early nineties. Yes, this happened well over thirty years ago.

I'd never been asked the sort of questions Salah asked me that day. I'd never basked in the attention of someone so focused on my inner core. It was like speaking with the most illuminated and curious therapist in the world, though the offer of a wonderful home-cooked Lebanese meal was certainly part of the allure. I was thousands of miles away from my mother's kitchen and, at that point, Toronto was not the culinary mecca it is today.

Salah makes you feel at home with yourself, no matter how far away that home might be. And it's not about exotic locations or a physical journey. He has the unique ability to make you feel that in his presence you might finally be able to resolve something about yourself that you've never understood. He has that magical ability to offer a hidden key. This gift comes from his having one of the most generous hearts in the world.

This is what all the famous people detailed in this wonderful book are responding to. When you meet someone who's so phenomenally giving, you want to give back. The sense of friendship and intimacy that informs these stories is the result of an extraordinary sense of alchemy that Salah generates—the feeling that you could be doing more. His munificent spirit is the gift that never stops giving.

This book is a rich journey through many lives. Through Salah's life, through moments in the lives of the countless actors and celebrities he's met, and, perhaps most evocatively, through the lives of the people whose experience has been transformed by the charities and causes Salah has supported. I encourage you to read this book slowly. You are meeting many stars and cherished popular figures you think you might know. You're about to know them a whole lot better, in ways you could never have imagined.

One of the most moving portraits here is of my idol, the American playwright Edward Albee. I couldn't believe what I was reading, that I was privileged to have this unbelievable access to a person whose work has had such a huge impact on me. When I was in high school, I played the role of The Young Man in his play *The American Dream*, and this experience transformed me. When I read Salah's words in this incredible chapter, I was transformed once again. I have no doubt that each reader of this book will find such a particular moment as they re-meet these luminous figures.

We have all been so deeply influenced by the books we've read, the movies we've seen, the writers and actors and directors who made those indelible works. Salah's great achievement here is to remind us of how important these people are to us, as he also reminds us how committed so many of these magnificent human beings have been to making the world a better place through their contributions to charities and social causes. This book is a wake-up call to the responsibilities we all have to use our respective platforms to effect change. If one kid from a village in Lebanon has done it, you can do it, too.

I don't have a copy of the interview that came out of that first meeting with Salah over thirty years ago, but I have the clear memory of a precious origin story to a long friendship. Salah made me feel very special that day, as he continues to make so many people feel cared for and cherished. You are about to read some unbelievable stories, but you must remember they are generated by an unbelievably unique man.

Salah is the patron saint for all of us who are full of curiosity, hungry for celebration, horny for fun, and who won't stop until every need is fulfilled. His appetite and passion for life is voracious. His ability to transform those passions into making life better for others is even more impressive.

ATOM EGOYAN

Prologue

I have known I was gay since I was eight years old, but I only realized I was Arab at age twelve, when I was over at a school chum's house and his dad asked, "Why is that dirty Arab here again?"

It could be that people in my new country identified us with camels and deserts, neither of which we have in Lebanon. In the part of Lebanon where I was raised—until my family moved to Canada in 1965, when I was ten—we described ourselves as Lebanese and as descendants of the Phoenicians, not as Arabs.

All my life, I have sought out community. That is what I remember most from my childhood in Lebanon—the sense of belonging. I remember a day when someone who was poor came to our house, and my mother and grandmother gave away half the basket of pita they had just baked, along with everything from clothing to jam. This was typical. While my middle-class family had money, we also had what everyone there had without question, rich or poor: community. My family, my true heroes, always made room at their table for those in need.

In a small village, everyone knows everyone. The world is your friend. My first-grade teacher was like a godmother to me. My second-grade teacher lived next door. My third-grade teacher was my uncle. My mother's father, Nicolas, was the mayor.

Everyone took care of everyone, or so it seemed. When someone died, the whole village went to the hospital to bring the family home and mourn with them. The entire village went with us to the airport when we left to join my dad in Canada; it was one of the first times a family of our size had left. Mom carried with her a wicker basket of figs from our garden, a taste of home.

There is a big difference between being an immigrant and being a refugee. A refugee often has no choice but to flee disasters, deadly threats, and war zones, waiting sometimes endlessly for a place at the table. For most immigrants, leaving is a choice. My family came to Canada on our own terms. It was still a difficult transition, and Lebanon is in my blood and always will be. The language, the people, the ways of small villages, the olive groves I still own and return to often. The Lebanon of old has changed—the civil war changed it, sowing mistrust and sectarianism that has only grown over the years. But the romance and longing of the place is still there for me, even if it is no longer my community. It is illegal there for me to be gay, despite my having partied with closeted Lebanese politicians or with their openly gay kids in Paris and London. As Anthony Bourdain said of Beirut, "There's no place else even remotely like it. Everything great and all the world's ills in one glorious, messed-up, magical, maddening, magnificent city." But the fact that some militant faction over there can simply pick me up at any time is not lost on me.

On April 13, 1975, Lebanon descended into civil war, which lasted from 1975 to 1990, with Syrian troops continuing to occupy the country until 2005. There were more than 120,000 casualties, and more than a million people fled this tiny country on the Mediterranean Sea. Needless to say, phone service and other communications were nearly non-existent. For a while, we lost contact with my grandparents and other family members. Which is why I could not imagine *not* visiting during that time.

We went to titanic efforts to get there. I relied on the connections and generosity of my uncle Chawki Choueiri, who was at different times Lebanon's ambassador to Greece, England, and the United Nations. I often traveled with my cousin Nicholas, carrying our suitcases through the rubble from the airport for a few kilometers to get a safe distance away from the checkpoints. Sometimes we took a ferry from Cyprus to North Lebanon when the airport had been bombed, or we would go through Syria or Jordan and drive a few hours to get in another way.

I depended heavily on my cousins Nouha and Adnan Makary, who would pick me up and take me to the old village and drive me around in Lebanon, and extricate me from potentially life-threatening situations and arrests. A couple of times, we fled our village immediately upon hearing news of an impending attack, but my cousins always assured me that it was relatively safe where we were. We would sit in bomb shelters and underground parking lots, the discussion turning to what we wanted for dinner, as if nothing were amiss.

Both of my grandmothers refused to leave during the war. Their thinking was, *What would those people want with an old lady anyway?*— and someone had to stay behind to protect the houses. They also took in fleeing families, especially those with kids, avoiding praise for their largesse by claiming it was because they wanted company.

Checkpoints were everywhere. Sometimes I was able to get through. On several occasions, the soldiers apologized for the inconvenience with, "Sorry, Father"; they must have thought, based on my beard and black clothing, that I was a Greek Orthodox priest.

On October 19, 2012, my husband Jacob and I were heading to our hotel in Beirut. He would be flying out the next morning, and I would be returning to the village for a few days. At the last minute, Jacob decided we didn't have enough gifts for our daughter, Ivy, so we asked the driver to take us to a local department store. By veering off to shop, we narrowly missed the street near our hotel where a car bomb exploded at that same moment, killing several people, including the Lebanese security official whose investigations had implicated Syria in the 2005 assassination of Lebanon's then president, Rafik al-Hariri.

One thing that never leaves me is the memory of how, wherever you looked in our village of Kfarhata, you saw olive groves.

Lebanon is better known for its majestic cedars, and the olive tree's flowers are hardly the showiest; for that, you can look to the almond tree that flowers in February and signals the end of winter, or the numerous other fruit trees and shrubs—plum, pomegranate, climbing jasmine. When my grandmother Anissa, at eighty-three, boarded her first flight to join us in Toronto, we drove along the highway as I pointed out all the sights of our new land and all she could say was: "Where are the fruit trees? Why don't they plant more fruit trees?"

Of all the fruit trees, the olive tree is the most dependable. It can live hundreds of years, with some lasting much longer. Its roots spread and establish themselves. It survives drought, frost, and often fire. Sometimes, just when you think an olive tree is dead, the roots rejuvenate.

The olive harvest was kind of our Thanksgiving. It marked the end of the harvest season and we planned everything around it. My cousin Salam and my ninety-one-year-old aunt Selwa still oversee it. The same seasonal workers returned each year and went from family to family to help pick and process. We cooked with olive oil and used it on everything. We made olive oil soap to last all year. Olives plus a bottle of olive oil were always on the kitchen table and still are. I loved a simple sandwich of homemade pita bread with olives, cheese, and either lemon grass, fresh marjoram, or green za'atar from our garden. I went on in later years to give olive oil as a gift to friends, clients, and a few celebrities, with the unintended outcome that they would remember and think of me, as the bottles sat in their kitchens a long time. A bottle of olive oil became my calling card.

I am the fourth of five children—including sisters Grace and Anissa, and brothers George and Ziad. We come from a well-educated bunch. Our uncles on my mom's side included an engineer, an ambassador, a doctor, and two schoolteachers. Our paternal grandmother, Anissa, who lived with us, was one of the first educated women in the village and spoke perfect Russian, as taught to her by the Russian Orthodox Church.

When I was little, I would sit on the steps of our house with my grandmother Anissa as she helped me with my arithmetic and spelling. She was the first huge influence on me. She saw something special in me that she wanted to nurture.

I assumed everybody in Canada spoke French and English, which of course is not the case in Toronto, but the only English phrases I knew and would use on the plane over were "Excuse me," "I love you," and "Rolls-Royce."

My dad's father owned land in the village, some of which my grandmother had to sell when he left for Brazil. He stayed there for over thirty years and left her a single mother of three—my aunts Adama and Daad; and my dad, Hanna, or John—during the Depression. It's not like you could drive anywhere back then. My grandmother's family supported her, and my dad found odd jobs from the time he was eleven. My aunt Adama died during childbirth. My maternal grandmother, Saide, a cousin of my grandfather's, would help Anissa when she could, long before she, too, was married.

I sometimes wondered what drove my grandfather away. Was it his sexual orientation? Was it mental illness? A combination of the two? When he finally returned, he had no place to stay. Despite everything, my parents took him in, and he and my grandmother lived together yet alone, in separate parts of our house, when the rest of us immigrated to Canada. My grandmother still cooked for him and took care of him. He died first, and when she passed away, a cousin of my grandfather's refused to allow her to be buried in the Bachir family crypt, with its monstrous headstones—even though my dad had given that cousin the land next to us to build a house. It was my grandfather's village, and yet the cousins treated his wife after her death as an outsider. Maybe they recognized that she was better than they. I know it would not have mattered to her, but it still stings. I have since built a garden around the main church there in her memory. Although I am not religious, I wanted to please my parents and fit in with their community—even if I didn't see myself as part of it anymore; I was the major contributor to building the largest church in the area, with the sole caveat that they build a community hall as well.

Over time, I would begin to identify with Lebanon in the same way the Québécois poet Gilles Vigneault identifies with Canada in the song "Mon pays": "My country is not a country, it's the reverse of a country that was neither country nor homeland." My romance with Lebanon was becoming more complicated.

Mom wouldn't marry Dad until he built his own house. He was living in his family's house with my grandmother, but my mother wanted a place of their own, even though my grandmother moved in with them soon enough to help raise us—including for the five years when my father, until then a contractor in the Persian Gulf, scoped out Canada as a place to move the family should a brewing civil war erupt, which it eventually did.

I bonded with other new immigrants in my ESL class in Canada, but it took time to create or feel like part of a community there and in the larger world. Society has many litmus tests—weight, sexuality, nationality—to determine who gets to go on the field and who gets relegated to the sidelines. While outsiders just want to fit in, others speak about them as if they are not there. They say we talk too much or too loudly or that our food smells. I grew up in my new homeland with a lingering sense of being an outsider, someone not quite welcomed into certain exclusive enclaves—the private schools and golf and country clubs where the elite forge early alliances. At the same time, I didn't want to be swallowed up in what we in Canada proudly call a cultural mosaic. Where in this tapestry was my bright, shiny pink fabric?

For a while, I led a double life; I was out to some but not others, and had learned to hide, like so many people I knew. I sometimes wonder if a small part of my attraction to befriending the larger-than-life people who appear in this book was a way for me to disappear into their shadow. They offered me affirmation and confidence and influenced my life, but the spotlight stayed on them and freed me up, in a way, from having others categorize or compartmentalize me. For the longest time, no one really knew what I did for a living. I had these different pockets of people who never overlapped, and each one knew me in a different way, like the parable about the blind men encountering different parts of an elephant but never getting the full picture.

My life is one of light and shadow, of fierce pride mixed with uncertainty, a kaleidoscope of hiding and revealing. I wanted to be known, and I wanted *not* to be known. I think this is a dilemma for famous people, too, particularly those in the performing arts, where fans think they know all about you, where they have seen you so often on screens or in concert that they hallucinate a kinship beyond mere appreciation, one that is likely to shatter the moment they encounter their idol on a bad hair day, or in a snippy mood, or just trying to enjoy a quiet dinner. Many who go into showbiz shine before the camera but are quite shy in real life; it's part of what draws them to that career, the ability to try out another way of being once a script is in hand, later reverting to form behind closed doors.

The celebrity experience is not unlike the immigrant experience. Who are we when we are not playing a character people expect of us? A Black celebrity is held up to represent all Black people. A Lebanese child stands in for all Lebanese, and perhaps all Arabs. A single person is called to account for "our people." Our behavior reflects on the behavior of everyone of our supposed "type." We are some things to some segments of society and other things to others. We fit in, and we don't.

I am fortunate to have cultivated friendships with extraordinary people over the decades. The ones you will read about in this book happen to be famous, but that was never the reason we bonded, and fame was never the glue that held us together.

I met some of them through chance, others through introductions, many through my work raising funds for charities and the arts, but mostly it all started with having unprecedented access to them through my connection to the entertainment industry—specifically home video, which was a new and exciting field when I took it on in the early 1980s.

I didn't have a long-term plan in mind when I managed my brother George's Toronto store, Videoland, the first consumer video store in Canada. I didn't go by the name Salah when I worked there; I told people I was a Steve, a holdover habit from my university days and a name I might have decided on from an old high school crush. There was so much porn and piracy in the industry at the time, and I was not going to have anyone connect my name with its seedy reputation. Also, too many people had trouble pronouncing my name (though it's not that hard to pronounce!), and I hate the shortened "Sal."

My brother George and I branched out into publishing *Videomania*, Canada's first magazine devoted solely to the new field, from the store's basement. I went on to publish a succession of entertainment magazines in English and French—*Premiere, Famous, Cineplex*, and *Star Cineplex*—but it started with that first one, which was a real seat-of-the-pants enterprise. I'm in touch with many of the people I worked with from the beginning; they have supported me and loved me over the years. Friends such as Cathy Prowse, Shane Carter, Janet Billett, Angele Abromaitis, with whom I started out in the early video days.

I was lucky enough also to have friends such as Cindy and Elliott Kosher, Felice Fleisher, John Bailey, Randall Erickson, Lance Novak,

Nancy Lockhart, Jim Gormley, and Dan Tau. I met Dan in 1982 when I ran Videoland. He would later sell me his office and warehouse, not charging me any interest on the mortgage.

Home video quickly became a cash cow for the studios, so they made their stars available, along with fat advertising budgets to spend on magazines like ours. They went out of their way to arrange meet-and-greet junkets in Hollywood and beyond to help get the word out about new films, which would later get a second boost with a video release. We'd get access, plus bonus advertising dollars for cover stories, providing we held those interviews until the video release date six months later.

In our magazines, we tried to keep the focus on the art and pleasure of film, not on celeb gossip, which made us popular with both studios and stars. This would eventually pave the way for a lovely synergy between my video life and the world of charity.

In 1982, Moe and Lorraine Himmelfarb walked through the doors of Videoland with a poorly shot tape of their daughter's wedding. Moe asked if there was any way I could color-correct it. We struck up a conversation about home video and then about musicals in New York. He was a big Jerry Herman fan, while I was Team Stephen Sondheim. He took my recommendations, rented a few videos, and returned them the next week, asking for more. The Himmelfarbs introduced me to the international children's charity Variety Club, which began as a sort of showbiz social-club-cum-carnival, where Moe was chief barker, and boasted many major entertainment and advertising industry executives as members. The Ontario chapter was one of the largest in the world, and I became involved with them in raising money through monthly celebrity luncheons and several galas with stars who happened to be filming or performing in town at the right time.

Known as "the kid" for my relative youth, I quickly became a member of Variety's inner circle, one that included brewery head and former football star Reg Bovaird, and Warner Brothers publicity director Al Dubin. I would also meet Gino Empry, who managed the Imperial

Room as well as publicity for Mirvish Productions' Royal Alexandra Theatre. Everyone who was anyone played the Royal Alex.

From this ever-widening circle of connections, it felt like a natural next step for our magazines to begin hosting Lifetime Achievement Awards as a way to kick off our annual trade show and raise funds for such charities as Variety, numerous hospitals, and the Canadian Foundation for AIDS Research. As I took more to fundraising and got better at it, I reached out to another place of natural interest, The 519, a Toronto community center that has grown to encompass everything I stand for, with its counseling services for refugees and for people coming out, with its food and housing security services, and with one of the leading transgender support programs in the world. I am a lifetime patron, and it now has a wing named after me. Not that I did any of this to see my name on a building, but it does give me joy.

Although the characters you will come across in this book are among the most famous people of all time, I was not interested in their celebrity, per se, but in what they did with it—the causes they championed, the good they did in the world by using their platform, the resilience they showed in handling not only fame but the vicissitudes of an amplified life.

I admired them. I learned from them. I valued them. But I did not fawn over them or ask what it was like to be "them," to have worked with other big names, or who they slept with or didn't. I was horrified to think I might come across as part of a chorus line of sycophants. I have always said that the only autograph I want is on a check, and the only photo I want is art that belongs on a wall.

Instead of having "celeb encounters," I found refuge in people who got so much attention they naturally wanted to hide from it. I finally got what Garbo was talking about when she said, "I want to be left alone." And that was before email! Like me, in some ways, they were in fear of discovery. We're afraid of what's behind it all. What image do we need to keep up? Can we truly speak our truth?

Immigrants, on the whole, want a chance to succeed because they saw their parents get out of one situation and enter another, learn a new language, deal with racism and all the other trials and tribulations of transplanting one's life so they could pave the way to a better existence for their children. Once, at a Woolworths, my mother asked someone how much something cost, and the lady said, "Speak in English"—even though my mother *was* speaking in English! She spoke three languages, asshole. To this day, I still get the sneer, the dismissive eyes. The haughty tone. I never did escape homophobia or the feeling of being invisible in the business world, no matter how successful I became. I was called "one of the family" by people who simultaneously tried to undermine me and take credit for my work.

I wanted to succeed, and I have. I have the highest honors that Canada and Ontario give, the Order of Canada and the Order of Ontario. I am a little embarrassed to wear the medals on my lapel, and seldom do; they make me feel as if I've been singled out from thousands who have done the same as I've done, if not more. I think we need to open up the order and give it to many more people each year. Since 1967, only 7,600 have been invested in the Order of Canada. The motto of the Order of Canada is "They desire a better country." And, really, who doesn't?

I have also received numerous other awards, including five honorary doctorates—although I never actually finished getting my B.A., and I don't believe sheepskins are a measure of a person—but while many think of me as a philanthropist or an art collector or a magazine publisher or whatever, the thing I most like to do is help if I can. It's that simple. If I get a lot of recognition, it's only because of the other people who often go unheralded. Many people volunteer in hospitals and food banks, knock on doors, and stuff envelopes, and they don't get their name on a building, even if nothing would have happened without them.

With my first freelance check, in 1980, I bought a friend's piece of art because I knew she couldn't support herself. I really needed that money, but she needed it more. That's okay, because money isn't capital. People are capital. The world is powered by social relations. Today, I support and encourage many artists, but I can also call people and get something done. I am never afraid to ask for help. Maybe the shy immigrant has found his voice. I ask for money and don't take no as a rejection; I will ask again next month. That is how I have chaired or co-chaired upward of one hundred galas—they call me Gala Salah—and raised hundreds of millions of dollars since 1980 for arts, culture, social justice, health, and numerous humanitarian causes and organizations worldwide. And I assure you that a Salah gala is one without long-winded speeches or live auctions. It ends by 10 p.m. Give them good food and entertainment, and people will come back next time.

Many of them came back. So many more became a fixture in my life: true friends. You will meet some of them in this book, in no particular order, as our lives became woven together in weird, wonderful, and entirely unexpected tapestries.

Why, then, if people are the coin of my realm, am I always first to leave the party?

When I was younger, I wanted to be the *last* to leave the party. Dance, drink, drugs! Let the carnival never stop. But I was afraid of what happens when we lose control, as I had seen so often.

Over time, I began to envy the ones who firmly yet gracefully left early. The conversations were still flowing and so was the wine, but that was the point—leave on a high note, not after people get drunk and nasty or you run out of things to say or wear out your welcome. Leave while it's all still aglow. Leave them wanting more of you, and you of them.

My friend Robbie always left events at 11 p.m., no matter who else was there, no matter what was going on. My friends Diane and Yvonne were out the door by 10:30 p.m., whether they had been sitting by the pool at photographer Herb Ritts's house or whether Liza was up next, or Chaka Khan. I admired their resolve. "We have to go walk the dog." Once I finally had a dog of my own, I understood how true that was.

Leaving the party early soon became my thing as well. A party is a luxury I do enjoy, but I'm letting you know right now that, much as I love you, I am leaving early. And I no longer go to openings or opening nights. The commotion. The frenzy. It is not a time to see art or interact closely with friends.

The same goes for guests coming to my place. It doesn't matter who the dinner is for, whether Salman Rushdie, Kim Cattrall, Dori Tunstall, or Margaret Atwood. If the invitation says 7 to 11 p.m., out you go by eleven. My caterers pack up and there's no one left to serve you a drink. How many drinks do you need in one night, anyway? Perhaps don't answer that question! We can always continue that scintillating conversation another day when we are both sober and without forty other guests around.

I can't say diabetes had nothing to do with it. I've lived with diabetes since 1980. It led increasingly to kidney disease, which plagued me for some thirty years and culminated in kidney failure in 2010. That led to dialysis three times a week and a kidney transplant on July 17, 2019. Not to mention other surgeries and serious complications—sepsis, and an ileostomy and its reversal. I have had to relearn to walk three times in the span of three years.

I used my time in dialysis to notice what hospitals needed for making patients, including cancer patients, more comfortable, and dreamed up a "non-gala gala," in which I asked people *not* to dress up or do anything fancy, and I offered them nothing in return—I just asked them to send me money. We collected $220,000 for better TV sets, family waiting areas, medications, and other amenities for St. Joseph's Health Centre in Toronto. Now there are two dialysis clinics in the Toronto area named after me and Jacob, and our families—the Bachir Yerex Dialysis Centres. We have also helped improve dialysis centers in other areas of the world, including Lebanon, through the generous support of many friends.

The night before my family departed Lebanon for Toronto—we left on my tenth birthday, October 3—my aunt Afaf gave me five dollars, truly a fortune for a kid back then. My mother immediately made me put it in a box at the church convent overlooking the Mediterranean. "You will make it back a thousand times over," she assured me.

As usual, she **was right**, although she was off by a few zeroes.

Marlon Brando
stops by for a barbecue

"What can I get you?" my mother asked Marlon Brando. She wasn't exactly clear on who he was, other than being some kind of actor and a new friend I had brought over for a backyard barbecue.

What could she get him? She would have asked the same of anyone. In our family and in our Lebanese culture, one of the ways we show love is with food. A lot of it. Lots of love, lots of food. It wouldn't have mattered if my mother had known who Marlon was, because she treated everyone with the same courtesy and hospitality—and anyway, to my mom, her kids were the stars. No one shone brighter. Whether I brought over Ginger Rogers, Douglas Fairbanks Jr., Elizabeth Taylor, Ella Fitzgerald, or any of the celebrities I befriended over the years, to her I was always the main attraction. The only time I shared the spotlight was when one of my siblings or their kids were also on hand.

True, my mother didn't bring out the good china for Brando; but then, she never used her good china with anyone, no matter how exalted. She had it there on display in the dining room buffet, one of those grand wooden pieces of furniture crafted in the old style, but I never saw her use it. She had a set of everyday china, a set of "better" china, and the "good" stuff that never saw the light of day. The home-made food was the main attraction, not the plates.

Marlon sat near the picnic table on one of our folding lawn chairs (the tubular metal variety with a fabric-strip seat), the pear and peach trees on one side and a wall of flowers on the other, with vegetables growing to disguise the chain-link fence that separated our house from its neighbor. Our vegetables were heavy on tomatoes, Lebanese cucumber, and kousa—similar to zucchini and also known as Lebanese squash. There was also plenty of marjoram, sumac, and the summer savories one can eat green or add to salads, and when dried go into za'atar, a Lebanese spice blend that is suddenly all the rage everywhere but has been here all along.

Ours was a regular three-bedroom house—with a carport, behind a strip mall, on a dead-end street that connected to another little circle—in a working-class neighborhood in north Toronto called Rexdale. At the end of the street was the Humber River, where my two sisters and two brothers and I played out our Tom Sawyer adventures. There was a cedar hedge alongside the house and a big shed out back where Dad kept his tools.

My father knew Brando from *On the Waterfront*, but perhaps he was unaware of the stature of the man for whom he was pouring a glass of arak near the flowering fruit trees.

"Did you know that your name is English for the Lebanese name Maroun?" he asked Marlon.

"St. Maroun, yes! I love that," exclaimed Marlon, to everyone's amazement. "The patron saint of the Maronite Church."

It was not the first time Marlon surprised me by coming out with something seemingly obscure, but he was a sponge for information that intrigued him. And virtually everything intrigued him.

"We're not Maronites, we're Greek Orthodox," my father clarified over tabouli and fattoush salads.

"We're not here to talk religion," I interceded, heading that off.

I don't think my parents would have acted any differently had they known their guest was one of the most revered actors of all time, a two-time Oscar winner for *On the Waterfront* and *The Godfather*—not that I put much stock in awards. Who's to say who is "the best" of anything? We were all instantly in love with Marlon anyway. He put everyone at ease and tasted everything Mom made, complimenting her lavishly. A couple of times he asked, in French, for the names of certain foods in Arabic.

It seemed that Brando was up for just about any conversation, no topic off limits, but I purposely steered the talk away from his fame and acting career. It's all on screen anyway, and I figured he'd enjoy a break from the endless questions—what was it like doing this or that or with this one or that one.

I also had no need to ferret out his secrets, sexual or otherwise. In the end, though, he learned all about mine.

It had always been Brando for me. He was one of the most exciting film actors to watch. I had heard Elizabeth Taylor say that everyone who met him, male or female, straight or not, felt the attraction. And in many cases, Marlon was up for it: from Laurence Olivier, Richard Pryor, and James Dean to Marilyn Monroe and Rita Moreno—just a few of the names linked to him over the years. Playwright Arthur Miller wrote that when Brando appeared in *A Streetcar Named Desire* on Broadway in December 1947, "it caused such a sensation that he seemed like a tiger on the loose. A sexual terrorist. Brando was the brute who bore the truth."

At the moment, the brute was in my childhood backyard in Rexdale, slouching and talking horse racing and cards with my dad, eating my mom's homemade mamoul and fruit jams for dessert, calling them Mr. and Mrs. Bachir.

Brando famously did not do interviews, but Fritz Friedman, then the head of publicity at Columbia Tristar Home Video, had called to tell me it was an outside possibility that I could have Matthew Broderick for the cover of *Premiere*—the Canadian home video magazine I published—if I visited the set of the new movie the two were filming, *The Freshman*. In that 1990 comedy, Broderick plays a strapped New York City film school student who takes a job with mobster Jimmy the Toucan smuggling a rare Komodo dragon hither and yon. The running gag is that Jimmy the Toucan bears a suspicious resemblance to Brando's mob boss Vito Corleone.

For *The Freshman*, Brando played a Mafia chieftain. A selection of Asian water monitors stood in to play the supposed Komodo dragon that Broderick lugged around for the majority of the movie.

Fritz told me with regret that I would have to get myself somehow to this unknown, misbegotten corner of Toronto where the movie was filming—maybe I could look it up on a map—called Rexdale.

Rexdale!

That's where I had grown up from the age of ten, when my family first came to Canada. It was where as a teen I'd held a succession of summer jobs that will sound familiar to most youths who grew up around there at around that time. I worked several part-time gigs after school and in the summer at one of the three area warehouses of Simpsons-Sears, a partnership between the Canadian department store Simpsons and the American behemoth Sears. The factory was on Rexdale Boulevard, and I was in what they called Department 42, which sounds like one of those government-suppressed UFO enclosures but was something much more mundane—it was where they repackaged the stuff that came back, like toilets and bathtubs and hardware items.

I also worked on the potato chip conveyor line at Humpty Dumpty and spent one summer at Labatt Breweries. After those experiences, I lost all desire for chips and beer.

The Freshman would go on to shoot at several locations dear to my heart—including a particular gas station, now a Petro-Canada, where the Komodo dragon breaks loose; the Woodbine Centre mall on Rexdale Boulevard, where I often dropped my mom to go shopping and where in the movie the creature swims with the bumper boats at the indoor Fantasy Fair amusement park; near the Woodbine Racetrack, which my dad frequented a little too often and where the Royal Family regularly attended the annual Queen's Plate—the oldest continuously run horse race in North America, funded in 1860 with the blessing of Queen Victoria; and at the Weston Arena, where I played goalie in hockey and lacrosse, and where Marlon was unhappily and unsteadily learning to ice skate for his role.

With my meeting with Broderick secured, I then used every contact I had, called in every chip, to get some face time with Marlon, too. The interview with Matthew never actually happened, but something better did: Marlon and I hit it off right away and we began spending time together. Like friends.

I know, it sounds ridiculous. *Me*, friends with Brando? I don't think so. Who was I to be palling around with him?

When I first met him, I approached it almost like a date. There was a nervous sexual energy to it, like when you're going out with someone new. Although it wasn't romantic, it felt the same, that anxiety you get when you don't want to screw things up or overstep your welcome. I didn't want to blurt out, "Hey, Marlon, how ya doing?" as if we were childhood pals.

I took care not to commandeer too much of his time—and he later gave me shit for it! Every couple of weeks, I'd receive an unsigned gift from a shop not far from the hotel where Brando was staying. One time, my mystery gift-giver sent a letter opener with a bluebird of happiness on it made by the Danish designer Georg Jensen. Another time he sent a Steuben candy dish. When I called Marlon to thank him, he'd lace into me: Why hadn't I called to see if he was free?

It was also, frankly, easier for him to dine out and relax when he was with me, because if he paid for dinner with a credit card in his name, that would mark the end of whatever blissful anonymity he might enjoy for the rest of the evening. I always gave my credit card on the way into the restaurant so Marlon wouldn't have to pay and thereby reveal his identity. As we went around together, I always introduced him as my cousin. At some of these places I received preferential treatment—as I was well known in those parts, and this big guy was simply "cousin George from Lebanon." On a couple of occasions, people said, "Yes, I can see the resemblance"—because at the time I did look somewhat like him, enough so that friends who later saw the skating scenes in *The Freshman* would swear it was me. Except that I'm a good skater. Marlon and I even joked that I could serve as his stunt double. Maybe it wasn't a joke, because Marlon, although he made a valiant effort, really could not skate at all.

From the moment I met him, we talked about everything—politics, olive oil, Indigenous rights, Lebanon . . . the guy was a walking encyclopedia, and not just of dry, lifeless information, but of limitless curiosity and a deep appreciation for things you would never guess he'd heard of. He was familiar with Indigenous Canadian painters. He had a keen appraiser's eye for sculpture. So that I wouldn't embarrass myself, I nervously boned up on Canadian art the night before I took him to art galleries. Luckily, I knew the director at one, and he walked us through the galleries showcasing landscape art of the Group of Seven; they, more than other artists, are how the world identifies Canada. At the end of the tour, the director said, "I hope your cousin George enjoyed his trip here."

Marlon and I wound up having many talks and dinners while he was making *The Freshman*. I took him to my favorite restaurants, and a few times to an Indian buffet in Rexdale. When I mentioned there was a gay village in Toronto, he was keen to see it. "Is there any particular bar you like?" he asked. I didn't really go to bars or strip clubs; they were depressing last resorts. But I took him to a coffee house frequented by bears—larger-sized gay men—on Church Street in the village for coffee, and another time for lunch. We sat outside on the patio, where people dropped by our table to say hi to my cousin George.

Friends of mine who knew it wasn't actually a cousin I was showing around my hometown often wanted to know one thing—what was

Marlon Brando really like? Well, he was charming and engaging, as you might expect. But who is to say what any of us is really like? People can spend nearly a lifetime with a person, either in friendship or marriage, and one day wake up to realize they never really knew them. You know, they were double agents or axe murderers, that kind of thing. The question of what anyone is "really" like is a double-edged sword. I mean, what is each of us bringing to the table? Are we engaging enough that we bring out the best qualities in others? Are we late or do we come unprepared and then blame a lackluster meeting on the other person? What false expectations do we bring that we then feel are unmet, through no fault of the other?

The real question wasn't what Marlon Brando the famous actor was like. It was about who he was as a person, not as a function of his day job or weight fluctuations or sexual history or reputation on the set.

Brando was a person who somehow invited others to confide. I learned more about myself even as I was learning a little about Marlon. It's weird, but sometimes there's a sense that you'd tell a stranger something you wouldn't tell your closest friend, and I found myself opening up to Marlon about body image.

"I thought I looked too pretty as a young man," I admitted to him. "I think subconsciously I put on weight to feel uglier to people."

In the eighties, I was afraid of contracting AIDS and almost welcomed rejection. Some of my eventual weight gain was about looking less desirable. Also, I had been sexually assaulted previously, and had also experienced a few uninvited incidents in a doctor's office and at the barber. I still find it awkward when someone takes my blood pressure, and I can't have a barber put a hot towel on my face to trim my beard. It's hard for me even to sleep alone in a house.

Marlon clearly understood when I told him how I had packed on weight as a kind of counterbalance to the dangers of the AIDS crisis—the fear that I would get into trouble if I remained too attractive to other men, if I happened to go someplace where I didn't have control. Weight can be a protective device. He and I had this in common; we had both been in great shape at one point. Marlon's weight famously ballooned over time, and it cost him in his career. He wanted to do a lot more, but Hollywood no longer offered him the good parts. Here he was, considered one of the finest actors of his generation, and he couldn't get work because of his size! Like with so many of us in the world, the powers that be judged him by the pound. It was the same for Orson Welles and Elizabeth Taylor. Size became a source of huge rage for Marlon; he hated how people chose to define him in a way he could not change or control.

He asked a lot of questions about when I'd realized I was attracted to men. Was I totally gay? What about the woman I'd once been engaged to?

I explained how that engagement had been more about my desire to have children. Also, the woman really was a lot of fun, and I genuinely loved her. He got this. He seemed to love the sense of family he saw in my childhood home—our unquestioned closeness. My siblings and I all stayed in Toronto, even once we were old enough and motivated enough to leave. When I had a major job offer in Los Angeles, I turned it down. "We didn't leave our land and homes in Lebanon and come here and learn a different language and do all those things just so one of you could leave," my mom said; I took this as common sense wisdom, not a threat. At one point, Mom and four of her five grown kids even lived in the same apartment building.

"How did they feel about you being gay?" asked Marlon.

"In a way, it was touching. My dad said, 'Don't tell your mom, she won't get it.' And when I admitted I'd already told her, he laughed. 'Why would you tell your mother first? I'm your best friend!'"

As for how my mother took the news, she told me: "All I want for you is to be able to have a child who has been half as nice to you as you have been to us."

When Marlon came for lunch in our backyard, my mom served him the same wide-ranging Lebanese menu she would have served any guest. In addition to barbecued chicken, there was kafta with ground beef, onions, parsley, and sumac. There were shish kebabs with barbe-cued onions, peppers, and vegetables. She brought out endless platters of her homemade specialties: pita bread along with apricot, quince, and fig jams, the figs all the way from Lebanon.

And good luck being vegetarian—which I was at the time—around a Lebanese family determined to feed you. There is always a selection of meats, because vegetables-only is a sign you can't afford stuff, so you never deprive a guest of meat.

Nevertheless, it was time for Mom's homemade mamoul, a pastry made with dates, walnuts, or pistachios. She also put out a platter of kaak, a sesame seed–encrusted cookie.

I told Marlon about publishing *Videomania* magazine in the base-ment of my brother George's store, and how things were so touch-and-go with that venture for a while that I'd moved back home to my parents' basement. My mother had saved up a bunch of money and hired a gay designer to do the bathroom down there for me.

"Show me," said Marlon, eager to see.

Marlon was incredibly supportive in a lot of ways. I was his equal—because he made me feel that way. Sure, I had heard about him sleeping with men and women, about his sexual prowess, about his physical endowment. I knew that he had slept with James Baldwin and Marvin Gaye . . . but I didn't want to go there. In a 1976 interview, the actor told a French journalist: "Homosexuality is so much in fashion it no longer makes news. Like a large number of men, I, too, have had homosexual experiences, and I am not ashamed."

I think if it were not for AIDS, perhaps men elsewhere in the world might have become like many European and Middle Eastern men who, though not gay, have flings with other men. Not that it didn't cross my mind that something could happen with Brando.

Brando was still hot in many ways, but more in the sense of how he had sturdy principles and was interested in and knowledgeable about so much. He could talk Indigenous art with my friend the museum director. Civil rights with activists. Horse racing with my dad. He was an olive oil aficionado and loved the special brand from my family groves, as well as the story about the Phoenicians delivering olive trees around the Mediterranean. He was eager to talk politics and Palestinian refugees.

That's why I get so furious with people who claim he was some kind of monster. To me, he just wanted to learn about everything. I think if he wasn't challenged, he'd get bored and kind of dismiss people, and those people who couldn't keep up with him would turn around and trash him, personally and professionally. They did it to recover their sense that they were all that, when Marlon probably knew they weren't. They did it to promote themselves by putting down someone more famous. So, you're just some two-bit actor and you were on a set with Marlon Brando and you think he was *mean* to you? *That's* your story to tell now? Instead of telling of your own achievements? I could mention names—the actors who rode on Brando's coattails in this sick, negative way—but why give them a shred of publicity?

Looking back now, I realize that Brando came into my life at a time of great uncertainty for me. There was AIDS and people dying. There was a stigma around being gay, and people were being fired or shunned for it. I still needed to find my voice and my confidence, and here was this icon of the twentieth century who was also struggling with body image and his place in the world, telling me he thought I was handsome no matter what size.

Over the years, I lost touch with Marlon. But one time, when I knew I'd be heading to L.A., I called and asked if he would be free for lunch, and brought him an Inuit soapstone sculpture of a bear, similar to the pieces we'd seen together at a gallery in Toronto.

"I missed you," he said. "Why didn't you stay in touch?"

But you are Marlon Brando, I wanted to say! *What could Marlon Brando possibly want with me?*

It occurred to me that maybe it wasn't just my parents who didn't know who Marlon Brando really was.

Ella Fitzgerald likes my mom's kibbe

Ella Fitzgerald would make me scrambled eggs in her kitchen—or I'd bring something over and we'd eat it in her backyard garden—but I think if I had known just how revered she was, I might not have been so relaxed around her.

When she performed, Ella would come out on stage in this ordinary dress, too long or large on her, and wearing glasses so thick you feared she'd trip before she got to the microphone. Then she'd begin to sing, and her voice would take over and fill the room alongside the sounds of a full orchestra.

Duke Ellington once remarked that he had "never seen musicians line up to hear a singer like they did with Ella." She had perfect pitch and a reputation for never doing a song the same way twice—except, of course, in the studio. Her Gershwin songbooks are an international treasure, rescuing show tunes from the heap of cultural flim-flam. Sinatra called her "the greatest popular singer in the world, male or female, bar none." He also said she was the only singer with whom he was nervous performing, because he kept trying to reach her heights.

I met Ella through a mutual acquaintance—the publicist, impresario, and all-around colorful character Gino Empry—who managed Tony Bennett for twelve years and also helped manage Ella in Canada. He booked her into the Imperial Room, a classic five-hundred-seat Toronto venue for big-name performers. Marlene Dietrich, Tony Bennett, Louis Armstrong, Tina Turner . . . in those days, stars who came to Toronto played the Imperial Room, which put on a first-class dinner and act. One of the infamous moments in the history of the venue was when maître d' Louis Jannetta refused entry to Bob Dylan for not wearing a tie.

"My uncle saw you perform in Baalbek in 1971," I told Ella backstage. The Baalbek International Festival—with its dramatic backdrop courtesy of the Temple of Bacchus's Roman ruins—is an experience no one forgets.

"You're Lebanese?" she asked me. "Tell me, where can I find good kibbe in Toronto?"

I certainly knew the answer to that question: "My mother."

Kibbe is one of Lebanon's and Syria's national dishes. It's made of meat and bulgur (cracked wheat), baked or fried, with finely chopped onions and pine nuts. Aleppo in Syria is famous for having more than twenty varieties.

Ella wanted kibbe? She would get it, and more. I asked my mother to make her some, and Mom went all out—not just kibbe, but side dishes to go with it, just like a Lebanese table spread out with mezze.

Everything she made for Ella, she made with a Lebanese twist. I saw to it that she used the finest ingredients, finer even than she would buy for our family. The fresh fruits and vegetables came from her garden, of course, but I canvased specialty stores for the best cuts of beef, organic this and that, and then sat in the parking lot peeling the price stickers off my purchases. My mother never would have paid even half of what I spent on pine nuts.

I also bought Mom new Tupperware on occasion, because Ella didn't always return the containers. The replacement containers didn't fool my mother for a moment, but she didn't let on at the time.

I brought Ella food most nights while she was in town; if she was doing a two-week run, I showed up with a different Lebanese dish seven or eight of those nights. She didn't like to eat right before a performance, but she needed to have a light meal, as she was diabetic. I knew that routine only too well.

Another thing Ella liked about Toronto was the maple syrup, but you can get that anywhere in Canada. The best kibbe . . . for *that* you have to go to my mom.

It's funny to reflect on it now and remember how I was bringing kibbe to Ella Fitzgerald at the Royal York hotel the way others might bring a photo for a star to sign. I didn't always stay for the show—sometimes I went off to play hockey—but I managed to bring my parents several times to see Ella perform. Louis Jannetta would whisk us to the best seats in the house and refuse to take money, but I'd bring him some kibbe, too. Does it count as a bribe if it's food your mother cooks?

Sometimes Ella would come over to the nearby apartment I kept in Toronto and just hang out after one of her performances. There was a privacy to it for her, I think, a feeling of relaxing rather than having to hold court at her hotel. She would sit around the table with a few friends and I would do a Lebanese dinner. We'd have music blasting; I'd play Joni Mitchell's albums *Clouds* and *Blue*. Sometimes I even played Ella's music. "I sounded good back then!" she would say with a laugh.

As I got to know Ella over the years and built a connection with her, I found myself wanting to defend her when people said or assumed things that were not true—that she only played for white audiences, for example, or didn't experience the pressure her good friend Billie Holiday did in the entertainment business. It wasn't my battle to fight, but it felt personal.

She was happiest when singing. "The only thing better than singing is more singing," she was known to say.

With Ella, I was a little different than I was with most people. She was so approachable that I broke my own rule and sometimes asked about the famous people she knew. She seemed happy to talk about the jazz legends, some of whom I'd met—Lena Horne, Sarah Vaughan, Louis Armstrong, Billie Holiday, Miles Davis, Pearl Bailey, Rosemary Clooney, Oscar Peterson. Ella thought Janis Joplin would have made a fine jazz singer.

She also talked a lot about her dear friend Marilyn Monroe—about Marilyn's humor and intellect. She felt people had wildly misunderstood Marilyn. Underrated her. Dismissed her as a mere sex kitten.

When Ella was still an up-and-coming singer, it was tough getting gigs. The racism of the era meant that certain clubs wouldn't take her because of her skin color, or at least were hesitant on that score. The hot, Latin American–themed Mocambo in Hollywood, where Sinatra made his Los Angeles debut, had featured Black performers before, including Eartha Kitt—but didn't want to take a chance on Ella. The owner reportedly thought Ella was too much jazz and not enough glam.

Marilyn called the Mocambo in 1955 and promised the owner she would take the front table if he booked Ella. Because Marilyn showed up every night, so did everyone else—and that's how Ella became a sensation.

Ella never forgot Marilyn's kindness. And she loved the ill-fated screen siren for far more than that. They often got together, with Ella cooking a meal for the two of them. They bonded over their miserable and not dissimilar childhoods—although Ella was the more reticent of the two when it came to discussing that period of her life.

The Canadian director Atom Egoyan should make a movie of their friendship. Hey, I'll produce it! I think Beyoncé or Queen Latifah would be perfect.

It's a mystery why there hasn't been an important movie about Ella's life. Hollywood loves a tragic background for its biopic subjects—witness

Billie Holiday. It's always bugged me that people assume Ella had a picket-fence upbringing and therefore doesn't have either the glamour or the crash-and-burn narrative to rate a major movie. She was locked in a New York State reformatory after her mother died, and then did a stint with her possibly abusive stepfather. She danced in tattered castoffs on street corners for spare change, and even ran numbers. She was always self-conscious about her looks—"I used to wish I was pretty," she said—yet boldly entered the entertainment field, which prizes beauty and discards pretty much everything else. About jazz drummer Chick Webb, who had a spinal deformity, turning Ella down to perform with him because she was not beautiful or glamorous enough, Margo Jefferson wrote in the *New York Times*: "Too ugly, said the bandleader with the tubercular spine."

Perhaps because of her difficult childhood, Ella loved performing for children. She would have the Royal York bring a thousand inner-city kids to the Imperial Room to see her; she wanted to make it a real outing for them, and give them a chance to appreciate the acoustics. She did many fundraisers on behalf of diabetes and children's charities, with numerous appearances at Variety Club lunches.

If Ella was in town, I knew she would agree in a heartbeat to appear at any fundraising gala I proposed—but I never asked her, for that very reason. Knowing she would say yes, and also that she would not accept payment, I was embarrassed to impose. And she was already doing so much for so many good causes.

She repaid the hospitality I showed her in Toronto many times over by cooking for me at her grand and lovely home in Beverly Hills, just north of Sunset Boulevard. She had a warm, joking relationship with her housekeeper; Ella credited laughter with getting her through so much in her life. I loved her self-deprecating sense of humor. Once, when asked why she was singing at a Variety Club lunch, she said, "Well, I am a singer and I am in town, and they are a charity and they promised me a free lunch. You know, most charities forget to feed the talent."

And on another occasion, when a reporter asked her what it felt like to be considered the greatest singer in the world, she responded: "Honey, you should go ask Sarah Vaughan."

At her home, she would make a barbecue for us, with honey-drizzled fruit salad for dessert—but she always checked the glycemic index of everything she served, for her sake and mine.

I named my first dog, a Tibetan terrier, Ella. The dog had separation anxiety and went with me everywhere. My dogs have always mirrored my health issues; Ella the dog had kidney failure when I had kidney failure. "I do hope that dog learns how to sing," Ella said when she learned of the four-footed Ella in my life.

I stayed in touch with the real Ella over the years as her diabetes took its toll, but she was always more concerned, in the best motherly way, with my own sugar levels. Late in life, she had both legs amputated due to diabetic complications and began refusing to see old friends. I called to see how she was, and in her true selfless way she just kept asking if I was keeping my sugar under control. "You know, if you get the best wines and scotch all you really need is one glass of it," she advised. "And keep away from the baklava!"

I could never figure out my fierce attraction to Ella. A friend asked whether I was like a son to her, but I don't think so. I loved to hear her sing, of course, but it was more than that. She made all of us feel special and equal. There was none of the glamour and the trappings one might expect with the First Lady of Song. Some of those who have criticized her for playing it safe, or for catering to white audiences, do not know her history and all the racist taunts and backlash she faced in her career. She often gave credit to her manager, jazz concert promoter Norman Granz, who sought to integrate jazz audiences and who was arrested along with Ella, Dizzy Gillespie, Illinois Jacquet, and Ella's personal assistant Georgiana Henry, in Houston, Texas, in 1955. Granz had been in the wings while Gene Krupa's band was onstage, and he rushed to intercede when undercover vice was busting everyone in Ella's dressing room. Granz blocked the bathroom door and was threatened at gun-point, but he didn't want to budge and give them time to plant drugs they could then "discover" later. They all were later released on fifty dollars bail, and with the cops asking the stars for autographs, but Granz spent $2,000 of his own money fighting the charges. He won. It wasn't a safe or easy road to travel, trying to integrate audiences or to perform at a time and in parts of the country where injustice was rampant and the disparity between the races was wide.

After Ella died in 1996, my friend Randy Erickson bought one of her purses at auction and gave it to me as a present. It was the one about which Ella had joked, "That purse has gone with me everywhere, more so than any man, and more dependable in every single way."

I keep it close.

"IT'S BAD ENOUGH THAT PEOPLE ARE DYING OF AIDS,
BUT NO ONE SHOULD DIE OF IGNORANCE."

Elizabeth Taylor

Elizabeth Taylor tries on my pearls

Elizabeth Taylor was one of us girls. I never called her Liz. And, for the record, do not call me Sal.

It wasn't about talking to "Elizabeth Taylor"; it was more like having a girlfriend over. She was glam, courageous, and generous, but she was also funny, caring, and a keen businesswoman. Like many stars, she put on an Oscar-winning act when that was what the situation called for. But when we went around Toronto checking out art galleries, it became clear how knowledgeable and savvy she was. She knew her art really well. Her father, Francis, had been an art dealer with his own gallery at the Beverly Hills Hotel, with clients that included Greta Garbo. She introduced me to the work of the Welsh artist Augustus John, whom her dad had represented. I knew she had several of John's pieces, along with a Degas, a van Gogh, and some Warhols, but I only discovered how vast her art and jewelry collections were when Christie's put them up for auction after her death and the pieces brought staggering prices. She collected many classic works of art with the same passion she devoted to her huge and wise investments in jewelry. One of the necklaces Richard Burton bought her in 1969 for $37,000 went for $11.8 million in 2011—in part because she was known to have worn it. Some of the proceeds went to her AIDS foundation.

Just to have a bit of freedom and get away from her celebrity, she would dress as if she were in her garden, so no one would notice her. She wore headscarves—and not Hermès, which might have tipped someone off—and big dark sunglasses, with dark or white jeans. Disguised her voice. We cruised an antiques market where she paid cash to buy me a couple of Lalique candlesticks, with no one recognizing her or seeing her name on a credit card, or forcing her back into being on-brand. You may be surprised to know how often I brought Swiss Chalet rotisserie chicken to the Four Seasons—and not just for Elizabeth.

The first time I met Elizabeth was in 1983, when she was in Toronto with Carol Burnett filming *Nobody Makes Me Cry*—called *Between Friends* in the United States—and I went to pick her up from her suite for an appearance at a Variety Club event. I found her sitting on the sofa, huddled in a mink coat, unwilling to go out and be "Elizabeth Taylor." She felt she didn't look good enough. It wasn't because she was a diva or mercurial. It was because insult comics, particularly Joan Rivers, had been digging in the knife about her weight, as if Elizabeth were immune to the derisive laughter, the careless jokes on late-night TV. As if she weren't a sentient human being!

I sat with her and tried to soothe her. I told her how the charity event was on behalf of kids with special needs who struggle with similar problems of self-image, of not fitting in. I also talked about how my own body image had changed over time, about how I had felt like I was on the outside of everything, but decided at some point to throw myself into the *middle* of everything, while not revealing all. Even the positions I played in sports—goalie in hockey and lacrosse, quarterback in football—were positions that are key to making other things happen.

Every time I ran into Elizabeth after that, I would say something unassuming, like, "Hi, I don't know if you remember me . . . " and she would cut me off: "Of course I remember you. How many times do you have to ask me?"

Even though I was very careful not to underestimate Elizabeth Taylor, I think we all underestimated her—how radical and smart she was. There was an incredible intelligence behind that soft voice. People made fun of her for all the wrong reasons, because they couldn't or wouldn't take her seriously, not even after all the incredible work she did to raise funds and awareness to fight the spread of HIV/AIDS. Instead, they'd make jokes about how she was really a gay man in a woman's body. Or about how her White Diamonds perfume was superficial, insignificant—about mere beauty—instead of being a smart business decision that played off of what so many people wanted from her.

The playwright Edward Albee said she discussed every aspect of her role in *Who's Afraid of Virginia Woolf?* with him. We tend to box certain actors into being glamour stars, to think of them as airheads, but Albee always spoke of Taylor's brilliance. I'm not surprised she managed to make the transition from *National Velvet* child star to sex symbol while also doing serious, Oscar-winning roles. While many people thought she was just a soft-spoken shrinking violet with violet eyes, she really went for it—and all in spite of an astonishing number of health problems and near-death experiences, including back pain, surgeries, stints in rehab, a tracheotomy, hip replacements, a benign brain tumor, skin cancer, and congestive heart failure. She was in so much pain all the time that I often brought her, at her request, codeine/paracetamol tablets, which were available over the counter in Canada and not in the United States.

At an early event for amfAR (the Foundation for AIDS Research), someone at my table jokingly asked her whether she was more like her misunderstood "slut of all time" character in 1960's *BUtterfield 8* or the struggling stateswoman in 1963's *Cleopatra*.

"There are days we all feel like the woman in *BUtterfield 8*," she replied with a laugh.

I would have to agree. Who wouldn't want to sleep with an angry, brooding Laurence Harvey?

People made fun of her for getting married eight times, as if that were a slut-of-all-time move, when it was, in its way, quite old-fashioned, especially at a time when the gay men around her juggled numerous partners. "In my day if you wanted to sleep with someone," she famously said, "you married them"—although that was not the whole story, as we later found out when Peter O'Toole revealed their affair.

Elizabeth was in Toronto to promote White Diamonds when she admired a particular brooch and pearls I was wearing. This led to a discussion of vintage jewelry, something in which we both invested and for which we shared a passion. I had a safe full of jewels: antique clips, pearls, and some diamond and sapphire necklaces I had designed.

"You should come over one day for coffee and try on some jewelry," I said.

"Why not?" she responded. "How about tomorrow morning?"

I hadn't expected such an immediate response.

"Um, sure . . ."

First, a word about my pearls.

Back when I co-owned Famous Players Media with Viacom and contributed hugely to their bottom line, their finance people told me I could not talk to the investment community, that they would not take me seriously. Because I wore jewelry. But my pearls are my badge of courage. And everyone can recognize me by my pearls.

So. Elizabeth Taylor.

The next day was a Saturday. That meant I had to get up early and do everything—go to the market, whip up something special, clean the place to within an inch of its life—but I only had time for essentials. Which meant flowers.

Elizabeth took a cab from her hotel to my downtown Toronto

condo, where the concierge didn't recognize her in her white pants and big sunglasses, her hair hidden beneath a scarf. It was just a fun outing for her, as rare as that can be in a star's life. An escape from being handled all the time. A time to have fun and talk about nothing in particular, and certainly not about what it was like working with and twice marrying Richard Burton.

Elizabeth sat at my dining room table with an espresso while I opened the safe. Once the jewelry came out, there was no more talk of art or philosophy. Jewelry was serious business, and she devoted her full attention to it, trying on piece after piece. I tried on her necklace, too, but I was not going to tell Elizabeth Taylor to hand over her earrings.

She had a keen eye. She knew about cut and clarity. She understood the provenance of antique brooches. She often bought such items for her own pleasure—but also as a savvy investment. "Sometimes all you need is to throw a stunning piece of jewelry on top of a plain dress," she said. "They only notice the jewelry."

She said she didn't feel comfortable traveling with her good jewelry, and that sometimes, the pieces she traveled with were fakes made expressly to match the originals. "You can't really tell," she insisted. And who would ever think Elizabeth Taylor would wear a copy? However, when it came time to wear a Chopard necklace, "Of *course* that's going to be real! If I'm going to wear a Chopard, it's not going to be fake." She did not wear her jewelry or clothing as some sort of brand advertising or on loan for an occasion. We girls wear our own jewels, and sometimes we even help design them.

Elizabeth had a natural affinity for gay men, and they for her. She came out for gay rights in the fifties and early sixties—a chance she took that people of her generation usually didn't. She sheltered and loved and was associated with gay people in the industry.

"They kept asking me why I had an AIDS foundation, why I cared? I wasn't gay and I didn't have AIDS," she told Larry King in 1990. "And

I told them that the only reason anyone knows who I am in this world is because of the support and efforts made on my behalf by gay people. They believed in me when I didn't know how to believe in myself. Take away all the paintings, all the music, all the dance, all the films, all the theater, all the architecture and design, all the science, all the books; everything that was created by gay people. There would be so little left that what was left wouldn't even matter."

At that early amfAR event, one of my friends asked her if she had known Rock Hudson was gay when they were making the 1956 movie *Giant*.

"You're probably too young to remember, but there was an old line that if you wanted to squelch rumors about a star's sexuality, you put him in a film with me," she said of her history of gay co-stars, including Laurence Harvey, James Dean, Sal Mineo, Rock Hudson, and Montgomery Clift.

"Have you seen the French poster for *Giant*? The art director had fun with it," she added. "A very homoerotic design. I'm looking up at James Dean like I'm about to give him a blowjob. He's holding a cigarette suggestively near his crotch, and Rock is in the background staring straight at him. No mystery there!"

The studio ultimately decided such an ad campaign was better "for the French." The American campaign opted for something safer. "It's like we were all kind of in on the joke," she said. "Or maybe we were all having a joke on the world."

After that, I began looking for auctions of original film posters. Among others, I acquired several that Taylor had mentioned as being of note, including the original German poster of Liza Minnelli in *Cabaret* and the original one of Catherine Deneuve for *Belle de jour*. I have an original *BUtterfield 8* poster hanging in my office, and an autographed photo of Montgomery Clift hanging in one of our bathrooms.

Finally, the prize: I was able to land a life-sized original of the smoldering French poster for *Giant*.

That is the best part of curating art. It can mean different things to different people—bringing back a memory, or a story. It always means something special to those who live with it, the how and why they acquired it. I can't walk past that *Giant* poster without a smile. I get it. Sometimes a cigarette is not just a cigarette.

Katharine Hepburn turns me down

Katharine Hepburn was a tall, patrician presence who didn't take guff from anyone. She did not try to hide her fiery intelligence or quick wit. Some mistook that innate dignity for arrogance, but she was truly lovely and approachable, a rarity in tightly corseted, male-dominated old Hollywood.

Like the rest of the world, I was a fan. I often stayed at an empty apartment that my cousin offered for my use on Manhattan's Forty-Seventh Street. I would see Hepburn doing that brisk walk of hers near her townhouse at 244 East Forty-Ninth Street, where she lived for over sixty years. I would say hi and make eye contact, and she would say hi back. Yes, in New York, where allegedly no one talks to strangers!

I was not the only person to run into her in the historic Turtle Bay Gardens neighborhood in those days. In New York, it's possible to run into famous people pretty often. But I admit I was watchful on her street, and not just to take in the design of the graceful wrought-iron balustrade on the second floor of her townhouse; there was always the hope of catching a glimpse of the Woman of the Year. I loved her independent feminist streak and how she wore trousers to work at RKO in the days when women faced arrest for "masquerading as men" in public. I loved how she didn't care for the red carpet and wasn't about to turn herself into a billboard for the latest au courant designer, even though she had played Coco Chanel in her only stage musical.

She gave huge performances, as in *The Lion in Winter* and *The Trojan Women*, without insulting the audience by changing her accent. Anyway, why would they speak in ancient Troy like modern Greek immigrants in The Bronx? It would be an insult to the audience and the culture. The screenplay and performance should be what captivate you, not concern over enunciation gymnastics. I'm not interested in seeing a showboat who can do an accent fifteen ways from Sunday, like juggling hoops of flame on a variety show. It's not as if Laurence Olivier did *Hamlet* with a Danish accent or gave Romeo an Italian accent. Should Elizabeth Taylor have used a Ptolemaic Egyptian accent to play Cleopatra? Excuse me, but this whole accent thing drives me crazy. I want to see the actor acting, not worry about whether they are about to trip up.

Hepburn was Hepburn was Hepburn—and yet she carried an incredible mystique, which I believe she loved and cultivated. None of this Hollywood marketing and gossip and photo shoot crap. Always on her own terms. The haughty goddess, seemingly out of character, even shared her favorite brownie recipe with the public. In a dessert cookbook by *Food & Wine*, step one tells us to add the eggs and vanilla to the melted cocoa and butter mixture and "beat it all like mad."

It's always a matter of who you know and who *they* know. In this way, I eventually found myself at a luncheon in Hepburn's backyard, with Douglas Fairbanks Jr. and some film students the two were encouraging toward boldness and taking chances. She referenced her neighbor Stephen Sondheim—"He has a *special friend*"—to let me know she was with it when it came to gays. She had a well-known history of working with them, though I wondered whether she was hinting at a kind of confirmation of the rumors that she, too, was open to having "a special friend."

She spoke frankly about making *The Lion in Winter* and called her otherwise-beloved co-star Peter O'Toole "a pig" for taking any role that came along and for all the sex and drinking. She thought O'Toole was a rare talent but wished he had chosen his parts better. He was of the "it pays the mortgage" school, but Kate thought he would have been a bigger star, in addition to being the acting icon he was, if only he had been more strategic in his choice of roles.

She spoke movingly about making *Guess Who's Coming to Dinner* in 1967. She knew it would be the last film for the love of her life, the much older Spencer Tracy, who by that time could work only a few hours each day. She was proud that he could end his career on a movie about racial tolerance, and surrounded by her, Sidney Poitier, and her niece Katharine Houghton, who was named after her. Tracy died of a heart attack at age sixty-seven, just seventeen days after his final scene wrapped.

Kate's own last film was *Love Affair* in 1994, with Warren Beatty and Annette Bening. She was eighty-seven and showing pronounced effects of Parkinson's disease, defying expectations that she should just hang it up and keep her Parkinson's to herself. Again, our Kate, breaking down barriers.

At the time of that lunch with Kate, the video industry was in its prime. I filled her in on the medium and how it gave new generations the opportunity to discover the classics, and proposed giving her a lifetime achievement award as a way to honor her entire body of work.

I thought she said yes.

She loved Toronto, she said, and seemed quite interested in hearing about video and film rights and changes in content delivery. She seemed willing to accept the honor, with the money going to charity, but perhaps it was my imagination. What was I thinking, anyway? This was a woman who'd had twelve Oscar nominations and won four, and never once showed up to the ceremony unless it was to honor someone else.

I have two items on my office wall to remind me of her—one is a portrait by the Hollywood glamour photographer George Hurrell. The other is the note Hepburn laboriously typed out to me on an old-fashioned Underwood and personally signed after I followed up with her about the details of coming to Canada for her award.

Dear Salah Bachir,

I'm grateful to you for telling me that I have won an Award.
At the same time I have to say to you that I don't go to these celebrations. I think you should give it to someone who would love to attend because I am unwilling to pay that price of fame.
Thank you anyway.

Katharine Houghton Hepburn

"ONE MOMENT SHE WAS A DISCIPLINED GODDESS AND DIVA,
ADEPT AT CREATING BEFORE MY CAMERA THE ILLUSION OF IMPOSING
MAJESTY BEFITTING THE OPERATIC HEROINES SHE PORTRAYS.
THE NEXT, RELAXED AND AT REST BETWEEN PHOTOGRAPHS, SHE WAS
DISARMINGLY GIRLISH, ENTHUSIASTIC, AND FREE OF PRIMA DONNA
PRETENSE. SHE SPOKE OF HER MAGNIFICENT VOICE ALMOST AS A
SEPARATE ENTITY—A UNIQUE, GOD-GIVEN GIFT—TO BE CARED FOR,
PROTECTED, AND, WHEN NECESSARY, MOLLIFIED."

Yousuf Karsh, photographer

Jessye Norman
makes a pact with me

I am embarrassed to admit that the first time I had lunch with Jessye Norman, I had no idea who she was. I was much more excited about having met Lawrence Taylor of the New York Giants a few days earlier.

When this woman entered, this vision, people began to clap one by one as she made her way to our table. Such beauty and grace! So effortless!

I was there at Lutèce, which became one of my five favorite restaurants ever, at the invitation of my uncle Chawki, Lebanon's ambassador to the UN at the time. I was nervous as he introduced us, and I blurted out, "I don't know who you are, but you are obviously loved!"

Then, to break the ice and have it melt all over my shoes, I stupidly told Jessye Norman that I could imagine wearing everything she had on.

"Maybe when I'm done with *them*," she said, jokingly referring to the tableful of UN dignitaries my uncle had invited.

I worried that I had embarrassed my uncle, whom I adored, but

Jessye rescued me immediately, and that told me all I needed to know about her. "Oh, this is going to be fun," she said with a laugh.

I could trust Uncle Chawki to choose the wines with our meal, even though he was one of those puzzling people who tasted food but never really ate it. The same, apparently, went for the size-two Chanel-suited ambassador's wife sitting across the table. I feared that if I left the ordering to them, I'd wind up stopping for a pretzel from a street vendor after lunch. So, when chef André Soltner came to our table to exchange pleasantries and ask what we were thinking of having, I blurted out: "*You* are the chef, monsieur. Feed us!"

Before anyone at the table could berate me, Soltner said that those were the words every chef loves to hear.

Perhaps it was no coincidence that the two larger-sized people in the group bonded over food, but that's what we did, and the "just feed me" line was one I went on to use on top chefs all over the world until dialysis eventually curtailed what I could eat.

But I hadn't finished putting my foot in my mouth and chomping away! When the woman who dominated La Scala, whose voice was "a grand mansion of sound," per *New York Times* music critic Edward Rothstein, asked me if I liked opera, I decided it was a swell time for brutal honesty: "Opera wasn't exactly something we did on a Saturday night in working-class Rexdale when I was growing up." Nevertheless, by the end of that first lunch, I had promised Jessye that I would learn about opera and give it a shot. We made a pact that if I could learn to love opera, she would happily perform in Lebanon.

We both kept our promises.

Jessye got me tickets to the Met, probably to make sure I kept my side of the bargain. I didn't care for the supertitles at first—although I grew to love them, as they helped me follow the plot—but I was smitten with the sets and the power of the costumes, the music, the whole atmosphere of people really dressing up, the fantasy of it all. It reminded me of those British miniseries where everything's good, they all live in a castle, no one mentions slavery or the evils of the British Empire, and even the servants are glamorous and have wonderful clothes and sleeping quarters.

Jacob and I became regulars at local opera and ballet, and at the Four Seasons Centre for the Performing Arts, where we eventually purchased season tickets and joined the President's Council. There's an old Marxist saying, "relationships are capital," and I have to admit that all this upscale hobnobbing was good for my business, even though it was not at all why I was doing it. I was doing it for Jessye. Later, when I really got into it, I was doing it for me. Opera is an overarching experience, and it includes the audience. There is a huge amount of fantasy, an even bigger diversion.

As for Jessye, she performed at the Baalbek International Festival. She later said it was one of the most magical places she had ever been.

A friend once described Jessye as La Pasionaria, the passionflower, a common reference to the Spanish Republican and anti-fascist Dolores Ibárruri, but in this case in reference to her unending joy in people and life. The night after that first lunch with Jessye at Lutèce, I phoned two friends. The first was the Canadian philanthropist Nada Ristich, and when I told her I had met this beautiful, stylish, lovely woman, an opera singer and recitalist by the name of Jessye Norman, she screamed, "What do you mean you don't know who she is?!"

The second friend demanded that they take my gay card away.

But I think I more than made up for it. I saw Jessye again on several occasions, the last time in 2018 when she traveled to Toronto as the first woman to win the Glenn Gould Prize. Every time we saw each other we would end by saying, "Can't wait to see you again." I wanted to see more of her, but by then my dialysis schedule would not permit. I promised we would catch up in New York soon, and she was excited that I was working up to a kidney transplant.

One of the last times we spoke, in September 2019, I told her that I blasted her version of the gay national anthem "Somewhere" at the hospital whenever they were changing my stoma bag. It brought back the occasions when she had put her index finger to her lips and looked directly at me in the audience while she performed that song, and I would melt.

"At least you survived sepsis," she said. "But it must be torture for you if the food is terrible."

That night, I could swear Jessye was singing "Somewhere" to me in person, lulling me to sleep all the way through the PA system squawks, a solid night's sleep for the first time since I'd been in the hospital. The next day, I called her back to check if maybe it had really happened.

She laughed and said, "Honey, you would *know* if I sang you 'Somewhere'!"

A few weeks later, on September 30, I received several calls from a number I didn't recognize. When I finally picked up after the third or fourth try, my friend Nick was on the line, sobbing. He said Jessye had died at seventy-four from septic shock and multiple organ failure, an outcome of a spinal-cord injury she had suffered in 2015. The poignancy was not lost on me as I lay there in the hospital with sepsis of my own.

That entrance so many years ago at a small restaurant, so casual but with such presence, beauty, and grace, will stay with me longer than any entrance on the grandest opera stage.

Eggs Benedict with Tennessee Williams

In October 1980, three years before his death at age seventy-one, the stupendous American playwright Tennessee Williams came to Vancouver for a spell. He was hardly at the top of his game while he served as writer-in-residence at the University of British Columbia, mounting a failed production of *The Red Devil Battery Sign* at the Vancouver Playhouse, but he could be quite charming, as rent boys must have found when he reportedly had them strip to their underwear in his hotel room and read to him from the Bible. I do wonder which passages, but as far as scandal goes, it sounded pretty tame compared to what I recall reading in the Bible.

When a friend heard I was going to be in Vancouver, he suggested I look up his gay cousin, who was involved with the Playhouse. You know how it is sometimes—well-meaning friends set you up with the only other gay person they know. And why not? I took the bait. Innocent enough, right?

On my second outing with the cousin for a perfectly delightful brunch, he brought along none other than the man himself. Needless to say, Tennessee Williams was the best third wheel imaginable.

"I'll have the eggs Benedict and fruit salad on the side," said Williams. Not quite up there with "I have always depended on the kindness of strangers," but I was impressed enough to order the same, even though I had never tasted eggs Benedict before and wasn't entirely sure what they were.

The restaurant was one of those places with a commanding view and breakfast menus that were long and laminated. Williams had notoriously fallen prey in his later years to alcoholism, but at brunch that day he was enormously entertaining and told the best stories. In the middle of one, a woman approached our table and asked for an autograph.

He fixed her with an imperious glare. "How do you know who I am?" he commanded in his Southern drawl.

"*A Streetcar Named Desire* is one of my favorites," she burbled, not at all cowed by being in the presence of a literary lion.

"Kind of you to say," said the literary lion.

"Yeah, a helluva movie!" She did not realize the enormity of her faux pas. "Ever consider writing a sequel?"

Williams signed the laminated menu for her quite cordially, despite how long and unwieldy it was, and signed over a napkin as well before she returned to her table.

"A *sequel*," he blasted after she left. "A SEQUEL!"

The more he chewed over the idea, the more impassioned he became.

"Good lord, can you imagine doing that now? Who would be Stella? Bella Abzug would be Stella!" he said with a hearty laugh. "Brando, all three hundred pounds of him, and two hundred and fifteen pounds of Bella!"

Then, recreating Brando's famous "Stella" line, he brayed: "BELLLL-AAA! Get me a beer!" He followed that with a line that fell somewhere between "I'll have the eggs Benedict" and "What is the victory of a cat on a hot tin roof," but it's one I'll always remember: he declared that in a statement for feminism, "Bella will slap Marlon on the cheek and say, 'Go fucking get it yourself!'"

I refuse to line up for much, but I would have lined up for that one—along with the rent boys reading from the Bible. Double bill, anyone?

"IN A SERIES, YOU LIVE WITH ONE CHARACTER DAY IN
AND DAY OUT—AND YOU ONLY HOPE IT WILL BE ONE
THAT WILL NOT DRIVE YOU CRAZY."

Elizabeth Montgomery

Elizabeth Montgomery bewitches, bothers, and bewilders

When I was in the hospital in 2019, I asked Jacob to download a few TV shows to help me take my mind off things. One of them was *Bewitched*, which holds up quite well—still campy and fun, and still relevant with its LGBTQ-ness. It was a distraction from the sepsis and ileostomy that followed my kidney transplant.

In the sitcom, which ran from 1964 to 1972, Elizabeth Montgomery plays Samantha Stephens, a witch who tries to put aside her spellbinding ways to lead a normal life with her normal husband (it was a mixed marriage!). But, you know, *she just can't help herself* . . . so whenever a situation calls for a little witchy magic, she twitches her button nose to the sound of tinkly plinks and does her best to intercede in human affairs—whether it's to help her husband land an advertising client with a clever campaign or to stop her magical meddling family from sabotaging her husband's non-supernatural suburban dream.

Of the major characters on *Bewitched*, most were played by actors who later identified as gay or at least had what it took to count as gay icons: Dick Sargent, the second actor to portray Sam's husband, Darrin, after Dick York left midway through season five with a back injury; the imperial Agnes Moorehead, who played Sam's imperious mom, Endora; double-entendre master Paul Lynde as the prankish uncle (everyone should have a gay uncle like Uncle Arthur, IMO); Maurice Evans as Sam's urbane warlock father; and Alice Ghostley as the frequently disappearing nervous Nellie housekeeper Esmeralda. A mostly gay family frolic if ever there was one! Here is a woman living a double life, trying to keep her true identity secret, and who also has a wild side—as expressed in the character of Serena, also played by Montgomery as a fun-loving, devil-may-care twin cousin and convenient alter-ego. Obviously, we were all in on the joke.

I was always bewitched by Elizabeth Montgomery, an active feminist and supporter of gay rights; she and Dick Sargent were grand marshals of the Los Angeles Pride Parade in June 1992. Elizabeth's father was Robert Montgomery of *Here Comes Mr. Jordan* fame, and she said she grew up in a household chock full of her dad's gay and lesbian showbiz pals.

So, when a chance presented itself to attend a Los Angeles fundraiser where Montgomery would be, I bought a table in hopes of running into her. I also began calling around to see if someone could score me a meeting or the possibility of an interview.

She agreed to a meet-and-greet, which turned into a leisurely lunch. She was not on board for a formal interview, but I prepared Brian Linehan–style anyway. Martin Short brilliantly satirized Linehan's famously meticulous research before interviewing celebrities with his "Brock Linehan" character on an *SCTV* parody. I knew the only way to achieve this level of prep myself was to go directly to the source, and Brian did not disappoint.

"Ask her if she slept with Elvis and JFK and Gary Cooper," he instructed me.

She probably would have answered, "No, *they* slept with *me*," but I knew I would never ask her such questions. It was her business if she did. And holy fuck, who wouldn't?

"Ask her whether Agnes Moorehead was a lesbian."

"Uh-huh." I was far more impressed, though, that Moorehead was the first woman to co-host the Academy Awards.

"Did you know that Elizabeth's great-grandfather, Archibald Montgomery, was a sixth cousin once removed to Lizzie Borden?" Brian asked me.

"The axe murderer?"

"She was acquitted," he said. "But Elizabeth played her in a 1975 TV movie without knowing they were related!"

When I arrived at the lunch, my Brian Linehan training went out the window. All I wanted was to pour out how important Elizabeth had been to me and how much her show had changed my life. I told her how I'd already known as a young boy that I was different, and what an unexpected joy it was to turn on the TV and welcome into my childhood home Paul Lynde reading people to filth, as RuPaul might put it, or Agnes Moorehead with the fabulous outfits that made both designers and drag queens swoon.

I told Elizabeth how when I first came to Canada, my ESL teacher Mr. Mackenzie from The Elms public school told me to watch certain shows, including *Bewitched*, to pick up local expressions.

"So, I have to thank you, all these years later," I said.

"Maybe you should be thanking Mr. Mackenzie," she said with a laugh.

Although I was the one who had prepared with Brian Linehan for our meeting, Elizabeth easily turned the tables and began interviewing me. She showed keen interest in my Lebanese childhood and was curious about whether I had come out to my parents and whether I'd been bullied.

It was a wonderful lunch, but I felt sheepish afterward for acting the fan. I've met some of the most important people in the world and I didn't gush like that! There was a glow to her—internal, ethereal—that even some of the biggest celebrities lack. People were drawn to her, and I didn't want to be part of the scrum jostling for her attention, basking in it, rudely sucking up her energy. So, when Elizabeth sent me one of those "if you're ever in town give me a call" notes, I was too shy to respond and I put it off for too long. Elizabeth Montgomery died on May 18, 1995, at the age of sixty-two, just eight weeks after learning that the colon cancer she thought she had licked had returned and spread to her liver.

By then, she had spent years devoted to social and political causes, giving freely of herself to champion gay and women's rights and to enable activism on behalf of people with disabilities. At the time of her death, there was still so much more she wanted to give and do—but what a spellbinding legacy she left us with just a twitch of her nose.

Aretha Franklin doesn't disappoint

"Are you a jeweler?"

That's how Aretha Franklin greeted me the first time we met. It was the same question several people have asked, and it was understandable under the circumstances—I'd come backstage to meet the Queen of Soul dressed all in black and in a full-length sheared black mink coat with sable collar and quite a few strands of black pearls interspersed with diamond rondelles.

Wherever Aretha performed, I always bought tickets. She was one of the best performers I have seen live. Her energy and vocal range exhausted you, and those performances were usually in the best concert halls—not some monstrous sports stadium designed for a football game, where simply getting to your seat is tiring enough. A few times when I could no longer attend, I bought tickets anyway and sent friends and played Aretha CDs during dialysis, as if she were singing just for me.

I met Aretha at a few events, where we chatted about her life and career, ranging from *The Blues Brothers* to her involvement with

Martin Luther King Jr. and the civil rights movement, but our meetings were sporadic. The second time I went to see her backstage after a show, I said, "I don't know if you remember me . . ." (I have now stopped using that line; I simply introduce myself in case there is any doubt.)

"You are NOT a jeweler," she said, to my delight. "But I see you dressed up for me."

We were both a bit overweight and loved jewelry and, at the time, fur—I'm not sure I would wear fur anymore—and it was the start of a kinship. Over time, she'd always end our discussions with a nod to my choice of jewelry, saying: "You didn't disappoint."

I saw her perform at the annual Elton John AIDS Foundation fund-raiser in November 2017 in the cavernous, transporting space of Manhattan's Cathedral Church of St. John the Divine. By then, she was riddled with pancreatic cancer, but it didn't affect her performance. Even as a shadow of her former self, she was as powerful as ever. She still had the room at her beck and call. Respect.

I went over to where she was having dinner after the show with her bandmates and backup singers. She could see I was wearing emeralds. "You didn't disappoint," the Memphis-born Queen of Soul said, using our secret code.

"Neither did you," I replied. "You were fabulous."

She gave one of those "give me five minutes" waves.

"We'll catch up later," I said, not wanting to interrupt.

I assumed there would be a later, but that would be Aretha's final public performance.

Eartha Kitt is not for sale

I can't listen to "Santa Baby" without feeling a bit bittersweet. I adored Eartha Kitt—generous, intelligent, fierce, wickedly funny. Sharp memory and keen attention to detail. Listening to that song today brings sadness that she is gone, but also so many memories.

I met her in the 1980s through the Variety Club. After that, I saw her every chance I got, in Toronto or New York, and we developed a warm friendship.

One night after a performance, Eartha admired my black pearls and told me I reminded her of Orson Welles, who was a champion of hers and helped launch her career. In 1950, at age twenty-two, in one of her earliest stage roles, she played Helen of Troy in *Time Runs*, a Welles adaptation of *Faust*. She adored the man and his passions, his charm and his genius. In what way could I possibly remind her of him?

"It will take more than incredibly generous compliments to give you a strand of my pearls," I joked, which belied how touched I was by her attention. When I did offer her the pearls sometime later, she would not accept.

She was one of the first supporters of gay marriage and rights, even before many of us had embraced the idea of marriage. "I feel very close to the gay crowd because we know what it feels like to be rejected," she once said. "We're asking for the same thing. If I have a partner and something happens to me, I want that partner to enjoy the benefits of what we have reaped together. It's a civil-rights thing, isn't it?"

At a lunch at the Lyndon Johnson White House in 1968, she turned to the First Lady and said: "You send the best of this country off to be shot and maimed" in the Vietnam War. "No wonder kids rebel and take pot." The encounter reportedly reduced Lady Bird to tears, and made front-page headlines: "Eartha Kitt Denounces War Policy to Mrs. Johnson." And, bam, Kitt was virtually unemployable in the United States for the next decade. The blacklisting extended to the CIA keeping a dossier on her, portions of which the *New York Times* printed. She would say it was the gays who kept her alive in the public imagination during those dark times, through their loving imitations of her and also in the sense of lifting her spirits.

She was beyond generous with her time and her soul. In 2014, she kicked off the capital campaign for The 519, one of the most prominent gay community centers in the world. The night before, we stayed up until 4 a.m., chatting. I had the suite next door and only left because she had to rest up for a show, but those late-night chats became a habit when we saw each other. She went down into the audience and sat on the lap of well-known financier Jim Fleck, getting an extra $10,000 donation from him by crooning her signature song, you know the one, about the old-fashioned girl just looking for an old-fashioned millionaire.

I asked her once if she would sing "Santa Baby" over the phone to a potential donor for an AIDS charity.

"How much are you getting?" she asked.

"Ten thousand dollars."

"Tell him I'll do it for twenty-five K."

"Wonderful. How much of that do you want?"

"Oh, don't be ridiculous!" she chided me. "I am not for sale."

I tried to reason with her. I told her people are always asking artists to do stuff for free, but no one ever expects that from other professionals, like dentists and lawyers.

"Fine," she said. "If you ever get a dentist to donate their services for a year, I'll take it."

We got the $25,000, and she wouldn't take a penny. I hope they kept a recording of it somewhere.

Eartha once asked whether I had anyone in my life, someone to whom she should be especially nice. It was the same way my father, in his roundabout way, used to ask about my love life—although Eartha didn't need to know the nature of any of my relationships. She had gone around for so long pigeonholed as this or that; she would not inflict that on someone else.

I told Eartha about Lance, a special friend who had done wonders for my self-esteem. "You'll meet him tomorrow night," I assured her. When the time came, I was too busy running around to bring Lance backstage, but at the end of her performance, Eartha went to the edge of the stage to shake his hand from the audience. "I want to meet the people who make you happy," she told me.

We stayed in touch, and she even telephoned after I lost my father.

"It will be a tough Christmas for you this year," she acknowledged. "But know that he loved passionately and was loved in return, which is all we need to have." This from a woman who never knew her father but who counted the world as her family.

Eartha Kitt died on Christmas Day 2008 from colon cancer at the age of eighty-one. We had a huge family gathering at the house that day, with "Santa Baby" on heavy rotation.

Trim the Christmas tree with decorations from Tiffany's? We had long believed in her. The house was decorated with silver and ornaments and Christmas plates, all from Tiffany's.

"I STARTED AT THE TOP AND HAVE BEEN
WORKING MY WAY DOWN EVER SINCE."

Orson Welles

Orson Welles
gives a master class

Orson Welles was the only interview I agreed to pay for, although I had no need for it. He didn't have anything new to promote, but I had studied *Citizen Kane* and *Touch of Evil*, along with the rest of his film career, and I needed to meet the legend.

In 1975, he was the third winner of the American Film Institute's Life Achievement Award. The first went to director John Ford and the second to actor James Cagney; this was the first time it went to someone who was both an actor and director.

But by the time we met in 1983 or '84, he was the butt of jokes and had trouble getting any real work. Everyone ridiculed him for his weight and his soused Paul Masson wine commercials. Joan Rivers savaged him, as did critics with an axe to grind—such as Pauline Kael, who made her own bid for relevancy in 1971 with her fifty-thousand-word essay "Raising Kane." The piece damaged his reputation, even though it was full of half-truths or outright lies, which also tarnished the gleam of the *New Yorker*. Kael had not interviewed key players; nor, apparently, had the magazine thoroughly fact-checked her claims.

The 2020 Netflix movie *Mank*, largely based on Kael's shoddy essay, further denigrated the contributions of Welles, who co-wrote, produced, directed, and starred in what is largely considered the most important movie ever made. *Mank* has a revisionist script by Joseph L. Mankiewicz—who claims that his father, the screenwriter Herman J. Mankiewicz, was the true force behind *Citizen Kane* and that Orson had little to do with it. *Mank* received ten nominations at the ninety-third Academy Awards, a reminder that Hollywood still has a complicated relationship with the genius of Orson Welles, a man who never wanted to cater to that community anyway.

Once again, Hollywood was judging talent by the pound, as if all their good works weighed nothing in the balance. Imagine what they would have said if Katharine Hepburn's weight had ballooned to three hundred pounds, how that would have been the lasting narrative about her, overriding everything else.

I picked up the tab for my lunch with Welles, of course—but his people had asked me to pay for the interview on top of that. Orson pitched a fit once he heard that his handlers had charged me. He demanded that the maître d' bring a phone to our table—yes, that is how it was done in olden times—and he yelled at them to tear up the check I'd sent, although I hadn't minded paying if it was the only way I could get a few hours with Orson Welles.

I even prepared for the interview in depth, studying up for weeks, as if I were going for a doctorate in film studies, but ultimately there was no need. I've never met anyone who talked pure stream of consciousness like Orson. The lunch, originally booked for an hour, went to two hours, then three, then four.

"This was a force of nature that came in, a creation that wiped the slate clean from the type of films that preceded him," director Martin Scorsese once said in an interview about Welles's creative influence from just that one movie. "There was never any gray with him. He told *Kane* cinematographer Gregg Toland, 'Let's do everything they told us never to do.' The low angles and deep focal-length lenses, the structure of the story, the flashbacks, the overlapping images—no one had ever seen anything like it."

I gave his people a pretext for the magazine interview: some of Orson's classic movies were just coming to video. If I had needed further pretext to talk to him, I could have used the news hook of Steven Spielberg recently buying the "Rosebud" sled from *Citizen Kane* for $60,500 at a Sotheby's auction. It was one of three balsa wood prop sleds made for the ending of the 1941 classic. Spoiler alert: The balsa models were for burning in the huge fireplace of Xanadu, the fictional estate of the massively wealthy but forever-wanting and forever-empty protagonist Charles Foster Kane, for the final scene, the "big reveal." Apparently, the second sled burned so nicely that Orson decided they had all the footage they needed, so the third sled survived—barely. A studio watchman rescued it from a trash heap outside the studio prop vault. He sold it to RKO chief archivist John Hall, who in turn put it up for auction in June 1982, where it made its way into Spielberg's collection for the next few decades.

Star Wars mogul George Lucas also reportedly had his eyes on that slice of film history, but gallantly stepped aside to let his pal Spielberg bid, and Spielberg thereafter claimed it was his favorite bit of memorabilia, more precious than artifacts from his own movies. He kept it for more than three decades before donating it in 2018 to the planned Academy Museum of Motion Pictures in Los Angeles.

Despite the gossip about Orson's drinking, he and I shared but a single bottle of red during our four-hour lunch. It was a French red, not a California wine like the Masson variety he shilled for; those TV ads were just a job, pretty much all he could get while he couldn't obtain funding for the many projects that endlessly bristled in his brain.

Meanwhile, the finger food we had ordered sat largely untouched.

We simply talked; or, I should say, it was mostly Orson doing the talking: Marlene Dietrich. Rita Hayworth. His films, his process. The man never stayed on topic. He spoke in his resonant, mesmerizing voice, with his beetling brows forming punctuation marks. "It's not about cinema, it's about the story . . . ," he boomed, sucking me in, before spinning vertiginously down rabbit holes of thoughts and ideas. I hung on for dear life to his verbal roller coaster. I was relieved when he came up for breath so that I could collect my thoughts and process his last sentence. He was furiously intelligent, furiously creative. It was an amazing conversation, my own private master class. I tried my best not to show that I was in awe of him, but I was in good company, as the trail of people in awe of him went way back to Kenneth Tynan and François Truffaut being starstruck by Welles's earliest creative output. He went—according to David Thomson in *Rosebud: The Story of Orson Welles*—"from being what Hollywood saw as the naughtiest boy, deserving of rebuke and comeuppance, to being the most lastingly influential of American filmmakers. For in his willful stress on genius, independence, and mercurial mystery, he offered a treacherous beacon to generations of young people seeking to make more movies."

Welles was bitter about his increasingly negative reception in Hollywood. As Bette Davis would also complain: "They're reviewing me, not my work."

"Temperamentally averse to compromise, to getting along with the sharks and minnows in show business, Welles could move with awful speed from arrogance to wounded lament," wrote Thomson. "He comes, more and more, to be a man known not just for his works but for the things not done, the plans announced."

Welles died at age seventy on October 10, 1985, just a few hours after giving a final interview on Merv Griffin's talk show. He left behind innumerable unfinished projects.

Legendary director John Huston—whose first film, *The Maltese Falcon*, was released in 1941, the same year as *Citizen Kane*—may have summed up Hollywood's tortured relationship to Welles best in his memoir *An Open Book*:

"People are afraid of Orson. People who haven't his stamina, his force or his talent. Standing close to him, their own inadequacies show up all too clearly. They're afraid of being overwhelmed by him."

Phyllis Diller's business plan

Once, at a charity event, someone tried to coax Phyllis Diller to tell jokes while we were relaxing in a club room before the show. She cut him down swiftly yet gently: "Darling, Phyllis is on at seven thirty."

There were two Phyllis Dillers. The one onstage with the fright wig was not the one I dined with before a *Premiere* video industry gala I did with her in the mid-eighties. The creature who was waiting alone for me at the table was a beautifully dressed and groomed woman, perfectly coiffed and done up, wearing a pink Chanel suit with a single strand of pearls and a butterfly brooch. I barely recognized her, despite numerous previous encounters—but that was the brilliance and beauty of the comic persona she had created. It was so powerful, singular, and unforgettable that it was easy to overlook the complicated individual underneath.

I wanted to introduce her to one of my favorite restaurants in Toronto, with one of my favorite chefs—the world-renowned Jamie Kennedy, who received the Order of Canada for his promotion of

Canadian cuisine and his use of organic, sustainable, and locally sourced ingredients. I joined Phyllis at the table and, to my delight, the woman who always acted the clown and made a living putting herself down, belting lines such as "You know you're old if they have discontinued your blood type"—this woman began schooling the sommelier.

"I suggest a nice Chablis," said the wine steward. I hate it when restaurant staff recommend something when they haven't been asked, or hustle an item on the menu without first knowing your tastes, allergies, or dietary restrictions.

"I prefer something red," she replied.

"I'm sorry, madame, but red does not go well with halibut."

"What makes you think so? Why do you follow these silly rules?" asked the woman who had refused to follow them all her life. "A light burgundy or a mild merlot is perfect with halibut. It brings out the acidity."

The real Phyllis was funny but not self-deprecating when the spotlight was off, with no need on her own time to be the alter-ego she had so brilliantly invented for the stage. I asked before the show I was emceeing whether she needed hair and makeup done; she opened a closet that held three garishly beaded dresses, two wigs, and "normal" clothing as well. She had come prepared. "But my wigs aren't so wild anymore," she pointed out. "Tina Turner has been copying me, HAAAAA!"

For her final joke the night of that gala, Phyllis mentioned then prime minister Pierre Trudeau as being very handsome. "For the record, I haven't slept with him, HAAAAA," she told the audience, to much laughter.

As I took the microphone to thank her, I cracked, "For the record, Phyllis, I haven't slept with him either." And that was how I came out to my advertisers and supporters in the video and entertainment industries. No doubt many of them had guessed already, but it is a testament to the headiness and confidence Phyllis could instill that I chose this moment, or it chose me.

I hadn't always been comfortable onstage—far from it. Although I did events from an early age, I was usually more in the background, organizing them, booking talent, writing notes for others to speak, crafting introductions for illustrious guests. I made so many notes that I realized I was actually the best person to emcee because I could recognize people without needing notes like these, supplied by someone else. I wouldn't screw up their names. But I had severe stage fright and had to down an Ativan with a glass of red wine before I could get myself up to the microphone. It made sense for me to be there as a way to make events run smoother, but it wasn't my favorite thing, especially knowing how much I stood out from others. I was always worried about possibly saying the wrong thing. I was sensitive to being judged. Well, darlings, my fuck-you attitude was just developing, on stage at least.

Sometimes, after a huge event that ended with everyone telling me how wonderful the evening was, how well I'd done, I'd go back to my hotel feeling lonely and empty. Even when stars complimented me, it didn't help—because sometimes they meant it, and sometimes it was just something to say, and how could I know the difference? "I'm so glad to be able to do a favor for my old friend Salah," Tony Bennett once said so graciously onstage. It was such a high, getting adoration and praise, and then I was back to facing the four walls of my hotel room. (Okay, eight walls if it was a suite.) These were the same feelings one gets with an addiction, that nothing else in life can provide that high.

At lunch the day after I'd killed with my follow-up joke about Pierre Trudeau, Phyllis chided me in a motherly way: "Never upstage your talent." But she was quite lovely about it. "I've always thought you are funny," I am delighted to report she told me. "Ever think of doing stand-up? You should come on the road with me!"

"Sure," I responded. "If my career doesn't work out."

"And what is it you do, exactly?" she asked. "They tell me you're big in the oil business."

That's what some of my friends would say, making a joke out of how

I still had a hand in the family olive oil business while doing so many other things that people were never sure just who or what I was.

"Yes, darling, I am in the oil business. Olive oil, that is, and I give it away to family and friends. Not much of a way to make a living."

She gave a lovely chuckle and held my hand—and all I could think was, *My god, Phyllis, I adore that ring you're wearing!*

Everyone knows Diller's body of work: the self-deprecating "housewife" humor, the wild hair and zany clothing, the braying voice, the bejeweled cigarette holder, the eccentricity. Unlike the insult comedians, she did not mean to offend: "People come to me to escape their problems, not for me to insult them." She was a trailblazer at a time when female comics were few and far between, among the first to become a household name, and you can see her influence on Joan Rivers, Roseanne Barr, Lily Tomlin, and Margaret Cho. In the early sixties, Barbra Streisand was her opening act in Greenwich Village; today, Lady Gaga's crazy couture takes a hanger from Diller's closet.

Less well known is that Phyllis was a music conservatory alumna who had studied to become a concert pianist and later compared her rapid-fire comic delivery to music: "One joke followed the other with a flow and a rhythm . . . Everything had a natural feel to it."

She was twice married, twice divorced, bore six children, and was primarily a housewife until she started doing comedy bits—but she also spent a decade in the seventies as a piano soloist traveling with symphony orchestras under the stage name Dame Illya Dillya, and receiving seriously good reviews. The *San Francisco Examiner* called her "a fine concert pianist with a firm touch."

Each time I encountered Phyllis, she managed to surprise, with conversation flowing easily from philosophy to wine to abstract art.

She was a writer. A self-taught painter who worked in acrylics, watercolors, and oils. At university, she studied literature, history, psychology, and philosophy. Although her jokes made her sound like a terrible homemaker—"Housework can't kill you, but why take a chance?"—she was actually quite versatile in the kitchen and in 1987 even licensed her own chili recipe.

I got a better chance to discover the real Phyllis when she later invited me to her stucco mansion in Brentwood. The former conservatory student had two grand pianos and a custom harpsichord. She had an entire room devoted to file cabinets stuffed with tens of thousands of jokes she had written over a lifetime; in 2003, she donated them all to the Smithsonian.

Also, Phyllis had one of the best entertainment-industry business minds I'd ever encountered.

"What brings you to L.A.?" she asked me.

I told her I was there to see friends, but I was also packing in some business.

"Good for you, you should always work," she said. "People will forget you if you're not out there. Take it from me."

"You must be kidding," I said. "You're a legend!" I couldn't fathom the idea of anyone ever forgetting her.

"It's not the money. It gets me out of the house and keeps me current and on people's minds. It also gives me the whole joy of working and being out there. That's my business plan. Even if there's two weeks where I have nothing booked, I find a way to appear somewhere. It keeps my brand alive."

It was true—she kept herself constantly in the public eye. When she wasn't doing stand-up, she was a regular on TV shows such as *Hollywood Squares* and *The Match Game*. When she wasn't on TV, she was in movies, and when she wasn't in movies she was writing, and when all else lagged, she took up painting.

She was always more than just her comedy, but her comedy was special—subversive, really. There was a subtlety to her humor that was lacking in attack comics like Don Rickles and Joan Rivers: "His finest hour lasted a minute and a half."

In some ways, she really was revolutionary, and she knew it. Many was the time we spoke about the tragedy of people trapped in bodies they didn't want to be in. She did not feel attractive ("My photographs don't do me justice—they just look like me"), and she became a big proponent of facelifts and cosmetic surgery, loving that it was available, that she could afford it, and that the change in her appearance brought her much pleasure. She admitted to having fifteen procedures over the years, starting when she was fifty-five. After lunch one time at the Variety Club, she even left money for a mutual friend to get a nose job. She had done the same thing with Gino Empry after a performance at the old O'Keefe Centre. That time, she left a check. This time, she left cash in an envelope on the table, like leaving a tip. In a way, it *was* a tip.

Although she worked it into her comedy and, as usual, made herself the butt of the jokes, secretly she reveled in looking better, and never went off the deep end with plastic surgery the way others have. Her philosophy was that if you can find a way to change yourself to a version you'd rather be, why not do it? And she worked her ass off to afford it.

"Phyllis Diller" was to Phyllis Diller what the Little Tramp was to Charlie Chaplin, a creative device through which she could criticize what she could not if she were simply some lady, especially in those times, railing against the whims of the fashion industry or the sexism of the "Take my wife, please" comics.

To aid in the deception, she invented Fang, an imaginary, long-suffering husband. It started off as an ad lib, "old fang-face," and developed into a persona. Her first husband, Sherwood Diller, proudly told people Fang was based on him—but it was not, and Phyllis actually didn't want Sherwood taking credit for it, undoubtedly knowing all too well the restrictions that come along with being mistaken for a farcical construct. It was Fang that allowed her to go further with her humor than she would have gotten away with otherwise. As she said about a woman of her time doing stand-up, "You gotta have a husband."

In this way, with her jokes about a mythical husband and her purportedly rotten looks and housekeeping, she was quite a feminist, deftly developing a platform and audience she might not otherwise have had. If she had simply embraced cosmetic surgery as something she loved, something she reveled in, the audience would have turned on her. Instead, she paved the way, in her own way, for the idea of taking ownership of how you look and who you are. She was doing the work at a time when women still weren't supposed to be working, and she was writing and amassing more than fifty thousand jokes, too.

Who did she look up to? She loved Lucy. No surprise there. Lucille Ball built her own studio (as did Mary Pickford), but people still saw Lucy as the zany redhead and Mary as America's Sweetheart. Phyllis, too, did not want to wreck the mystique of the zany blond, even as she was building her own empire.

Although she officially "retired" from stand-up in 2002, Phyllis continued to appear in movies and as a guest on late-night talk shows. At age eighty-six, she invited me to one of her well-publicized art shows, where people came to her Brentwood home and bought her paintings. It was like an opening, with waitstaff serving champagne and canapés. I never did get to try her chili, but I sampled her cupcakes and an apple coffee cake she made.

As for her art, I was glad she had two other careers to fall back on. And if she could hear that remark, I'm sure she would crack her famous cackle, the one she added at the end of each gag—HAAAAA—to make sure everyone else was in on the joke.

Princess Margaret lights my cigarette

"Oh, you must have gotten the memo."

That dose of dry humor came from Princess Margaret, upon surveying the lunch arrayed before her: cold salmon atop salad greens, dressing on the side. White rolls. Boiled asparagus. Don't ask me why the British like to leach the taste out of perfectly good food. For dessert: strawberry shortcake and coffee. I was not sure why they had asked me to sit next to her. My charm? My devil-may-care attitude? Darling, you may be a princess, but I am a queen in these parts.

The Variety Club had indeed gotten the memo. This was the meal the palace had advised serving when the Countess of Snowdon came in 1988 for the ribbon-cutting of a new aquatic wing at Variety Village, a huge facility and sports center catering to disabled children. I was on the board and one of their top fundraisers.

Margaret is generally seen as a complicated woman with many times the personality of her older sister, Elizabeth, who unexpectedly became Queen of England at the age of twenty-five and died in 2022 after reigning for more than seventy years. Margaret, four years younger and therefore second in line to the throne after the 1952 death of their father, George VI, at fifty-six, was forever stuck between a rock and a hard place—always expected to behave in a certain way and not make a comment or have an opinion. And that was just the tip of the iceberg. The real activities of the Royal Court are no doubt more tawdry and cynical than anything a tabloid can dream up—even though the tabloids are pretty good at going at things with gusto, with knives out, like running Princess Diana into a tunnel, and to her death.

The seating arrangement was doubly mysterious given that I had made no secret of my feelings about royalty and "titles." Soapbox alert: I am all for taking down statues of old-time enslavers. I am for truth and reconciliation. I am for renaming streets. But but . . . shouldn't we also look at the bigger picture of who we bow our heads to? The British Empire reportedly shipped more than five million slaves to the Caribbean and North America before the United States even existed. Why is that not part of our national dialogue? The British press is now talking about the crimes of the British Empire in Africa, India, Ireland, and elsewhere, but Canada has remained virtually silent. Hell, even Charles has mentioned Britain's role in slavery.

So, please indulge me, Your Worship, Your Eminence, Your Honor, Your Self-Appointed So-and-So, but no titles recognized here. No kings, queens, princes, or princesses. No dames or sirs. No titles allowed. Everyone is welcome, so take a seat—and you can call yourself blue cheese if you are indeed blue cheese, all veined and moldy. My grandmother always told me that everyone is important, and no one is important.

So, you can see how mystified I was as to why they would seat me, of all people, next to a "royal."

Margaret, however, broke the mold. I was wrong about her. I saw that she simply had to do what "The Firm" told her to do, yet she managed to do it her way, in her own inimitable style, and that was what made dining with her that day such a pleasure.

"I'm dying for a cigarette," she said after the main course. We had time before the festivities began, and she saved this diabetic from an awful-looking strawberry shortcake. At one point, she had smoked sixty Chesterfields a day. She began when she was fifteen and only quit, cold turkey, in 1991, but the habit had taken its toll, and she eventually died as a result of it.

"I'll join you," I responded out of courtesy, and to protect "Her Royal Highness" from intruders and well-wishers.

Outdoors in the Scarborough suburbs of Toronto, with a tall, handsome security agent in a fabulous uniform patrolling nearby to make sure no one got too close, the princess offered me one of her ciggies. She used her elegant cigarette holder. Non-smoker though I was, I took it in like a pro!

She asked me about growing up in Lebanon and uprooting to Canada in 1965. My father had scoped out Canada for us in 1960, just two years after the United States landed fourteen thousand infantry and Marines at the Port of Beirut and Beirut International Airport.

A lovely, well-meaning woman approached us as we smoked, chatted, and managed to avoid part of the kind of luncheon Margaret could conduct in her sleep.

"I just wanted to thank you," the woman said. "I've had cancer and my brother has had cancer, and we both went to Princess Margaret Hospital, and we're both fully recovered."

Margaret was passionate about many causes—she supported the arts, particularly music and ballet—but the woman who approached us that day was confusing the real Margaret in some happy, grateful way with Princess Margaret Hospital (renamed in 2012 as Princess Margaret Cancer Centre), the largest cancer hospital in Canada and among the best in the world. The princess graciously said she was pleased the woman's family was well and seemed quite comfortable with this sort of outpouring of gratitude. Afterward, she turned to me and said, with that wry sense of humor again, "Oh dear, I hope she knows I had nothing to do with that!" And we took another puff of our cigarettes. Although The Firm does dole out its members' names as a way of showcasing its good works, such as hospitals, and although Margaret's father had died of lung cancer and she herself had had part of a lung removed to determine whether she had the disease, she didn't have a personal connection to the hospital that bore her name.

I've often recalled the conversation Margaret and I had that day about Lebanon. I'm glad I didn't end up trapped there during the war—and glad, as well, that my only real experience with being trapped came in business situations where people reacted badly to my sexuality. But I imagine Margaret often felt trapped by her royal role, albeit with the trappings of wealth and prestige to comfort her. It wasn't quite the same as being stuck in Lebanon during wartime, but she was straitjacketed by The Firm into a life she didn't choose. It seems like we are all trying to play a role, each of us reading the appropriate lines, but at least Margaret did it with style and originality.

There was no pretense with Margaret, the original "spare" of our time, long before Prince Harry came along. She was funny, charming, and carried out her duties with care and attention. It was a duty, after all, and the price she had to pay for living in that palace, but there was no hint that she resented it or was counting down how many appearances she had left to make the rent, as it were.

I will always remember her lighting my cigarette with her gold lighter, both of us making the best of it. She changed my perception of what it could mean, at least in this brief encounter, to be royal yet at the same time second banana.

"HAVE YOU ALWAYS BEEN A NEGRO OR
ARE YOU JUST TRYING TO BE FASHIONABLE?"

Lloyd Nolan as Diahann Carroll's doctor boss on Julia

Diahann Carroll makes me break into song

Diahann Carroll doesn't always get all the credit she deserves. She was too perfectly coiffed and glamorous for some. Her portrayals of authentic Black characters disturbed others. Interviewers were more interested in her affairs and marriages, which diminished her achievements and legacy.

I had been a fan of Diahann's long before I finally met her in 1995, when she was so brilliant in the Canadian production of the Andrew Lloyd Webber musical *Sunset Boulevard*. She played Norma Desmond, the grande dame first made famous on film by Gloria Swanson. They had faces then . . .

I can probably make my way blindfolded around that concert hall in North Toronto, the old Ford Centre for the Performing Arts, in part because I must have gone to see Diahann play Norma at least fifteen times. She was spectacular, and word quickly got around; I would have friends from L.A., New York, and London fly in just to see her.

I often sent her flowers with a note either backstage or to her hotel. After the third or fourth time, she had someone from Garth Drabinsky's production company, Livent, call me and invite me to a lunch. She showed up with two well-dressed people, a kind of "muscle" in case I was an axe murderer, although she laughed and clarified that it was an axe murderer "who sends the most gorgeous flowers."

Diahann had a wicked sense of humor and used a line I have since co-opted: "If you insist on sending me flowers, *these* are the flowers I like," specifying exactly which kind. She didn't like lilies or a lot of greenery padding out the arrangement. I hadn't realized my florist had included hydrangeas; she said yes to the roses, no to the hydrangeas. We settled on roses and peonies for future bouquets. Which would have been my choice in the first place.

She always looked stunning, with no wrinkles until late in life. She traveled with several elaborate wigs. She always wore a suit, such as a jacket and skirt—and had the thinnest legs I'd ever seen! Thanks to her sunglasses and scarf, you'd never realize it was Diahann Carroll wafting through the door of Bistro 990.

There was no denying she was a trailblazer: the first Black woman to win the Best Actress Tony in a musical (for *No Strings*, a 1962 play Richard Rodgers wrote especially for her). She first appeared in *Carmen Jones* (1954), with Dorothy Dandridge, the first Black woman nominated for a Best Actress Oscar (Diahann would have to wait for her own nomination until 1974's rom-com drama *Claudine*). Then there was *Porgy and Bess* (1959), the first major Hollywood picture to feature an all-Black cast. Playing a widowed nurse and independent single mom in *Julia* from 1968–71, she was the first Black woman to star in a TV series, and without having to play a household drudge! She wore a nurse's cap, not a maid's apron, which in itself was ground-shifting. *Julia*'s debut was lauded on the cover of *TV Guide* as part of what the magazine awkwardly dubbed the "Year of the Negro."

It always pained Diahann when some people carped that nurse Julia "wasn't Black enough," or that *she* wasn't Black enough. They assumed she had landed in the right place at the right time, as if it were happenstance, thoroughly ignoring her previous body of work and failing to anticipate her future gambles, including going against type to play a welfare cheat in *Claudine*.

Although Diahann's career evolved over time, it was an uphill climb. "I'm living proof of the horror of discrimination," she said when testifying in 1962 before a congressional hearing on racial bias in the entertainment industry.

She maintained her sense of humor about it, though. She joked that she needed to look her best when marching for civil rights alongside Marlon Brando, Sammy Davis Jr., Paul Newman, and Sidney Poitier.

But she was no "token Negro" in the parts she played. For *Dynasty*, in the 1980s, she wanted producer Aaron Spelling to write the role as if the character were a ruthless rich white man. "I want to be the first Black bitch on television," she said of playing Dominique Deveraux, the surprise half-sister of John Forsythe's millionaire Blake Carrington, amid a lily-white cast—which made her the only Black actress with a recurring role on a nighttime serial, as well as the first major Black character on any prime-time soap. "I certainly wasn't researching the number of Blacks on TV, but how could you fail to see they're not there?" she pointed out.

She was born Carol Diann Johnson in The Bronx to a subway conductor father and a mother who was a nurse, and grew up in Harlem as a musical prodigy who modeled for *Ebony* by the time that she was fifteen. She always considered herself a New Yorker, even when she went on to live in Los Angeles; it was Brando who goaded her into returning to New York in the 1960s to do "some real acting," and for a time, she lived at the Plaza Hotel with her daughter, Suzanne Kay— her first marriage had collapsed by then—and did as Marlon said.

Fashion model, actor, activist, dancer, trailblazer. She was determined to do it all.

She was married four times, but the relationship that blazed was with Sidney Poitier. For nine years they were Hollywood's most prominent unmarried couple—at least, unmarried to each other—but it was not a secret. They attended the 36th Academy Awards ceremony together.

She spoke about it with me several times, and also later wrote about it in a memoir, *The Legs Are the Last to Go*, about how most people assume the relationship ended because he changed his mind about leaving his wife. Actually, he had wanted for them to live together—in a ten-room apartment he bought for her on Manhattan's Upper West Side—in a six-month trial arrangement that did not include her daughter; it was something about him not wanting to exit one family situation only to plunge full-bore into another.

Naturally, Diahann refused, and from there it got messy. Ultimately, though, they remained friends for life, and over time she would wax ever more complimentary about him, telling me how smoldering hot and generous he was.

We met for meals a few times in Toronto and later at Diahann's condo at the Sierra Towers in Los Angeles, and at restaurants in New York. In 2010, twenty-five years after our first meeting, I asked her agent if Diahann would come and do a benefit for the capital campaign for The 519. The agent said Diahann would love to do it, especially because she wanted to revisit the city and see old friends. Moreover, she would do it for free. I argued that we always pay our artists and even had a sponsor lined up to cover the cost. In the end, Diahann reduced the fee I negotiated with her agent by half.

No surprise, she sold out the Four Seasons venue in just a few days and turned her forty-five-minute set into a full-on ninety-minute show. Everyone ate it up. When a friend asked why she still did these relatively small events—a fundraiser for five hundred people instead of a bigger venue for thousands—she said she always felt the love from the gay community, and that the intimacy was what had opened the door for her to have a career at all. Pure class! I once asked another entertainment legend, Cicely Tyson, whether Diahann was always this nice, and she said: "When you're that talented and confident, it's easy to be nice."

But the answer is yes, from what I could tell, she was always that nice. I would call her every year on her birthday and she would joke, "Of course you remember, because it's your favorite Ella's birthday." (She meant my Tibetan terrier, named after my *other* favorite Ella, Fitzgerald.)

Ms. Carroll could do anything, and she did it on her own terms. Don't be fooled by that perfectly coiffed hair or hold it against her, darling—it's a wig.

The lady on stage would tell you that nothing ever came easy for a Black woman, then or now. I like to remember that to nab the role of the demure nurse Julia Baker, the notoriously glam Diahann Carroll went to her screen test in a very plain dress.

It was Givenchy, but still.

Doris Day,
my secret love

I was changing in the school locker room after a lacrosse game when we all started chattering about our favorite TV shows, past and present—*Sonny and Cher*, *Hawaii Five-O*, *Mannix*. Mike Connors, of Armenian descent, played Joe Mannix, and the show often had him speaking fluent Armenian, a point in its favor around my household, as there is a huge Armenian community in Lebanon. The opening credits showed tough-guy former mercenary Mannix in a montage of running, leaping, throwing punches, and hopping a ride on what looks like a grain conveyor belt. He put the man in Mannix.

"Oh, and I just love *The Doris Day Show*," I blurted.

Crickets.

The other boys simply moved on as if I had not said a thing. It was like the board meetings I would one day experience where the agenda is already set and no one is prepared to entertain a differing point of view.

After that locker room incident, my handsome lacrosse coach made the unusual offer of driving me home, when I lived within easy walking distance.

He cleared his throat. "You're my all-star goalie," he said.

"Oh, thank you," I replied.

"And I want to keep it that way."

"Uh, okay." This was all very baffling.

"So, I'm just telling you for your own sake that no one needs to know you like Doris Day. Okay? Because people might take it the wrong way."

Huh? I had no idea what he meant, although later people would say the same thing about my love for Elton John. I was early to the game, but late to the lingo. I also never really understood the phrase "friend of Dorothy," the *Wizard of Oz*–derived euphemism for homosexual.

Why did my love for Doris Day have to stay in the shadows? What person could not swoon over those opening credits? Doris—driving to San Francisco in her pink bucket hat and matching coat. Doris—pertly leaning against the banister of a circular staircase. The show ran for five seasons, from 1968 until 1973, and was to me in retrospect a delightful mash-up of *Bewitched* and *The Mary Tyler Moore Show*, with Doris's single, career-gal character moving gaily among an often gay or gay-ish supporting cast of strapping young men. There was a same-sex couple (Alan Dewitt and Lester Fletcher) that lived next door in season two, surely a first for prime-time TV. There was openly gay actor Billy De Wolfe playing nemesis neighbor Willard Jarvis. De Wolfe was a good friend of Day's going back to when they met on the set of the 1950 movie *Tea for Two*.

Interestingly, I ran into that same high school coach many years later when he was attending an AIDS fundraiser arm in arm with his partner. "I should have known," I said dryly.

It seemed that it was never the right time to admit to liking Doris Day, at least not after her mass popularity wore off after the late fifties and early sixties. Those were the years when she starred in so many chaste romantic comedies, often opposite closeted actors such as Cary

Grant (*That Touch of Mink*, 1962) and Rock Hudson (*Pillow Talk*, 1959; *Lover Come Back*, 1961; and *Send Me No Flowers*, 1964). The renowned and highly opinionated film critic Pauline Kael dismissed it as "the Doris Day routine of flirting with bed but never getting there," and I argued that very point with Kael when I visited the *New Yorker* offices to interview her for one of my video magazines.

"Then what are you looking for, porn?" I asked. "Did Katharine Hepburn make out with Humphrey Bogart in *The African Queen*?"

(I made a friend of Kael, but putting her on the cover of the magazine was a huge mistake. It became the worst-selling issue we ever ran. But she did give me a tour of the *New Yorker* offices. When she introduced me to the famed editor William Shawn and described me as a young man publishing a video magazine, Shawn asked me how to work his newfangled VCR so he could record a program he wanted to watch.)

Doris Day's movies were how I first fell in love with her—not so much the Rock Hudson bagatelles as with Alfred Hitchcock's 1956 suspense thriller *The Man Who Knew Too Much*. There, she plays a mother who finds her kidnapped boy—it's a convoluted plot—by singing "Que Sera, Sera" at full throttle, both dread and hope on display.

If I came to her through her movies, though, it was her measure as a person, as a champion of the rights of people and animals, that kept me addicted. The best thing? She did something magical in those early days—she humanized AIDS. She showed people not to be afraid of the deadly disease that was killing millions worldwide.

July 15, 1985: President Ronald Reagan was still ignoring the growing AIDS crisis, and wouldn't even mention the word for another two years. Yes, that Reagan, the one with whom Doris Day once had an affair during their Hollywood years. On that day in 1985, Doris held a press conference in Carmel, California, to announce her return to television with *Doris Day's Best Friends*, an animal activism talk show on the Christian Broadcasting Network. Her first guest was a true best friend of hers—Rock Hudson, with whom she had stayed close long after they made their string of popular romantic comedies. Hudson taped the TV episode a few days before the press conference that was to be a photo-op reunion of the two stars.

The studio had always worked overtime to mask Hudson's sexual preference, not to mention his recent AIDS diagnosis, but all that fell away when the actor showed up as promised—to a collective gasp of confusion. He looked frail, gaunt, almost unrecognizable. Day greeted him warmly and snuggled against him, planting a deliberate kiss on his cheek. No matter how he looked—face fallen, eyes sunken—he was still the Rock Hudson she had known and loved as a friend for decades.

Spurred on by the relentless coverage of the press conference, Hudson soon became one of the first celebrities to disclose he had AIDS. His revelation, which put a well-known and loved face to a confounding condition, proved to be a critical turning point in the fight against the disease. Images of newly minted Christian Broadcasting Network star Doris hugging her friend went a long way: if America's sweetheart wasn't afraid, no one should be.

Hudson's guest appearance on the new show aired days after he died of AIDS-related complications on October 2, 1985, at the age of fifty-nine. Doris taped a special introduction to the segment, her voice choked with emotion, recalling how Hudson had always told her: "The best time I've ever had was making comedies with you." She felt the same way.

She also told the press and her audience that "if there is a heaven, I'm sure Rock Hudson is there because he was such a kind person." This was huge, and not only to a conservative, largely Christian Middle America. The hug and message played constantly around the world, especially on still-fledgling CNN. It was a message to all those uncomprehending parents who had turned their backs on family members, leaving their children to die alone of AIDS.

It was a cultural turning point as well. Hudson's death raised awareness of the disease and the need for research funds, while Day's public support of her friend sparked individual compassion.

I always thought people misunderstood and underrated Doris Day. Why didn't they see what Alfred Hitchcock saw in her? When she chided Hitchcock for not giving her enough direction on the set of *The Man Who Knew Too Much*, he told her that if he saw something he didn't like, he'd give her some. And, to Pauline Kael's point, he cast her in the first place because he didn't want a star who dripped sex but merely suggested it.

Doris was the number one star at the box office four times in the early sixties. The only other woman who had achieved that previously was Shirley Temple. She stayed among the top ten for an uninterrupted decade after that. She was *Billboard*'s number-one female vocalist nine times in ten years, from 1949 through 1958. I'm not sure anyone else has stats like that. If it seemed that she didn't get as many awards as others, part of it was that she was afraid of flying to accept them.

But the sixties counterculture could not separate the Doris Day onscreen from the real one. They rejected her as being too safe, too Goody Two-shoes. Her name, though lauded in pop culture references, also became a joke, as in the lyrics to "Look at Me I'm Sandra Dee," the *Grease* song bemoaning chastity.

It's true that she had an image to uphold, one the industry had assigned to her. She was also a product of the Hollywood mill, just like Rock Hudson, and they were both whitewashed in their own ways. In her personal life, Doris didn't mind dropping the occasional f-bomb or hanging with Frank Sinatra and Lauren Bacall, surely a fast crowd. She enjoyed numerous big-name affairs. Her life wasn't all *Teacher's Pet*. She was even Mike Nichols's first choice to play Mrs. Robinson opposite Dustin Hoffman in *The Graduate* in 1967, although it is unclear whether she turned it down or whether her husband, Martin Melcher—who did her no favors in many ways—ever showed her the script.

Though perceived as squeaky clean, she has always been a major gay icon, especially after the 1953 Western musical *Calamity Jane*, where she played the tomboy Wild West sharpshooter who, legend has it (but not some historians), was bisexual.

In the movie, wearing cowboy pants and a little bowtie, her blond hair pulled back nearly butch style, a holstered pistol on her hip, Doris goes from an almost-ladylike quasi–side saddle to swinging her legs and going full straddle by the end of the song.

"She's vastly underrated," Norman Jewison told me, validating my instincts.

Jewison—it was rumored he and Day had an affair—worked with her on *The Thrill of It All* in 1963 and *Send Me No Flowers* in 1964, early in the Canadian director's career. In 2011, he thanked her while presenting her with an L.A. Film Critics Association Career Achievement Award.

"Your support for me started my whole career," he said. "It was those Doris Day movies at Universal that really gave me my start in the business. After all these years, I look back on it and think of how much fun we had together and how much we liked each other. Whether you know it or not, you carry some magic in your heart, and somehow you reached out to the world . . . and you touched people's hearts."

Doris eventually settled in Carmel, where she purposely allowed her movie career to wind down while she amped up her work promoting animal rights. Although she found herself committed by Melcher without her knowledge to *The Doris Day Show*—not to mention that she needed money after it turned out that the louse had squandered her fortune—she'd pretty much had it with Hollywood following the insipid 1968 romantic comedy *With Six You Get Eggroll*, for which Vincent Canby of the *New York Times* skewered her: "I kept wondering how the characters played by Miss Day lose their husbands. Cancer? Suicide? Auto accident? There's never any hint. There are, however, some hints of the very real comic talent that has, over the years, become hermetically sealed inside a lacquered personality."

Doris began actively turning down good parts—including the title character in Albert Brooks's 1996 *Mother*, a role written with her in mind that subsequently went to Debbie Reynolds—because she was genuinely content right where she was.

———

The few times I visited Doris in Carmel, she often had several dogs and cats enjoying the run of the place, as well as of a pet-friendly hotel she owned. It was because of her that I first seriously entertained the idea of getting a dog, and dogs have been my companions ever since.

"Do you have someone in your life?" she asked me at that first lunch, even though I was there with a partner!

The problem was that I had too many people in my life, a revolving door of sex and partying and late nights that was getting out of control. My therapist had advised me to curtail having people unexpectedly drop in at all hours by moving away from downtown Toronto and, as I told Doris, by getting a dog. Having a dog is always a good excuse for when you need to leave the party early. "Sorry, I need to go home and walk my dog." I became so attached to my Ella that I took her every-where—to work, to restaurants. As she became increasingly deaf, I would say to everyone, "Don't step on my dog!" She was my therapy dog. She rescued me.

Prior to that, I hadn't understood the appeal of having a pet. I took a friend to New York one time and gave him a whirlwind tour, dinners with Patricia Neal, Douglas Fairbanks Jr., and a slew of famous musicians, and all he could say on the flight home was how much he missed his dog, Charlie. You just met Patricia Neal and you miss your *dog*? It was something I never understood until I had one myself.

Doris talked about the joy animals brought her, how refreshing it was to be away from the moviemaking industry and taking long walks with her animals in the fresh Pacific air. She made it sound simple and idyllic.

It was through her love of animals that I got to meet her in the first place. I had persuaded my wealthy friend Mark to donate to Doris's pet foundation, as that was a foolproof way, at the time, to get a chance to meet her during my visits to Carmel, where I began to collect Peter

Max paintings at Hanson Galleries. I am sure she would have argued that the money for the paintings would better have been spent on an animal shelter, just as she had once told dog-lover Elizabeth Taylor how many dog shelters she could open with the Harry Winston necklace Liz was wearing.

It came full circle for me in 1996, when I was asked to walk the runway at Fashion Cares, the extraordinary AIDS fundraising event in support of the AIDS Committee of Toronto. The theme that year was "Future Perfect," and I wanted to make my appearance all about same-sex marriage, long before it was legal, and to go as a bride—but not simply as a man in drag. We were talking about a *perfect* future, were we not? Therefore, I walked the runway in a silk broad-lapeled Hoax Couture wedding dress and bejeweled tiara, my moustache dark and proud. I hurled my bouquet clear across the room to land on the table of my friends, which led FashionTV host Jeanne Becker to describe me as having "the elegance of a bride, but the arm of a quarterback."

I was allowed to choose any song I wanted for my catwalk debut. I chose Doris singing "Que Sera, Sera," feeling in a way that I was picking up the mantle.

Now I was the all-American Doris, nabbing my version of Rock Hudson. And my secret love of Doris Day was no secret anymore.

Paul Newman and Joanne Woodward: inseparable, incomparable

From the bedroom window of my apartment in downtown Toronto's entertainment district, you could see the marquee of the handsome Beaux-Arts Royal Alexandra Theatre. In the spring of 1988, Joanne Woodward was in residence there for a six-week run of Tennessee Williams's *Sweet Bird of Youth*, in which she played a faded, middle-aged movie star. Fun fact: her husband, Paul Newman, starred as the fading Adonis Chance Wayne in the original Broadway production and in the 1962 film version. If you stretched your mind to think of the two productions as a kind of Möbius strip, his character of *then* romanced Joanne's character of *now*.

I caught Woodward's show a number of times—although not as many as Newman, who often stood at the back of the theater, both at rehearsals and performances, clearly entranced by his wife. To the many people I know who have hoped aloud that Paul was playing for our team—to which the enduring response was always, "You wish"—I have to say that the sexiest thing about Paul Newman was the way he looked at Joanne Woodward.

I got to know Paul and Joanne largely thanks to that downtown apartment with its view of the Royal Alex. It started with lunch, as I find many things in life do. Mutual friend Gino Empry invited me and one of my friends out with Paul while Joanne was at rehearsals.

That first time I met Paul, he was so confident in his own skin and, sorry, but he was . . . so . . . fucking . . . hot. You can imagine us at the table—Paul Newman and two gay guys; three if you counted Gino, whose closet-dwelling was still a matter of conjecture, at least to him. For expedience's sake, let's say three gay guys and Paul-fucking-Newman. But Paul was so down to earth and open and thoughtful that you quickly forgot about his sex appeal. Okay, not quite true, but you know what I mean. Being with him wasn't about being with Butch Cassidy or Hud or Cool Hand Luke or any of those roles he played. He was just this handsome man you happened to be having lunch with. We connected over his support of Famous People Players and AIDS charities, of which he and Joanne were early and vocal supporters.

It was one of those all-afternoon lunches. He started with a beer. I started with red wine. We both ended with double martinis.

What's more astonishing is that Paul and Joanne were so very much a couple—each so talented and charismatic in their own right but forming a perfect unit—that people who knew them didn't harbor a secret preference for one or the other. It was a single, delicious package. It was impossible not to love them both.

It was even clear that Paul considered Joanne by far the better actor of the two. The Academy of Motion Picture Arts and Sciences would seem to agree, as they awarded her an Oscar for *The Three Faces of Eve* in 1958, twenty-eight years before they finally caught up with Paul when they gave him an honorary Oscar in 1986, and then a Best Actor statuette in 1987 for *The Color of Money*.

But back to that first lunch. It wasn't the blue eyes I fell in love with, gorgeous as they were. In some ways he was such an unassuming man, with not a trace of star ego, yet his passion and intellect blazed from behind those eyes. It was that passion I fell in love with more than anything—for civil rights, gay rights, all kinds of causes, along with his fervent dream of a better world. He would let you know how comfortable he was playing gay characters and mentioned he had wanted to do a gay-themed film later in life with his *Butch Cassidy and the Sundance Kid* and *The Sting* co-star Robert Redford, but they never found the right vehicle.

"Where people put their dicks, it's not my business," was Paul's attitude, the foundation of his support for gay rights.

Two of his earliest films, both in 1958, established Newman as a star and had him playing gay characters, even if both movies bent over backward to please the censors—*The Left Handed Gun* and *Cat on a Hot Tin Roof*. The former, with Newman playing a gay version of Billy the Kid, was based on a play by Joanne's good friend Gore Vidal, for whom she had sometimes acted as a beard when Vidal, famously prickly on the semantics of his homosexuality, was in the mood to disavow his actual partner, Howard Austen London, with whom he stayed for fifty-three years, until Austen's death. Very early in their marriage, Paul and Joanne shared a house—Shirley MacLaine's beach house in Malibu, if you must know—with Gore and Howard.

The Left Handed Gun bombed in the United States, but four months later, *Cat on a Hot Tin Roof* opened, part of an enduring creative relationship among Paul and Joanne and the playwright Tennessee Williams. Newman played Brick, whose tortured sexuality is relegated to the subtext of the movie—something to do with being unable to get past the suicide of his best friend and football teammate Skipper. Elizabeth Taylor starred opposite him as the wife he ignores. Kicking Elizabeth Taylor out of bed? It's easy to read between the lines on that one.

Joanne would only have a light snack before curtain at The Alex, so she and Paul would leave the theater each night after the show ravenous both for food and a relatively quiet night to themselves.

"I live just down the block from the theater," I said. "You're welcome to hang out any time."

This was an offer I often made to people performing in the downtown area. My apartment was close to the theaters and venues, private enough that nobody would barge in for an autograph, and, if I may say so, well stocked. With everything. Art, wine, my mother's homemade jams. You name it, and if I didn't already have it, I'd order it in.

Paul said they might take me up on that.

Gino pulled me aside with a warning: Nothing fancy. Paul and Joanne liked things casual. At which I panicked. No chef? No server? I'm doing this myself? They lived a modest lifestyle, Gino insisted, considering all their riches; the extra, they gave to charity. Only a few years before, Newman and his Westport, Connecticut, neighbor, the writer A.E. Hotchner, had started Newman's Own, a line of salad dressing, popcorn, lemonade, and more, with Newman's face on the label, which donated all after-tax profits to good causes, including Paul and Joanne's Hole in the Wall Gang Camp for kids with life-threatening illnesses. They really walked the talk.

Okay, nothing fancy, I promised. I wasn't sure if Paul was going to take me up on the offer anyway.

And then, one evening, word came: tonight's the night.

Of all times for this to happen, I was low on food and wine. And with Ontario's then-archaic liquor laws, there was almost no way to get my hands on even a drop of alcohol. I wound up calling my friends at a restaurant nearby and having the kitchen send over cheese platters along with the finest wine. It was technically illegal for them to traffic in booze, so they hid the bottles in garbage bags. I had garbage bags of the finest French wines delivered.

Presentation is everything.

To the platters, I added my mom's homemade jams. I never ran out of those! I offered two types of quince jam and two types of fig jam. There are two ways of doing each one, since you asked. You can do quince as a soft paste, or you can dice and cook it, which is chewier. For figs, you can cook them green, which I really love, or sun-dry them, as we often did atop the roof of our house in Lebanon. Then you slice and boil, and add sugar, sesame seeds, and chopped walnuts or almonds. It's like a Fig Newton, but a hundred times better. The recipes will be in my next book!

Oh, and grapes. I added a bunch of grapes to the platters as well. Now I was ready for my guests.

Paul took one look at the spread, including all the bottles of fine wine I had painstakingly smuggled over in garbage bags, and said: "You got any beer?"

Beer? No, I did not have any beer. But it was okay. He made do with wine. Paul was easy.

Gino was right to tell me they were a down-to-earth couple. In 1988, designer water was still relatively new, and I had put out Evian and Perrier. But when Joanne wanted a glass of water, she went to the kitchen and drew one for herself from the tap, completely bypassing the snazzy bottled offerings. They did everything they could to make everyone relaxed, and they were grateful that I had gone to all this trouble for them.

Joanne had a fear of flying, or at least a reluctance, so whenever the two of them came up to Toronto from New York, they did so by land.

They had plenty of reason to be here. For one thing, they supported Famous People Players, a nonprofit black-light puppetry theater troupe starring disabled kids. Liberace had them open for him in Vegas for ten years, during which time Jack Lemmon caught the show and recommended it to Paul when it played at the Lyceum in New York. Paul and Hotchner saw it and added it to the list of beneficiaries from the proceeds of Newman's Own, and Paul became an honorary board director and liked to visit the group and its founder, my friend Diane Dupuy, when he was in town.

Toronto offered another draw for Paul—the Mosport racing track (now called Canadian Tire Motorsport Park).

"I'm not a very graceful person," he once said. "I was a sloppy skier, a sloppy tennis player, a sloppy football player and a sloppy dancer with anyone other than Joanne. The only thing I found grace in was racing a car."

I didn't really get it, but hey, it's Paul Newman. When he invited me to watch him race, I went, dragging along friends who also weren't much into racing but very into this particular racer.

Newman got the racing bug while training for the 1969 film *Winning* with Robert Wagner, and diligently pursued the new passion in a serious way, not in a movie-star way. He won respect at the wheel, and when he wore his sunglasses and cap around the stadium you could hardly tell it was him.

After seeing him race—he won many prizes and continued to gun it on the track until he was eighty—I still didn't get it. But that's me.

Everyone who comes to Toronto wants to see Niagara Falls. On a lovely spring day, Paul and Joanne were all set to hire a car and driver to take them there.

"Why don't I take you?" I offered, naively.

This was obviously not the first time I had made an impulsive offer. Here, I would be getting behind the wheel to drive a decorated racing pro. I could only hope I wouldn't get nervous and drive us all off the road.

At least, thank goodness, my friend Cathy had finally convinced me to get rid of one of my two gray K cars. The Chrysler K was cheap and not the most attractive conveyance on the road, and Cathy had insisted I needed something nicer for driving clients. I kept one of the Ks for transporting my goalie equipment—it had a spacious trunk—and sold the other, investing instead in a new Volvo. It still wasn't worthy of a renowned speed freak like Paul, but at least he and Joanne didn't have to wedge themselves in among my hockey sticks. Then again, the star who did his own skating in the 1977 film *Slap Shot* might not have minded.

The trip to Niagara was like taking any of my friends. Joanne wore a simple trench coat and scarf, and Paul wore a windbreaker. With both of them in sunglasses, no one gave a second look when we stopped at fast-food restaurants for bathroom breaks. I had catered sandwiches and treats in the car, but Paul and Joanne insisted on ordering at the franchises, probably because they thought it was wrong to use the facilities and not offer anything in return. The concierge at my Toronto pad called my place Party Central and was always on the lookout for famous faces, and even he didn't recognize them.

How down-home were they? Joanne was so sure she wouldn't win an Oscar for *The Three Faces of Eve*—she even voted that year for Deborah Kerr—that she made her own gown for the ceremony, using $100 worth of emerald-green satin. Who would ever see it? Later, Joan Crawford sniped about it, saying Joanne's Oscars dress set fashion back thirty years and griping that while Paul could have any woman in Hollywood he'd chosen "this Georgia redneck and her feedsack dress."

Well, Paul and his feedsack-dress bride and I had a marvelous time that day at Niagara Falls.

On their subsequent visits to Toronto, and mine to New York, I invited Paul and Joanne out to lunch several times. No matter how much I wished to treat them, Paul always left his credit card with the maître d' on his way into a restaurant to make sure the bill never touched down upon our table, even when I had invited my friends along.

They also had me out to their historic ten-acre riverfront spread in Westport a few times. What do you bring as a hostess gift to the couple who has everything? I was dating a lord's son at the time, and I asked his mom what she would want people to bring to *her* home. She said, "Bring what rich people always bring: just a jar of jam."

I smuggled across the border some jams my mom had made and some green almonds, so young they hadn't hardened yet. We had talked about them before and I wanted my hosts to taste some. If you keep them in cold water in the refrigerator, they stay fresh.

One time, I went to Sherry-Lehmann's in New York, where my diplomat uncle got a diplomatic price, and bought them a fine Bordeaux. But it was my bottle of Salah's Gold that most impressed them, despite the coals-to-Newcastle-ness of bringing olive oil to the king of salad dressings.

We talked about the health benefits of olive oil. After all, Jeanne Calment—who lived to be 122 years and 164 days old, the world's longest recorded human lifespan—said, at age 120, that the key to her longevity was olive oil. Not only did she use it liberally on her food but she also spread it all over her skin. "I have only one wrinkle . . . and I'm sitting on it," she famously said.

I was at a dinner one time at the home of John and Velvet Haney when one of the guests said, "Olive oil from Lebanon? I've never heard of such a thing!" Well, John was one of the creators of the game Trivial Pursuit, and he emailed us all later that night to inform us that the Phoenicians from our area of the world took olive trees along their trade routes all over the Mediterranean.

Joanne took to Salah's Gold immediately. She served it with homemade bread and a salad of fresh tomatoes, lettuce, cucumbers, and herbs from their garden.

One time, they also invited A.E. Hotchner. This is where everything intersects, or it did for me—Hotch had worked with Doris Day on her autobiography, *Doris Day: Her Own Story*. Knowing one person always led to knowing someone else, until all the worlds seemed to mesh.

Any time we talked about acting, Paul deferred to Joanne. I think there might have been a bit of guilt on his part, because Joanne had put her career aside to raise their three kids. She told me that "mothers can't be present all the time," an acceptance that there are trade-offs at home for everything a mother has to or wants to do out in the world.

"Initially, I probably had a real movie-star dream," she once told an interviewer. "It faded somewhere in my mid-thirties, when I realized I wasn't going to be that kind of actor. It was painful. Also, I curtailed my career because of my children. Quite a bit. I resented it at the time, which was not a good way to be around the children. Paul was away on location a lot. I wouldn't go on location because of the children. I did once, and felt overwhelmed with guilt."

Newman and Woodward were married for more than fifty years— until Paul's death at eighty-three, on September 26, 2008, of lung cancer. Joanne attributed the lasting power of their union to Paul's ability to make her laugh, while he attributed it to "some combination of lust and respect and patience. And determination."

They worked on sixteen films together, including when he directed her on several occasions, from his directorial debut on *Rachel, Rachel* to his final directing gig, *The Glass Menagerie*. Their last appearance together, and the last performance for both, was in *Empire Falls* in 2005, although he often said that he felt most fulfilled in life by his charitable work. But, without his film career recognition, there would not have been a Newman's Own.

They first met on a production of *Picnic*, where twenty-eight-year-old Paul was making his theater debut and Joanne was a twenty-two-year-old understudy. She said the blue-eyed actor, cool as a cucumber on an otherwise sweltering day, looked "like an ice cream soda ad," which she found "disgusting."

Newman was smitten on the spot, according to Shawn Levy's book *Paul Newman: A Life*. "She was modern and independent, whereas I was shy and a bit conservative. It took me a long time to persuade her that I wasn't as dull as I looked," Levy quotes Paul as saying.

By the time they co-starred in *The Long, Hot Summer* in 1957, they were both on the same page, although Paul was still married and shared three children with his first wife. Once he was able to untangle all that, he and Joanne were married, on January 29, 1958. Barely two months later, Joanne won her Oscar.

"Paul was an unadorned man," Hotch said in eulogizing his friend. "He was simple and direct and honest and off-center and mischievous, and romantic and very handsome. All of these qualities became the generating force behind him . . . He was the same man in 2008 that he was in 1956—unchanged, despite all the honors and the movie stardom, not a whisper of a change. That was something—the constancy of the man."

Paul and Joanne both went out of their way to let you know that there was nothing special about them. They would do the dishes after picking vegetables from their garden to make lunch. There was no need for a publicist or a hair and makeup person. It was not a fake, showy relationship they were promoting through a Hollywood prism.

There was no spin, nothing to massage or hide. It was a real love story.

"I REMEMBER WHEN I USED TO SIT ON HOSPITAL BEDS AND
HOLD PEOPLE'S HANDS, PEOPLE USED TO BE SHOCKED
BECAUSE THEY'D NEVER SEEN THIS BEFORE.
TO ME IT WAS QUITE NORMAL."

Princess Diana

Princess Diana
shows how it's done

Jacob and I have had many occasions to meet royalty, both in Canada and the United Kingdom, and we have always declined the invitation. I don't need to explain further why I don't think there is anyone "royal," or anyone who has the right to pretend to be. I did, however, get to meet Princess Diana's dad—not exactly by choice, but when her childhood home, the family estate of Althorp, was rented out for a party.

On a November 1987 trip to London with Orion Pictures to celebrate the fiftieth anniversary of BBC Television, whose library Orion had acquired, we were whisked off in Bentleys to Althorp, where Diana was born and is buried today. At the 550-acre estate, we met with Diana's father, John "call me Earl of Spencer," who gave us a tour of a few of the rooms. He told us he was known as "Diana's dad." Not to be cheeky, but I said I thought that was why Orion had brought us all the way out here in the first place, renting the place for an intimate dinner of twenty-four—just to see where Diana was born and meet her dad.

John Spencer could not show us the whole house, as some rooms were still being renovated, he said. More likely closed off, as they would have been too costly to heat. We sat in a beautiful dining room that featured stately portraits and more silver than I'd ever seen at Tiffany's.

After our dinner, the Earl of Spencer came back down from the upstairs chambers to make sure everything was going well. He sat in one of his Queen Anne chairs. If you insist on referring to them as Queen Anne chairs, I suppose this was the place to do it.

He started up a conversation with me about Beirut, of all places, before he turned my attention back to Althorp, an estate he clearly did not have the means to keep up on his own. He said he was pleased more people were visiting, now that Diana was the Princess of Wales, but told me about how much it cost to run such a place and keep up with all the necessary renovations.

Suddenly, he asked me if I would like to see a book he had written about his times in Japan, and get a personally signed postcard bearing a photo of the estate. *What a lovely gesture*, I thought. He signed it to Salah, mentioning something about good times in Beirut, and then he asked for forty-five British pounds. The freshly signed postcard was five pounds. "I'm sorry, I don't have any money on me," I said. We were on a junket, and on junkets, the organizers pay for everything.

On hearing of this, an aghast Paul Wagner, our host, rushed over and asked him to sign a postcard for everyone in the group; the post-cards and the books all went on the Orion tab.

I couldn't imagine how much money it took to keep up appearances on an estate like that. "The burden of property," a woman whose name was preceded by "lady" told me during another trip.

Several members of the group left their books behind in the hotel; they were the heavy coffee-table type, not suitable for transatlantic lug-gage. I did take mine with me, but I couldn't tell you which box in the basement we put it into.

Our collective fascination with the royal family continues. It sells magazines and newspapers, whether what winds up in print is real or pure fiction. We indulge in so much intrigue over costumes and castles and opulence that it's easy to lose perspective. There are journalists who use their pens (well, their computer keyboards) as cudgels to stand up for truth and reconciliation when discussing Indigenous Peoples or the Black Lives Matter movement, yet fawn over the royals in "fun" feature stories. They fail to look through a cold lens at the atrocities of the British Empire around the world—from India to the slave trade, from the Arab world to Rhodesia and South Africa. They admire the trappings while glossing over the history of stolen treasures: the Elgin Marbles, ripped from the Parthenon in Greece and "preserved" in the British Museum after sustaining millennia's worth of damage during transit and relocation; the provenance of the diamonds on various royal trinkets and tiaras.

A few months after that meeting with her dad, my impressions of Diana began to change. I came to see her in a different light, and not just as a style icon and HRH the Princess of Wales, or as the Windsors' latest attempt to hold onto all of their titles, palaces, and privilege.

In April 1987, at the height of the AIDS epidemic, this statuesque twenty-five-year-old opened the United Kingdom's first HIV/AIDS unit at London's Middlesex Hospital. The photos taken at that event have become synonymous with the People's Princess's legacy of compassion and kindness. Gloveless, she asked to shake hands with an HIV-positive man at a time when many believed, incorrectly, that you could "catch" the disease just through proximity, never mind touch, and amid a growing stigma that led some to avoid sick friends at all cost.

To put this into perspective, 1987 was the same year that the United States banned HIV-positive immigrants and visitors from entry. It was also the year that Larry Kramer founded the activist group ACT UP (the AIDS Coalition to Unleash Power). There was still widespread ignorance about transmission, and widespread uncertainty—even in the medical community—about the disease. Articles appeared about the dangers of drinking from the same glass or hugging an infected person. We were all terrified. *How do we get tested? Where do we go?* It was the same year I helped establish the Canadian Foundation for AIDS Research with Jack and Beverly Creed, Susan Davidson, Sydney Krelstein, Andy and Valerie Pringle, Bluma Appel, Chris Bunting, and a few other friends. The foundation was funded by the service industry, including Robert Mang and chefs Dinah Koo and Dufflet Rosenberg, Brian King, Michael Carlevale, who all donated their services. I chaired many of its initial events to raise funds for AIDS research.

That's why the image of Diana holding the hand of an AIDS patient amid this climate of ignorance and hostility reverberated around the globe, and still moves me today. That visit made corporate America and Canada take notice, and donations began to come in. Even President Reagan began to address the topic, if reluctantly. Here was one of the most glamorous people on the planet telling and showing the world that there was nothing to fear. In one simple gesture, she did more to humanize the disease than many thousands of us had been able to accomplish in all our protests and demonstrations.

In February 1989, Diana made her famous solo trip to New York. After the obligatory coverage of her parading in the latest designer duds, the press followed her to the AIDS unit of Harlem Hospital, where she picked up and hugged a seven-year-old patient. Diana knew exactly what she was doing, and again it contributed to lessening the fear and stigma surrounding AIDS. On several other occasions, she displayed her affection and compassion for people living with the then deadly disease—including in April 1991, when she visited a Brazilian hostel for abandoned children, many of whom were HIV-positive or suffered from full-blown AIDS.

After these high-profile trips that she made, everyone was lobbying to have a visit from Diana. Canada was no exception. Enter national treasure June Callwood, patron saint of many charities and founder of one of the country's most prominent AIDS hospices, Casey House, named in memory of her son. June announced at lunch one day that she had heard rumors of a planned Canada visit by Princess Di and was therefore going to phone the prime minister's office to turn the screws. You see, June liked to play left field, politically speaking, and she thought she might be able to convince Prime Minister Brian Mulroney, who played right and was a good friend of the Reagans, to get Diana over to Casey House. We had fought with June earlier when she aligned the AIDS hospice with the city's largest Catholic hospital. I told her I knew the local cardinal, Gerald Emmett Carter, and he upheld the church's homophobic values. June replied that every hospital in town had turned her down. "The cardinal may be a homophobe, but not the doctors and nurses," she said. "Besides, I went through the nuns to do this." The Sisters of Mercy had donated the land for building a hospital in 1876; somehow, they were still represented on the board, and June of course knew some of them.

We had doubted June before, and again I told her something to the effect of that she was out of her fucking mind. To which June politely explained that the prime minister had family of his own and would understand; besides, he was conservative, but "not *that* kind of American conservative."

I sent June the biggest flower arrangement I could afford at the announcement a few months later that Diana would come to Casey House on October 27, 1991. I went there that day, but did not try to get close to the media circus. Instead, I watched from far across the street. I didn't want anyone to see me, as then I would have had to go in. I did my best impression of Barbara Stanwyck in *Stella Dallas*, teary-eyed, with her face pressed against that wrought-iron fence.

Once again, the photos of Diana making the simple gesture of shaking a patient's hand while gloveless helped dispel the fear of what many were still calling "the gay plague." She was not there for photo opportunities or to advance her public profile. She genuinely cared. A couple of the patients didn't want to shake her hand—only because they feared they might infect her.

They refused to touch her out of love.

André Leon Talley
makes an entrance

André Leon Talley walked into a room like he owned it. Every patron at the Ritz in Toronto stared at our table, bedazzled by the longtime *Vogue* magazine creative director and larger-than-life fashion personality; we talked for hours, stopping only when André needed to get ready for a screening. He was sorry I could not accompany him, as I had a dialysis appointment.

"Do you always have to leave parties early because of dialysis?" he asked.

"No darling," I said. "Only when I'm bored." Or recoiling from the usual collection of obnoxious people who say the worst things and blame it all the next day on alcohol.

I met André in passing many times throughout the years, but truly connected with him at renowned philanthropist Suzanne Rogers's fourth annual fashion fundraiser in 2017 in Toronto, which featured André and the designer Diane von Furstenberg. I went up to say hello to the fabulously stylish hosts, Sylvia Mantella and Suzanne, and Diane immediately exclaimed, "We know each other from somewhere. I recognize those pearls!" She must have recognized them from the New York City elevator we sometimes shared in the early eighties when she was having a fling with Richard Gere and I was having a fling with someone else in the same building.

She quickly turned to André to introduce us, but André was quicker, saying, "Of course I know him. We see each other all over the place. I always admire Salah's jewelry and he always compliments whatever I'm wearing. We are planning to do an exchange someday."

André Leon Talley defined style for me. It was not about fashion, per se, but about art and history and context. Being with him, with his knowledge and intimate connection with beauty, was like hanging out with a brilliant little kid who came up with astonishing insights into the most intricate details. "Wearing clothes should be a personal narrative of emotion," he once said in an interview. "I always respond to fashion in an emotional way. I don't consider myself a slave to fashion, but a custodian and curatorial person of fashion."

I was never particularly interested in the fashion industry or fashion shows, but André was more than that, anyway. He had a vision for a more democratic fashion world. As *Vogue*'s first Black creative director, he helped transform the industry in the 1980s and 1990s by ensuring the magazine's pages included Black models, people-of-color designers, and garments that referenced the African diaspora.

In 2018, André was back in Toronto for the premiere of Kate Novack's documentary *The Gospel According to André*, an intimate portrait of the man that took viewers from his roots growing up in the segregated Jim Crow South to his role as one of the most influential tastemakers and fashion curators of our times. There was a Canadian Film Centre (CFC) dinner party in celebration of the film, hosted by CFC board member and philanthropist Kate Alexander Daniels. It was Kate who sat me next to André, and that was the only place I wanted to be, beneath a glamorous backyard tent filled with fifty or so big names.

I wore a long robe and a ruby-and-diamond necklace designed by Hoax Couture that evening in André's honor. He was in an extravagant black and red velvet Saint Laurent cape in honor of Laurent's longtime partner Pierre Bergé, who had died the previous week at age eighty-six. André laughed with delight at the sight of my humongous necklace, and we chatted about mutual friends and parties we had attended over the years.

"Why didn't I see you at . . . ," he would ask me of this or that fête, but I was never one to go out of my way—let alone halfway around the world—for a birthday party, no matter whose birthday or how spectacular the estate.

"Besides, how can you leave when you're on a private island and reliant on your host for everything?" I asked him.

"Oh, darling, not all of us can afford to ignore such events," André said with his glorious laugh.

In his position, there was an expectation to be places he could neither easily afford nor get to, especially when trying to find a comfortable airplane seat to accommodate his large frame, but he was beholden to others, in my opinion. The largesse his filthy rich patrons lavished on him often came with what I considered too high a price. He wrote about that, if tangentially, in *The Chiffon Trenches*, the memoir in which he famously threw shade at *Vogue* editor Anna Wintour, to whom he owed much of his career. He claimed he had lost his *Vogue* gig for being "old, overweight, uncool," and that Anna, far from being a true friend, had left him with "huge emotional and psychological scars," and that she was "immune to anyone other than the powerful and famous people who populate the pages of *Vogue*." He felt tossed aside.

While the press glommed on to the more negative passages in André's book, he also described it as "in many ways a love letter to Anna Wintour." More than that, he thought it was important to write *The Chiffon Trenches* for its message of empowerment and belonging. As he told *Time Out* magazine: "I'd like to be remembered as someone who made a difference in the lives of young people—that I nurtured someone and taught them to pursue their dreams and their careers, to leave a legacy. You cannot live your life in the elitist world of fashion and not step out or you're disconnected. You have to realize that fashion is not the endgame."

He is certainly remembered as a nurturer. Designer LaQuan Smith dedicated his autumn/winter 2022 show at New York Fashion Week to André, opening with a moment of silence for his former mentor. "This one's for you, André," said Smith before showcasing a sequins-and-mile-high-heels glamour collection that the man would have loved. Parsons and FIT had rejected Smith, but André certainly hadn't; he was the first to champion the young Black designer.

"There was no limit to the amount of support or guidance he gave," Smith told the *New York Times*. "When I was designing out of my grandmother's home with no team or money, cutting patterns out of newspapers, André gave me the money I needed to travel to Paris for the first time."

Under the tent that night, André and I talked about everything and everyone, from Andy Warhol to Yves Saint Laurent, and we quickly identified as outsiders looking in. We even talked about how he had managed to survive in a world that celebrates the gaunt and scrawny. "Well, darling, Miss Anna does not like fat people," he said—even though he was always quick to say he might forgive her one day for sacking him. The two eventually overcame their differences and resumed a guarded friendship in the months before André's death.

But people kept getting a lot wrong about André. For example, it wasn't that he had no money and relied only on the good graces of others—he had made oodles of money and had access to anyone in the fashion world and elsewhere. Okay, he went through the funds quickly and didn't manage his finances well, but he enjoyed spending down on whatever gave him immense pleasure. These spending sprees were purposeful acts.

And it wasn't true that he ended up "alone," as many have said, simply because he was "single." Alone is not the same as lonely, and André was never lonely. People always surrounded him, and he was in a very happy place when I knew him. If his romantic relationships didn't take, it was also true that he never tried to stick them out. Personally, I don't think he wanted a relationship with just one person.

André Leon Talley died from complications of a heart attack and COVID-19 at a hospital in White Plains, New York, on January 18, 2022, at the age of seventy-three. The last time I saw him, I gave him one of my favorite rings—a .70-carat aquamarine ring with little birds on the side with white and yellow diamonds. It was a big, bold, and stunning piece he had admired, and he knew the Paris designer who had made it for me.

For once, he was speechless. It was the perfect gift for this beautiful man who was a unique gift to the fashion world and to all of us.

"Thank you for giving us all the courage and style to be ourselves," I said to him. "Thank you for the endless inspiration and affirmation. Most of all, thank you for being fabulous."

I was happy to see he had kept the ring, and years later it appeared at auction at Christie's among his personal belongings, with all the proceeds going to charity.

"THE CASTING COUCH? THERE'S ONLY ONE OF US
WHO EVER MADE IT TO STARDOM WITHOUT IT,
AND THAT WAS BETTE DAVIS."

Claudette Colbert

Bette Davis towers over us all

By the time I met Bette Davis, quite late in her career, she was a tiny thing. She was never tall to begin with—five foot three in her prime—and had been weighted down with various health problems, including a history of strokes and a bout with breast cancer in 1983. She continued smoking right up until the end.

But what a towering figure she was!

At lunch, I chose a special red wine, and we sipped. I needed it more than she did.

"Young man, I heard you're a big fan," is how she launched into our conversation. She went on to grill me about the video industry, the cash cow that was keeping the studios going at that time—although, of course, actors were not seeing a penny of those profits.

I was nervous as well as thrilled, but I had prepared extensively—I knew she would appreciate that—and I just let her do the talking, let her lead as she had done so ably in the industry for over fifty years. For me, this was more of a pilgrimage than an interview.

There was a couple who used to stop by Videoland on the Queensway when I was running the store, asking if any Bette Davis movies had newly come out on video. There weren't many available at that time, but the couple invited me to their home to see *Of Human Bondage*, a 1934 title that had fallen into the public domain.

Well, I'd never seen anything like it! I knew a lot of movies from that era, but this one was different. There was only one question on my mind: This couple who had invited me over so enthusiastically, how could the husband like Bette Davis so much and still be straight? And yet, he was straight. Was I falling for the very stereotypes I detested? As vigilant as we may be, stereotypes repeat so often that they seep into your consciousness, kind of like an oil spill that spreads despite all the eco-friendly efforts to contain it.

Bette was continuing to work and had been doing a handful of films that went straight to video or cable, including *Strangers: The Story of a Mother and Daughter* (1979) with Gena Rowlands for Vestron (I actually think *Terms of Endearment* swiped its storyline from this), and *Right of Way* (1983) for HBO, where Bette paired with Jimmy Stewart to portray an elderly couple facing an end-of-life decision, a subject that was ahead of its time. The dam seemed to break when *The Whales of August*, a nostalgic 1987 movie with Bette and Lillian Gish as widowed sisters sharing a seaside summer house in Maine, came straight to video. With that, a slew of older, more classic titles was also, finally, heading to cassette from Warner Home Video. The older titles would help sell the newer one, and vice versa.

I really wanted to meet Bette Davis. And usually, if I want something I figure out a way to do it. Success in advertising and fundraising is often simply a matter of persistence. Because I ran Canada's largest video trade and consumer magazines, I had access to publicity luncheons and junkets in L.A. to meet and interview stars, but that wasn't enough—I wanted Bette all to myself! And I knew she wanted the publicity. She had always thought she would be the first actress to win a third Oscar, after all; she had won two by 1939, and was nominated eleven times over the course of her career.

I connived to get a private meeting. I used a connection with a well-placed L.A. studio executive and with Al Dubin, a retired longtime publicist for Warner Bros. in Toronto. I had them on speed dial, although I'm not sure speed dial existed back then.

My contacts finally came through, and they helped arrange a lunch. "Of course I'd have lunch with you. I heard you were paying!" Bette later joked. And like the veteran trouper she was, she wanted to promote her new, direct-to-video films as well.

I had no intention of "interviewing" her—at least not in the typical style of capitalizing on innuendo and gossip. Queer people know all too well the perils of that, and I didn't want to play into the way our culture diminishes everything the best actors stand for. Orson Welles, Elizabeth Taylor, Marlon Brando, Diahann Carroll, Bette Davis, and so many others . . . who cares about their sex lives and private habits if it comes at the expense of their talent and contribution to the world?

At my lunch with Bette, the conversation flowed easily and led, down the road, to several more lunches and a dinner. Over time, I learned that she was a fierce Democrat who referred to her *Dark Victory* co-star Ronald Reagan, who had ascended to the presidency of the United States, as "a fool then, a fool now."

Regrets, she had a few—particularly losing the role they had promised her of Scarlett O'Hara in *Gone with the Wind*, and only winning two Oscars (for 1935's *Dangerous* and 1938's *Jezebel*) and not for any of the other nine movies for which she was nominated. She felt Hollywood was holding her press clippings against her. As with so many strong, independent women who didn't always play by the rules, the media often reduced Bette to some monster on the set.

She was clear-eyed about it. "There are many who think I am difficult," she told me. "But when Kubrick or Hitchcock or Wyler reshoot scenes endlessly to get the right one, they call them perfectionists."

Also, "I was always prepared and never kept people waiting for hours," she said of how stories swirled that she was "difficult" or "a bitch," just because she was a woman who stood up for herself, like Tallulah Bankhead, whom Bette described as magnificent. "And she was a lot more temperamental than I was," said Bette, who had done several of Tallulah's Broadway parts in the film versions—*Dark Victory*, *Jezebel*, *The Little Foxes*.

She hoped Carol Kane would one day play her in the story of her life.

On her famous feud with Joan Crawford: there was tension between them, certainly, because Bette prepared for everything and Joan wanted to be more glamorous, wafting along with the aid of a gel lens— but it seemed from how Bette spoke about it that the feud was fanned mostly for publicity purposes.

Bette was as close to a gay man as you can get—not just because she had lived in the gay meccas of Laguna Beach and West Hollywood, but for her over-the-top drive, her unconventional personal life with its focus on freedom, and the way she never stopped breaking down barriers even when she wasn't getting proper credit. She had become so much a part of the culture that drag queens imitated her—but it was the fight in her that was so admirable. Although all of the actors who made it big back in the day tend to get lumped together as "stars," a rather bland way to describe and even dismiss them, Bette was a working woman. She was a working-class actor, as opposed to a glamourpuss or a Hollywood *thing*. She put an ad in *Variety* looking for work—"mobile still and more affable than rumor would have it"— which was so gutsy. She was the original LinkedIn!

She always showed up to the set at the top of her game, but what did they fixate on? Whether or not she drank! Whether she was a good mother! Famously pickled male actors got a pass, even when a Spencer Tracy or a Peter O'Toole showed up unable to work. And no one demanded to know whether Henry Fonda attended his kids' every dance recital or Little League game, or went on from that to rate his paternal skills and therefore his worth as a man. If you asked Bette's daughter B.D. Hyman—who scorched her mom in two memoirs—you'd get one view of Bette's fitness as a mother. But if you asked her son, Michael, you'd get the opposite.

When asked whether she had ever tried to be low-key, she once answered: "Never, never, never!" In the 1930s, she was not afraid to take on Warner Bros. and stare down what she referred to as "the contract slave system," wherein the studio forced her into "mediocre" movies that watered down her real achievements. Who DID that back then?

Put aside for the moment how she was the first actress to receive ten Oscar nominations for best actress (and two wins), the hundred or so movies she made, and all the rest—this tiny thing fought a studio; broke down the Barbie culture of Hollywood; and took on working-class roles, the kind you sit and watch over a beer.

Naturally, I wanted to get Bette to Toronto to honor her at a gala. "Can't have too many awards," she once said—and she agreed to come. But first, she flew to Spain to accept an award at the San Sebastián International Film Festival and was so ill with the return of breast cancer, now stage four and spreading, that she made it only as far as France. She died in a hospital at Neuilly-sur-Seine on October 6, 1989, at the age of eighty-one.

I have a photo hanging in my office of Bette Davis, taken by the eminent portrait photographer Greg Gorman, that still shows her, even after cancer and a series of strokes, with all the grace and stamina of someone who has done it all on her terms—and holding a cigarette, no less. Nothing was ever handed to her. Forget all the dumb stories about feuds and such; this tiny woman took on the whole studio system and scraped and scratched for her right to independence and a career.

"A LOT OF THE STORIES I'VE READ ABOUT MYSELF,
I DON'T EVEN RECOGNIZE WHO THEY'RE WRITING ABOUT."

Sacheen Littlefeather

Sacheen Littlefeather takes a stand

Over the years, it has become almost routine to hear political protest folded into acceptance speeches at the Oscars—whether it's Vanessa Redgrave congratulating the Academy for standing up to Zionist "hoodlums" or Leonardo DiCaprio opining on climate change. But the first time such a thing happened it was a brave, bold move. No one saw it coming. Even today, it is a powerful reminder of how one person can inspire change and draw attention to an issue with a single courageous act.

The year was 1973 and the messenger was Sacheen Littlefeather, a Native American activist and actress born Marie Louise Cruz in 1946 in Salinas, California. Marlon Brando sent her in his stead when he was nominated for Best Actor for *The Godfather*. At the 45th Academy Awards ceremony, Littlefeather took the stage and, when presented with Marlon's golden statuette, she pushed it away.

"I'm Apache and . . . I'm representing Marlon Brando this evening, and he has asked me to tell you in a very long speech that I cannot share with you presently, because of time . . . [that] he very regretfully cannot accept this very generous award," she said with grace and humility. She explained that Brando could not accept the award because of "the treatment of American Indians today by the film industry."

The crowd interrupted her, with some applauding and some booing (the horror!). "Excuse me," she said calmly before continuing: "And on television and movie reruns, and also with recent happenings at Wounded Knee."

Wounded Knee, in South Dakota, was famously the site of a massacre of Indigenous people by U.S. government forces in 1890, and in 1973 was the site of a month-long standoff between Native American activists and U.S. authorities, sparked by the murder of a Lakota man.

Brando had been outspoken in support of civil and Native rights for years, and that evening Littlefeather read a portion of a statement he had written, the entirety of which the press later published. "The motion picture community has been as responsible as any," Brando wrote, "for degrading the Indian and making a mockery of his character, describing him as savage, hostile and evil." That statement was one of the reasons I had wanted to meet Brando in the first place.

Littlefeather endured mockery and physical threats for her words, but she stood proud and undeterred. She ended her speech by begging that "in the future, our hearts and our understandings will meet with love and generosity."

She certainly was not met with love and generosity backstage. She recalled people making stereotypical Native American war cries and miming chopping with a tomahawk. Six security men had to restrain self-professed white supremacist John Wayne from tackling her. (Wayne was likely responsible for slaughtering onscreen more Native American characters in his westerns than any other actor.) Clint Eastwood, up next to present the award for Best Picture to *The Godfather*, made light of her by quipping: "I don't know if I should present this award on behalf of all the cowboys shot in all the John Ford westerns over the years."

After Littlefeather's speech, the Academy banned the practice of award recipients sending proxies onstage.

I mentioned to Brando how in awe I was of that remarkable moment in television history, when Littlefeather stood alone on that stage to deliver an eloquent and powerful message on Hollywood's stereotypical treatment of minorities. The three of us had lunch in L.A. on a couple of occasions, and I also went to see her speak a few other times, chatting with her afterward.

Was she truly Native American? Some suggested after her death that she was not. Was she just acting? If so, she played the part extremely well. She had detailed knowledge of Native American history and conditions. She spoke deliberately and with confidence, while also being gently funny. But if she was only acting—and I do not agree that she was—it came with a price, because roles for her pretty much dried up because of her activism, and she continued to receive death threats over the years.

There was a power and eloquence behind Littlefeather's words whenever she spoke, and I wasn't the only one who felt it. When I look back at my encounters with her, I remember groups of people both young and old always surrounding her and telling her how that one act had inspired them to speak out. She encouraged them, like a teacher or an Elder, saying that every small gesture causes a ripple, and you don't necessarily need an audience of several hundred million—"although it helps." It's a perfect example of the power of activism and how crucial that is for creating the groundwork for change. It's a testament to how one person can stand tall and speak out against oppression.

Sacheen Littlefeather died on October 2, 2022, of metastatic breast cancer, but the disease had not taken away her grace or her determination to challenge the system. She talked about the end of life with the same composure and dignity she exhibited that night in 1973. "I'm going to another place," she told *The Guardian*. "I'm going to the world of my ancestors. I'm saying goodbye to you . . . I've earned the right to be my true self."

Donald Sutherland: a touch of caviar

Norman Jewison gave me a tip when he suggested Donald Sutherland— star of *Klute*, *M*A*S*H*, *Ordinary People*, and more—as a possible life-time achievement honoree for our awards gala: the key to Donald's heart.

Since the proceeds of the event went in part to the Canadian Film Centre, we made sure to include Canadians in the mix, such as Christopher Plummer, David Cronenberg, and Jewison himself. Sutherland was born in New Brunswick. The father of his second wife, Shirley Douglas, was the colorful politician Tommy Douglas, who was lauded as a hero for intro-ducing the continent's first single-payer universal health care system. Shirley and I would see each other at events and she would joke, "I went from being Tommy Douglas's daughter to Donald Sutherland's wife to Kiefer's mom," even though she was a fine actress and ardent activist in her own right.

Donald was sufficiently Canadian. Norman suggested I warm him up by sending him caviar. "He's at his cottage at the moment. I'll give you the address," he said. "Send caviar and drop my name."

The cottage was in Quebec's Eastern Townships. Although I did not expect the star to come to the door and receive the package himself, Norman gave me a P.O. box address, the kind that usually alerts addressees when a big package comes in. I sent $1,500 of high-quality caviar from Caviar Direct, packed in a freezer bag to keep it fresh for at least two days.

I never heard from Sutherland. Neither a thank-you nor a *merci*, for that matter. I finally ran into him some time later and asked him in person if we could honor him with an award. Sutherland, then in his early sixties, said he was flattered but turned it down. "I'm way too young for a lifetime achievement award," he said. "Try me again in ten years."

I told him that I had sent caviar in a previous attempt to get his attention, and then it dawned on him: I was his attempted murderer! It turned out that his assistant had not picked up the dry-ice-packed caviar in a timely manner.

"You're the guy who tried to kill me!" he bellowed.

But it could not have been me. How could I deprive the world of such film classics as *Space Cowboys* and *Beerfest*? Mais non. Maybe Kiefer or Shirley sent it.

Cesar Chavez
teaches me a lesson

I got my start fundraising for causes at age fifteen, when I'd go with a group of friends to stand outside supermarkets on behalf of the United Farm Workers and urge people to boycott California grapes.

For the record, grapes are probably my favorite fruit, to the point that my husband considers me a reincarnation of Bacchus—but that is not why I did it. I had begun going to protests against the war in Vietnam and apartheid in South Africa, but the plight of migrant farm workers held a special place in my heart. As an immigrant and the son of working-class and farming parents, I could identify. Part of the way our village in Lebanon made money was by harvesting tobacco, and I had long admired the labor leader and civil rights activist Cesar Chavez, who, with Dolores Huerta, co-founded the United Farm Workers.

The way it worked was that my friends and I would get a lift to different supermarkets—although more often than not I ended up at the Dominion store in the plaza near my house. I'd get the most donations there because that's where my parents and neighbors shopped. And I don't mind telling you that, as a bonus, a couple of neighbors who worked in the store would discreetly bring out a pastry for me, often a bear claw: a giant, semicircular confection filled with dates and dripping with sweet icing. I swear those things were the size of an actual bear claw.

We also had among our cadre what they called a liberal Catholic priest, and that gave us a little extra gravitas when making our pitch, as Chavez was a practicing Catholic and had a devoted church following.

In August 1973, a couple of years after I'd started raising cash for the cause, Chavez himself came to town. We went to picket California grapes outside Dominion in the morning so we'd have some cash to give Chavez when we met with him later. It was a busy day—lots of quarters and dollars in my cup—but I only managed to raise $100, which seemed paltry in the grand scheme of things. I kept telling anyone who would listen that I was on my way to see the great Cesar Chavez and hand the money to him directly, but $100 in one day was already pushing my burgeoning fundraising abilities. My father, a proud union man from Local 46 of the Plumbers, Steamfitters and Welders union, topped it off with an extra fifty dollars, but it still didn't seem enough. I felt I was going to let the big man down.

We were all invited to meet Chavez at a potluck supper—a type of event I'd never been to but on which I came to rely later at university when I was president of the International Students Association. It was a tool for introducing ourselves and our cuisine to the wider community, and it sold out every Sunday.

When I met the man, at that historic moment in my life, I sheepishly admitted: "I only raised $150!"

What Chavez did next taught me a lesson I carry with me to this day.

"But that's incredible!" he responded gently, his gorgeous bright eyes shining. "That is 150 more dollars than we had this morning."

He went on to explain in minute detail how that sum could change the lives of two families. The simple gesture of telling me how they would spend the donations and the good that money could do is central to my understanding of fundraising. I learned always to follow up with donors and tell them the specific uses in store for their lovingly donated funds, and how much any donation of any size matters.

That was back in my Salah days, when I was still green and new. I later realized that, while many people involved in the charity world will tell you how much they have raised, seldom do they mention how much they had to spend to get there. They never reveal the net amount or tell you exactly where the money is going.

In 2017, I received the Outstanding Volunteer Fundraiser award from the international Association of Fundraising Professionals (AFP) for helping to bring in hundreds of millions of dollars for different charities and capital campaigns, not to mention hosting or emceeing more than one hundred galas in my time. "A great volunteer fundraiser brings passion to his or her work—passion that is infectious and lifts up other people and inspires them to get involved," said Jason Lee, then president and CEO of the AFP. And I like that old adage regarding committee and board—give, get, or get off—but in a more modest fashion; I try to involve all of my friends and colleagues in the fundraisers and causes in which I'm involved.

Maria Dyck of St. Joseph's Health Centre in Toronto nominated me, along with some ten other organizations. So, Jacob, Maria, and I went off to San Francisco for the ceremony, where we were joined by one of my oldest and dearest friends from university, Christopher Jones, who lived nearby. Being there, I couldn't help thinking how proud my parents and grandparents—who had worked the fields—would have been. And maybe Cesar himself. See what a simple gesture can do? With Cesar Chavez, as with the other people I have met through life, a few of whom grace these pages, it was never about status or celebrity. Sometimes the simplest encounter can have the most powerful and lasting effect.

I was one of six honorees at the event. I sat backstage and had a chance to chat with another one, the extraordinary twenty-year-old Malala Yousafzai—the Pakistani activist for female education who was the youngest Nobel Prize laureate and only the second Pakistani to receive the award. She asked me for the secret to fundraising.

"Be passionate about your cause and always know where the money goes," I said with a smile. "But oh my god you are Malala. You lead by example."

"BE BRAVE AND BE COURAGEOUS.
AND DON'T BE AFRAID TO BE
CONTROVERSIAL OR IRREVERENT."

Norman Jewison's advice to a young filmmaker

Norman Jewison tells a story or three

We end our regular checkup calls with Norman and Lynne by saying, "We love you guys." And then it always hits me a few minutes later— holy shit, I've been talking to the legendary Norman Jewison as if he were my best friend, or even one of the family. Norman and Lynne are definitely chosen family.

There's a lot of "legendary" about Norman. Producer, screenwriter, and founder of the Canadian Film Centre. Nominated for three Best Director Oscars. Winner of several lifetime achievement awards and more. Not to mention receiving the Academy of Motion Picture Arts and Sciences' Irving G. Thalberg Memorial Award for "creative producers whose bodies of work reflect a consistently high quality of motion picture production." That ranks him in the company of Walt Disney, Alfred Hitchcock, and Ingmar Bergman, to name only a few film giants who have been so honored.

All that recognition is well-deserved, as Norman has directed some of the most important films of our times—including the Oscar winner

In the Heat of the Night (1967), and four more movies that garnered Best Picture nominations: *The Russians Are Coming, the Russians Are Coming* (1966), *Fiddler on the Roof* (1971), *A Soldier's Story* (1984), and *Moonstruck* (1987).

More than just an award-winning Hollywood director, Norman has fought over the years for social justice and an end to racism. As Canadian filmmaker Clement Virgo points out, Norman's life intersected with the civil unrest of the 1960s and it affected him deeply. He marched behind Martin Luther King Jr.'s coffin in Atlanta in 1968 and, later that year, was on his way to meet his friend Robert Kennedy the night Bobby was assassinated at the Ambassador Hotel in Los Angeles.

Clement postulates that an incident when Norman was in the navy at seventeen is what made this "white Protestant kid from the Beaches in Toronto's east end able to tap into the soul of social justice in his movies." While on leave, Norman was making his way through the American South, and on a bus in Tennessee, he went to sit in the back where the windows were open and it was cooler. As Clement tells it: "Five minutes into the ride, the bus driver stopped the bus, glared at him and barked, 'You tryin' to be funny, sailor? Can't you read the sign?' That's when Norman saw the sign in the middle of the bus that said: *Colored people to the rear.* He looked around and realized he was surrounded by Black people. The white people in the front of the bus all turned to stare at him. Norman got off the bus as a sign of protest."

I first met Norman in 1985 when I was invited to a boozy all-afternoon lunch with then *Globe and Mail* film critic Jay Scott. Norman's friends were critical of a biography of Jewison that Jay was planning to write. Norman had just finished filming *Agnes of God* with Jane Fonda, Anne Bancroft, and Meg Tilly—the latter of whom, Jewison reported, held her own with the two acting legends. It was one of those eighties lunches that began with a double martini and ended with a double martini. Anyway, the biography proved more difficult to write after Jay discovered through numerous interviews that the dashing young Jewison had conducted several affairs; he wasn't sure how and whether to work them in. Jay died of AIDS in 1993, and his version of the book never saw the light of day.

I often saw Norman around town at events and with friends, and a couple of years later, I felt comfortable enough to ask if he would accept a lifetime achievement award from the home video industry, with proceeds going to charity. He laughed at the idea of capping a career that was in full swing, and said, "I still have a lot of films I want to do, but yes." The price for his acceptance was that some of the charity funds had to go toward the Canadian Film Centre, which Norman notably founded in 1988 to help foster and finance new generations of homegrown filmmakers.

"You should come on the board of the CFC and I will help you any way I can if you need me to," he told me after the gala. It was one of the best deals I've ever made.

Norman has worked with just about everyone in his seventy-plus years in the business. The man directed *The Judy Garland Show*, which alone gives him honorary status, and has the singular distinction of directing Sinatra, Sammy Davis Jr., and Dean Martin performing a song with Judy. He lived up to his promise to me and made himself available as my calling card to people such as Doris Day and Gregory Peck. He sent checks to causes when I hadn't even asked him for a contribution, merely mentioned it at a board meeting. Checks from him simply appeared.

He gave of his time and personal energy as well. When a star didn't show for some event, he'd offer to step in at the last minute. On a few occasions, I would begin with, "I hate to ask, but so-and-so just canceled . . . ," and he would agree before I could even describe the event. He agreed to do things that, in retrospect, I'd think, *Oh my god, I shouldn't have asked him to do that*. I explained the significance of this to people who don't realize how important Norman is by saying it would be like running into Scorsese and him saying, "I'll do anything you want; where do you need me to be?"

Atom Egoyan likes to tell of how Norman changed his life, starting with the film version of *Jesus Christ Superstar*. "Other people will say that Norman has made much more important and socially significant films (and he certainly has), but seeing this glorious piece of cinema in 1973 when I was thirteen was mind-blowing," says Atom. "He brilliantly thought of staging it as a play within a play, so all the singers show up in the middle of the desert in a bus and then perform the musical. It was the most exciting thing I'd ever seen. It rocked me in a way that no other rock film ever had, not even the incredible movie of The Beatles' *Help!* by Richard Lester. So, I can honestly say that the movie that made me want to make my own films was by a fellow Canadian."

Atom, barely a teenager, wrote Norman a note about it. "Miraculously, he responded, and I still have his card from decades ago that says: 'Dear Atom, Thanks for the kind words,' before he went into some detail describing how he had made the film. Wow. For a young aspiring filmmaker, this was an amazing gift."

I can remember us sitting around on a beautiful summer night at Norman's beloved film center—a gracious estate in north Toronto—telling stories my friends still talk about today. He would always start off with, "I'm just a storyteller . . . ," and suddenly you're hanging on every word and we'd have to drag him away when a supposedly two-hour dinner began running toward midnight.

"Sidney Poitier was adamant that he would not film *In the Heat of the Night* in Sparta, Mississippi. He said he wouldn't feel comfortable in the South. We wound up filming instead in Sparta, Illinois—so we both got our way," Norman told us. Then it was on to *Moonstruck* and a story about Nicolas Cage throwing a chair across the room, followed by a story about how hard Denzel Washington worked in *The Hurricane*. "Denzel really wanted to capture Rubin Carter as a fighter. It's a story we both wanted to tell. He worked so hard and really learned how to fight."

Next, Norman was telling us about how he met Robert Kennedy while they were skiing with their families at Christmas in Sun Valley.

"There was a skiing race for kids and my second son, Mike, fell and broke his leg," said Norman. "Kennedy's son was also in the race and he also fell and broke his leg, so we ended up sitting in this tiny little hospital room together, waiting for our kids to get their casts. I looked over and smiled at him and he said, 'What do you do?' I said, 'I'm a filmmaker, Mr. Kennedy.' He asked what kind of films I made and I said, 'I'm making a film that's going to be very interesting, about a Black detective from Philadelphia.' In two seconds, I told him the story of the film: a Black detective, Sidney Poitier, goes to the South and falls under suspicion of murder. He stays on to solve the case."

Bobby was the first person to tell Norman that *In the Heat of the Night* could turn out to be a very important movie. "He told me timing is everything—in politics, in art, and in life itself," said Norman. "I'll never forget that."

The movie went on to receive seven Oscar nominations, winning Best Picture, and Best Actor for Rod Steiger. It cleaned up at other awards ceremonies, too, and marked the beginning of an important trio of socially aware Norman Jewison films, including *A Soldier's Story*, which starred a young Denzel Washington, and *The Hurricane* (1999), with Denzel again. Norman keeps claiming he's not a message filmmaker, but those films certainly sent a message. He was even up to direct *Malcolm X* (1992), bowing out for sensitivity over whether a white guy from Canada should direct it. Spike Lee ended up at the helm.

"Sidney Poitier was one of my screen heroes, as he was to many Black people," says Clement Virgo. "So, when the southern sheriff [Steiger] berated him by shouting, 'Virgil? That's a funny name for a n***er boy that comes from Philadelphia. What do they call you up there?' and Poitier responded with a defiant, 'They call me MISTER TIBBS!' it was a watershed moment for so many."

I, too, was a fan of Poitier's. At a dinner with Norman and Lynne, I gushed about him. Flash forward a couple of years and Norman asked me to a CFC reception. He insisted I show up early—and that's when he introduced me to the man himself. Norman and Sidney were born six months apart, and Sidney referred to Norman as his older brother.

Norman was so generous in his compliments, saying of me: "The biggest Lebanese heart of anyone I know." So generous that I didn't even recognize myself.

At those CFC fundraisers, I'd always spring for a dinner with Norman and Lynne, and invite my clients to hear his stories in a tent outside the film center with huge floral displays—and Norman holding court with his campfire tales, leaving my ad buyers spellbound. His stories also taught me how everyone in the film business is there to do a job; they work hard and make the best of the opportunities they get. It doesn't matter to Norman whether a movie is a box-office flop; he accentuates the importance of what the filmmakers, actors, and crew were doing and, ultimately, trying to achieve. Ever enthusiastic, with an infectious laugh and his trademark baseball hat (except on formal occasions), he would point away from perceived failure to the triumphs, big and small, of moviemaking.

I don't think there is anyone who has been a bigger ambassador for Canada and Canadian film than Norman. He even holds sugaring-off festivals at his farm north of Toronto, where he produces and cans his own maple syrup before packaging it and sending gift boxes of it along with pancake mix to everyone on his holiday list. Could there be anyone more suited to promoting all things Canadian?

Ginger Rogers makes a pit stop

After a gala in which the video industry paid tribute to Ginger Rogers and the Hollywood musical, I took Ginger to dinner at one of the top restaurants in Toronto, a place owned by master chef Jamie Kennedy.

"This is one of the best meals I've ever had," enthused Fred Astaire's former dance partner—and she put it in writing to Jamie on a napkin to make it official. I feted her by singing "They Can't Take That Away from Me," the Gershwin song Fred Astaire sang to her in the film *Shall We Dance*. Fred sang it perfectly, but I took my lead from the lyrics "the way you sing off key" to sing it the only way I know how—off key. No one can do off key like me. No, no, they can't take that away from me.

At the time, Ginger was in a wheelchair after taking a fall off a ladder on Ronald Reagan's boat—she co-starred in the 1951 film noir *Storm Warning* with the future president of the United States and campaigned for him during his political career—but as a Christian Scientist she would not agree to surgery, and so could not use the facilities one flight down at the restaurant. On the drive back to her hotel, she had us stop at the only other available option, a corner gas station. And not the best gas station at that.

I hopped out of the car and buttonholed the attendant.

"I've got Ginger Rogers in the car, and she needs to use the facilities. Can we just go in and clean the bathroom before she uses it?"

The attendant looked at me. "Right," he said, "and I'm fucking Fred Astaire."

A beat.

"Do you mean to say you *are* Fred Astaire?" I asked. "Or are you *fucking* Fred Astaire?"

The guy realized I was serious and quickly went to clean the toilets.

Ginger was gracious about the whole thing. She took the attendant's name and address and sent him an autographed photo.

Virginia "Ginger" Rogers made an astonishing seventy-three films and won a Best Actress Oscar for a dramatic role, not a musical one, for 1940's *Kitty Foyle*. The dress she wore became known as the Kitty Foyle dress.

Ginger and Fred lifted spirits during the Depression, and the dancing still holds up on any size screen. It can carry you far from the mundane. I came across a quote from the Dutch cancer researcher Hans Bos that brings Ginger Rogers wafting back into my thoughts:

"While I dance, I cannot judge. I cannot hate. I cannot separate myself from life. I can only be joyful and whole. That is why I dance."

"THE YEARS TOLD ME HIS SECRET. WHEN HE PLAYED
ATTICUS FINCH, HE HAD PLAYED HIMSELF, AND TIME
HAS TOLD ALL OF US SOMETHING MORE: WHEN HE
PLAYED HIMSELF, HE TOUCHED THE WORLD."

Harper Lee

Wooing
Gregory Peck

It would be silly to say I had a thing for Gregory Peck, but I did. I kept waiting for him to turn me away, to tell me this would never work, but with every encounter my affection and respect grew. I would call and ask if he was free, and was impressed that somehow his assistant would know or had been told to say he would love to meet.

I also fell in love with his lovely wife, Veronique, who graciously tolerated my broken French. I was always looking for willing victims with whom I could practice my poor French—only to find on my first trip to France that most Parisian cab drivers spoke Arabic. I would be able to find my hotel after all, bien sûr.

I first met Peck in 1987, when MCA Home Video cashed in on the twenty-fifth anniversary of the 1962 film *To Kill a Mockingbird* with a special home-video release. The companies were always doing that, commemorating anniversaries of the classics and thus extending the shelf life of those movies. Many actors and directors came out to help publicize the releases, which didn't earn them any more money but lionized their work and kept them in the public eye. The video arm of the industry suddenly offered up venerable actors for tie-in interviews, and Eldred Gregory Peck was perhaps the actor I chased hardest in a bid to pay tribute to him. He was also one of the most fascinating and engaging people I have had the good fortune to meet.

Our first meeting did not come about by happenstance. I cooked it up in cahoots with Janet Billett, the senior vice president of MCA Home Video in Canada, which later became Universal Home Video. We devised a foolproof plan whereby I would gradually lure Peck north for an award and shower him with every amenity Toronto had to offer. Janet and I pretended I was going to be in L.A. anyway, and she scheduled an interview for me with Peck to promote the video release; he had won an Oscar for playing the principled Southern lawyer Atticus Finch.

I booked the trip. What I neglected to do was actually watch the movie! Absurd as it may seem, although I was quite familiar with Peck's work, I had never seen *To Kill a Mockingbird*. Okay, spare me the grief. I caught up with it later, and meanwhile did a little research so I wouldn't be completely unprepared—somewhat, yes; but not completely. I am making up for it now that we watch it at least once a year, and I still cry at the same scenes.

Rarely if ever have I seen more reverence than when Gregory Peck walked into a restaurant. And this was Los Angeles and the Four Seasons, where people are accustomed to seeing just about anyone. Even popular political leaders have their detractors, but when Peck walked in, a hush descended. Mouths went agape in mid-chew. You could feel the reverence pulsing his way. It was like the scene I would later catch up on in the movie where everyone in the upper tier stands in respect as Atticus Finch passes through the courthouse, even though he loses the case. Respect, man! I later mentioned this to Peck, and he told me I have a vivid imagination.

The video publicist had cautioned that I should mostly discuss the film—yes, the one I hadn't yet seen. I struggled to come up with intelligent questions from reading the press kit and failed miserably. Here are a few mortifying examples:

"Hey, whatever happened to that young man who played Tom Robinson?" I had assumed the actor's only claim to fame was playing the wrongly accused guy that Atticus Finch nearly busts a gut defending. (Answer: I get a kind lecture about Brock Peters, a giant talent both before and since *Mockingbird*, and a strong singer as well. His supporting role as a gay gangster in 1964's *The Pawnbroker* was groundbreaking, and the Screen Actors Guild later awarded him a Life Achievement Award in 1990.)

"Hey, do you ever keep in touch with the girl who played Scout?" (Answer: I get a kind lecture on Mary Badham, who played his character's daughter—the narrator of the movie—and was nominated for an Academy Award, and who I later learned called him Atticus until the day he died.)

He spoke glowingly about everyone associated with the film. Fortunately, I didn't ask how that guy Robert Duvall was doing. Playing reticent neighbor Boo Radley was the Oscar winner's first film role.

Seeing that I looked a bit embarrassed trying to come up with questions, Peck asked me a bit about myself and my background. The more I told him, the deeper he probed. We talked about Lebanon and racism and raising funds for good causes and people we knew in common, and everything suddenly changed. It was like we were becoming friends, and he was becoming more Atticus Finch by the moment. If anything, Atticus had been a little detached, but Peck was full of encouragement and devoid of ego. As Joni Mitchell sang, "Help me I think I'm fallin' . . ."

And every time I thought *This man can't be this principled, this open-minded, this progressive*, he proved me wrong. Atticus Finch was just an opening act. Here was Gregory Peck: the quiet hero of American film who opposed the Vietnam War and supported draft dodgers, who marched alongside Martin Luther King Jr. and his friend Jane Fonda, who championed AIDS research.

He told the hovering studio publicist he was okay to spend more time, and my one-hour lunch became two. We met again after that on several occasions for lunch, for no real reason other than that I imagined I was still wooing him up to Toronto for an award.

"I'm developing a little crush on you," I told him.

"Well, you're a pretty handsome fella yourself," he said.

We got together on both coasts, and then one time when I was in L.A., I got a call at my hotel from someone at Universal asking if I was free to have lunch with Mr. Peck at the house.

Was I available? Yes! I scrapped my plans, sent flowers on ahead—always send them ahead so your hosts don't have to scramble for a vase; if they're really nice, they may bring out better champagne—changed into my best Sunday clothes, and took a cab out to Peck's nine-thousand-square-foot French-chateau-style mansion. Veronique put out plates of finger sandwiches on brioche—*They must have a French housekeeper*, I thought—and we dined outdoors in their landscaped, park-like garden.

We talked about his history of activism and how his movie *Gentleman's Agreement* in 1947 shined a light on the plague of anti-Semitism.

In his time, he had stood up to the House Un-American Activities Committee in 1947, championed AIDS research ("It just seems silly to me that something so right and simple has to be fought for at all"), denounced the war in Vietnam while attending rallies with Jane Fonda, and promoted everything from regional theater to literacy for kids. President Lyndon Johnson gave him the Presidential Medal of Freedom in 1969 for his humanitarian contributions. I thought, *This man cannot be this nice and handsome and progressive! How is it possible?*

Peck was also very allied with Irish patriot causes. I told him of my love for James Joyce, and quoted to him from *Dubliners*. He did not give me the hook and hustle me out of his backyard, but rather shot right back: "You just tell Norman Jewison that when we do that fundraiser, half can go to his Canadian Film Centre, and the other half has to go to the Irish Film Institute." (He had worked with Jewison on *Other People's Money* in 1991.)

So, it seemed all my hard work had paid off: he was coming to Toronto and I would give him his award!

Alas, fate intervened. We had our final gala in 1998, and I moved away from the video industry toward film the year after. He never did come to Toronto for his award, but I didn't need a ceremony to fix in my mind the Gregory Peck I knew. Harper Lee was just a bit off when she said he embodied Atticus Finch; actually, he was far more dashing and intense than one of the most revered movie characters of all time.

Stephen Sondheim: anyone can whistle

I would like to tell you about my Carnegie Hall debut, but first, here's a question: How do you ask one of Broadway's greatest composers and lyricists to lunch without seeming like a stalker?

Well, the way I did it was that I occasionally left flowers on Stephen Sondheim's doorstep after seeing one magnificent production of his or another—*Into the Woods* or *Sweeney Todd* or *Sunday in the Park with George*—along with a note that said I'd like to take him to lunch and that I wasn't a stalker and that this wasn't a date or a proposal. Maybe I lied a little bit about the last part.

I planned my New York trips around Sondheim. His Broadway productions were an event, a pilgrimage, even years later for lesser musicals like *Assassins* (1990) and *Passion* (1994). So that was a lot of flowers I left on his doorstep over the years. Maybe I *was* a stalker.

But, holy shit, it worked!

During a time when my friend Michael and I were between flings, we would vet prospective husbands with three questions. No, not how they were hung or whether they were a top or bottom—although it certainly helped if they volunteered the information. We were more concerned about the long term and not just the one night. Here are the questions that narrowed down my field:

1. Do you have a *J* in your name? A few "psychics" had told me I would work with and fall in love with people with the letter *J* in their name. It could have been a lucky guess on their part, but that kind of thing plays games with your psyche and you start paying attention. After all, my father's name was John, I eventually married a Jacob ("my Jacob," as explained elsewhere in this book), one of the most important business partnerships I had was with Viacom's John Bailey, and this book was written with Jami Bernard.

2. Do you love garlic? Because I do. And I don't like to kiss someone who finds it offensive. As a garlic lover, I got to sleep with a host of Middle Eastern and Mediterranean men. Garlic and lust transcend political and religious differences sometimes.

3. Do you like show tunes? More specifically, how do you feel about Stephen Sondheim?

Sondheim's songs were the soundtrack of our lives. The gay national anthem was "Somewhere." A place for us.

We played it as often and as obnoxiously loudly as some kid today blasting hip-hop through an open car window. We played it on birthdays and holidays and at fundraisers. When the clock struck midnight on New Year's Eve, our song was "I'm Still Here." At my wedding to Jacob-with-a-*J*, we had the Tony-nominated Louise Pitre sing "Being Alive" and "Losing My Mind." (Yes, "Losing My Mind" is a love song.) Patti LuPone sang "Being Alive" for my sixty-fifth birthday, and Barbara Cook embarrassed me one night by dedicating that song to me.

I could go on. I usually do. "In Buddy's eyes I'm young, I'm beautiful . . ." You get the picture, or the tune.

The point is that one cannot underestimate what Stephen Sondheim means to me, to us. So, when I would come to New York in the early eighties and stay with my cousin in Turtle Bay, I would walk around the neighborhood seeing the sights, saying hello to strangers (which immediately marked me as a non–New Yorker), and gravitating a couple of blocks over to Stephen Sondheim's townhouse at East Forty-Ninth Street.

Sondheim bought the Turtle Bay Gardens place in 1960 and called it "the house that *Gypsy* built," because his lyrics for the hit musical of that name were what paid for it. He was two doors down from Katharine Hepburn, who would accost him on occasion from both his front door and through the shared courtyard out back when his late-night musical interludes kept her awake.

As I passed the two doorways, I paid silent homage to the great Kate and sometimes left flowers and I'm-not-a-stalker cards at Stephen's front door. In today's world, you wouldn't do that, as people expecting Amazon deliveries have discovered to their dismay. You can't just leave packages unattended anymore. Back then, though, it was fine. *Psycho* star Anthony Perkins left Sondheim a bicycle. "I came home one Christmas Eve to find a bike outside my house on 49th Street, all wrapped up with a big red ribbon," Sondheim recalled. And who was Anthony Perkins to outdo me? I am not known to be a shrinking violet.

Also in those notes, I would leave my card with contact phone numbers in New York, Toronto, and Beirut, to show I was legit. A gay man of the world.

One evening there was a message on my home line: "Mr. Sondheim would love to have lunch. Let us know when you are back in town."

I raced back to town! I brought along my cousin Nicholas so I would look even less like a threat, and Stephen brought along the stunning Lee Remick, his close friend, perhaps to protect him. Along with Angela Lansbury, Lee was in the original 1964 production of Sondheim's

Anyone Can Whistle. They laughed together at all the right moments and finished each other's sentences. For years, Nicholas thought they were married. "So what if he's gay? I know happily married gay men!"

I chose Lutèce, the best French restaurant outside of France at the time, and that's where we met for lunch on several other occasions as well. Stephen was always curious, loving, and funny—aside from being brilliant, as we already knew. He had no need to perform for this young lunch partner whom he didn't even know; although I assure you, they were very nice flowers I sent. Still, I had no illusions that he was going to be my new drinking buddy or that we were going to be hanging out at wine bars in the Village, singing show tunes together. He was the god of musical theater! I was grateful for those lunches, and anyway, I could get all the Sondheim I wanted from his music.

After that, I would still drop off occasional items on his doorstep when I was in town—only now, along with the flowers, it was often DVDs of Canadian films I thought he'd have an interest in that weren't available in the States. He invited me in to watch some of those together, such as the 1996 John Greyson film *Lilies.*

On April 8, 1995, I was with two of my dearest friends from my Variety Club days, Moe and Lorraine Himmelfarb, along with some other pals, in the front row at the *Anyone Can Whistle* AIDS benefit concert in support of the "Gay Men's Health Crisis"—remember when AIDS was known as a gay men's disease? To many narrow-minded countries, it probably still is.

Angela Lansbury and Bernadette Peters performed, along with so many others. At the end, Sondheim took to the stage and lingered after his standing ovation. Seeing me in the audience, he waved me up onstage and we hugged and kissed. And I got an adoring hand on the cheek.

Darling, how do you get to Carnegie Hall? Connections. I didn't even have to practice, practice, practice.

Céline Dion
doesn't make the cut

There was one entertainer, a nice local Québécois singer, that Sony Music said they could get us for a reasonable price to perform at our annual Premiere Awards Gala. I was a fan of her early songs, but I wondered how a singer who sang mostly in French and was not well known at that time outside Quebec would go over with a mainly English-speaking crowd.

I met with her agent, who would later become her husband, in Montreal. I knew this René Angélil was Lebanese, and brought him a bottle of olive oil from our family groves back home. I also met with the two people who were producing the event with me, my friends and colleagues Cathy Prowse and Shane Carter, and we decided instead to go with another local talent, André-Philippe Gagnon, a popular comedian and impressionist whose claim to fame was that he could imitate all the voices from "We Are the World."

I would meet René Angélil again years later, this time bringing him Lebanese baklava. The meeting was set up by none other than Shane

Carter, who is now president of Sony Music in Canada, the label for the singer I had turned down—Céline Dion.

Courage. I admire Céline and all that she has done. She is the biggest-selling Canadian and French-speaking artist of all time. With grace, strength, and power, she has poured her heart out about her illness, and over the years has supported so many charities, including ones with which I have been involved. Shane and his wife, Linda, keep me abreast of her struggle with stiff-person syndrome, a rare neurological condition that gives people painful muscle spasms, among other symptoms, and which has no known cure. Céline's involvement has called attention to the disease, perhaps presaging a cure one day.

I have always loved the Edith Piaf song "Non, je ne regrette rien," but it's a fantasy. Not booking Céline is a huge regret that falls into the "what were you thinking" file.

Regrets? Yup, I've had more than a few. But my heart will go on.

"IF YOU ARE NOT PERSONALLY FREE TO BE
YOURSELF IN THAT MOST IMPORTANT OF ALL
HUMAN ACTIVITIES—THE EXPRESSION OF LOVE—
THEN LIFE ITSELF LOSES ITS MEANING."

Harvey Milk

Harvey Milk
sets me free

I never did meet Harvey Milk, but the day he was shot, everything changed for me. Suddenly, homosexuals were not just artists, authors, interior designers, and hairdressers. We were targets. Hunted. Everything became political.

I was twenty-three, a student at the University of Waterloo and a well-known activist on campus, arrested on occasion while campaigning for a cause. My interest in journalism began while I was part of a nine-month occupation of the student newspaper, the longest such in Canada. Although in high school I was relatively subdued when it came to politics, by the time I got to university I really wanted to do more to change the world, so I teamed up with others I believed were like-minded. We became involved in a quasi-Marxist group and marched against apartheid, racism, sexism, and cutbacks to education.

It became increasingly apparent that the group was not always on the same page as I was. Even though many of us were friends and had occupied the student newspaper together, we reported to a clique of stuffed shirts. The leadership was divisive, homophobic, and authoritarian. I still believed in community and belonging, while selling ads for the paper to keep it going—something that would serve me well when I later became publisher of several magazines—and demanded due process when the administration closed the paper for being taken over by "a Maoist fringe." Reinstate! Investigate! But due process was not what the group offered its own members. It denounced some of us for things we hadn't done.

I reached out to other progressive organizations that our group would go on to denounce and exclude. I always believed that we could have our differences while joining together on an issue. I thought we could all be in this bigger umbrella group. After all, it was Mao who said, "Let a hundred flowers bloom. Let a hundred schools of thought contend." Well, that may have looked good on a poster, but Mao obviously didn't mean it; even the most idealistic rabble-rousers tend to become unrecognizable once they seize power.

How can we ever achieve anything without allies? I thought I could have a voice and discuss ideas within the group. After all, that had been possible back when the group formed to protest the firing of three progressive teachers at an Anglican College at the University of Waterloo.

As president of the International Students Association, I was able to connect with different communities. I showed up to a meeting about reinstating the paper, armed with eighteen hundred proxies, while everyone else had fewer than three hundred. They shut down the meeting.

I also worked the night shift as a custodian in the math building—although they called us janitors back then—to help pay for my education and to recruit "working-class members," as our party branch wanted, workers who did not understand a word of the party's bellicose press.

It turns out that I was a lousy custodian. It took Jerry, a fellow janitor and one of two Chilean refugees I befriended who had escaped Pinochet's dictatorship—one was a chemist and one was a poli-sci professor, both making ends meet as janitors—to show me how, and to teach me more important things as well.

I was going to classes, occupying the newspaper, and then cleaning floors all night: study, occupy, mop. I asked Jerry who his hero was, the person he most looked up to in Chile. Was it Allende? Guevara?

He said it was Paul Robeson.

I was finally learning to mop a floor properly, but I was embarrassed that I did not know who Paul Robeson was. For the rest of our 3:30 a.m. break, we leaned on our mops, and when we were finished discussing world issues, Jerry explained how Robeson was one of the most admired and revered anti-fascist civil rights activists in the world.

The most I knew about Robeson, like many, was that he had been an actor with a deeply resonant voice that was perfect for "Ol' Man River." I had no idea about the many other things he'd accomplished before his death in 1976, and in so many fields. "As an artist I come to sing, but as a citizen, I will always speak for peace, and no one can silence me in this," said the man who spoke fifteen languages and who continued to use them to fight for justice and peace, even after the U.S. government stripped him of his passport for eight years during the McCarthy era. "Paul Robeson was the most persecuted, the most ostracized, the most condemned Black man in America, then or ever," said writer and Robeson biographer Lloyd Brown.

Chilean poet and diplomat Pablo Neruda, in his "Ode to Paul Robeson," wrote: "Light parted from darkness, day from night, earth from the primal waters. And the voice of Paul Robeson was divided from the silence."

I learned more in the janitor's lunchroom with my Chilean friends than I learned in our petty group, which always brings to my mind the Monty Python sketch from *Life of Brian* where the characters self-righteously split hairs over whether to call themselves the People's Front of Judea or the Judean People's Front.

When the student union changed the locks on the newspaper's office and evicted the student occupiers, Jerry said, "Why are you so depressed? You're a janitor!" He held in front of me the master key for the Campus Centre, which we were cleaning later that night. With it, he helped me sneak back in through a side door. Neil Docherty, who was editor of the paper and went on to become an internationally known documentary filmmaker, told the press: "We snuck Salah under the door."

It was during this time that I first became known as "Steve," because the group believed we were being bugged, but it was also easier to be a Steve at the clubs and after rallies and while picking up men, to distinguish me from Salah, whom everyone knew on campus. I was out only to a few close friends. The Three Faces of Salah. Being a closeted homosexual, one learns to play many parts.

And then Harvey Milk was shot.

Harvey Bernard Milk was the first openly gay elected official in the history of California, where he won election to the San Francisco Board of Supervisors. He served nearly eleven months, during which he sponsored a bill banning discrimination in housing and employment based on sexual orientation. The bill passed 11–1, and Mayor George Moscone signed it into law.

"It takes no compromising to give people their rights. It takes no money to respect the individual. It takes no survey to remove repressions," Harvey said in a 1973 speech during an unsuccessful first run for supervisor.

On November 27, 1978, Dan White, a disgruntled city supervisor, assassinated both Milk and Moscone. When I heard the news, I fell to my knees and screamed "No!" in the cavernous Campus Centre. Members of a nearby gay campus group came rushing over. They didn't know my sexual orientation, but there was a growing realization as we sobbed together and hugged each other that we were all in the same boat.

Despite his short career in politics, Harvey became a gay icon and a symbol for civil rights. He is still one of the most famous openly gay officials ever elected in the United States. President Obama posthumously awarded him the Presidential Medal of Freedom in 2009. His death shocked me into a new chapter of my life. I really came out, and I became more vocal from the day he died. I realized I needed to find my voice and use it. Living several lives at once wasn't working. Being out at times, or just for certain people, and sneaking around to have sex was no longer going to cut it.

I also realized that I needed to get back to Toronto and also go to New York, Montreal, and to Harvey's San Francisco. I wanted to meet like-minded artists, writers, and activists. I didn't have money then, but somehow, I made it work, and I have retained many friends from back then—those who recognized and accepted the Three Faces of Salah.

My goal was to build coalitions and break down barriers. And I still rely on many of my allies from those days. Strength in community. Including Neil Docherty, Christopher Jones, Tom and Gina Cody, Dianne Chapatis, Denise Donlon, and Michael Hollett.

Harvey Milk's murder made me realize that I couldn't help to change things from deep inside a locked closet.

"WHEN PEOPLE COME AND SEE MY SHOW,
I TRY TO INFUSE INTO THEM THAT THEY CAN WALK AWAY
FEELING LIKE THEIR LIVES ARE A VICTORY."

Ben Vereen

Ben Vereen
sings me a song

I was once at a café in Stockholm with friends when a British couple approached me and asked for an autograph.

"Who do you think I am?" I asked them.

"Why, Mr. DeLuise, we would recognize you anywhere!"

I didn't want to disappoint them, so I signed: *Love, Dom* (not Perignon).

A friend tells of how his then girlfriend asked Ben Vereen to take a selfie with her when she was so excited to spot him in an airport lounge. As they walked away, she told my friend: "I've got to call my mom and tell her I met Flip Wilson!"

When I told Ben that story, he broke out into that tremendous laugh of his.

Everyone gets mistaken for someone else at some point, but there is a big difference in the kind of fan base and treatment performers get when they are big stars on film and TV. Vereen, despite having been in *Roots*, is better known to Broadway audiences who saw him in *Pippin*, *Chicago*, and *Wicked*.

We were doing a gala for The 519 when our star attraction Chita Rivera came down with a sore throat and couldn't perform. Her management graciously offered to find us a last-minute replacement, and came up with Chita's pal Ben Vereen.

Ben offered to perform at a reduced fee, but you already know my hard-and-fast rule: We pay entertainers. Artists deserve to be paid. They are free to donate part or all of it back to charity, but that is their choice.

Well, Ben knocked it out of the park. The response in the room was electric, and he felt it too—it was like he was singing and dancing his heart out in his Broadway debut. He still had the moves!

"I just love 'The Candy Man,'" I gushed to him after he sang the song his friend Sammy Davis Jr. had made famous. "Who can take a sunrise, sprinkle it with dew . . ." (I actually have one of Sammy's rings, a blue sapphire with diamonds along the side, that Sinatra gave him. I bought it when his wife, Altovise, sold it at auction, and had it expanded to fit my petite fingers.)

Vereen delighted in my delight.

I asked him back to perform several more times for different charities. I often heard about what he was up to through a mutual friend, Linda Nash. He has had quite the long career: He's in the American Theater Hall of Fame. He's in the Dance Hall of Fame. He's in the Casino Legends Hall of Fame as a performer. He's had decades of Broadway and TV hits, along with numerous awards and accolades. He is also a humanitarian, with many awards and honors.

One night in the hospital, when I was struggling with all my kidney transplant issues, the phone rang. I was drugged up and had all kinds of different tubes snaking out of different places—oxygen tube, feeding tube, catheter—and I wasn't sure I heard right when I picked up the phone. There was that Cheshire laugh, and then I heard him serenade me. The Candy Man can.

"I know you love this song, baby," said Ben on the other end of the line.

I wasn't sure if I was dreaming. I vaguely recall him saying something about how I was important to him, important to God.

Throughout my stay in the hospital and in rehab, Ben would call and sing me a song. He did "I Don't Know How to Love Him" from *Jesus Christ Superstar*. Knowing I love Joni Mitchell, he did "Both Sides Now." He did the Stevie Wonder song "As," and then another one by Usher.

"*Usher*?" I said. "How the hell do you know who Usher is? I'm so impressed that you keep up with the younger musicians!"

"Of course I do," he said. "Also, he's my godson."

I've seen Ben perform often over the years, and every single time, he brings such joy and enthusiasm. It's an injection of happiness just being in the same room with him.

I know it sounds corny, but he can take the sunrise and sprinkle it with dew.

Sean Connery
takes it on the chest

This is how film junkets work, or at least how they worked in 1990 when I attended the one for *The Hunt for Red October*, with Sean Connery playing a defecting Soviet submarine captain (with his Scottish accent intact, as it should be) and Alec Baldwin as a CIA analyst who recognizes the rogue captain's honorable intentions.

At film junkets like these, the journalists sit in groups of about eight or ten at round tables in a hotel ballroom, and every twenty minutes or so one of the stars or filmmakers rotates to that table before going on to the next, facing pretty much the same set of questions from each group of journalists. Publicists skulk nearby, ready to rush in and perhaps douse the journalists with cold water (or subject them to an electrical shock?) should they veer into unacceptable territory—which would be anything not directly related to their latest pet project. Advancing the studio's marketing and PR agenda is the only reason they flew you in and put you up; it's a "who pays the piper calls the tune" kind of thing.

The journalists, aware of their short window of opportunity, may be full of bonhomie as they browse the breakfast buffet. But once the clock starts for the round-robin interviews, they're like a snarling wolf pack trying to get in their questions ahead of everyone else, and pushing forward their tape recorders (yes, tape recorders in those days) until the star is dwarfed by an array of blinking electronic devices.

This was long after Connery had finished his run as James Bond, and we were supposed to be asking only about *Red October*, but the other journos were peppering him with questions like, "What's your favorite Bond film?"

Connery looked at me after a bit and said, "*You're* quiet."

"Well," I said, "I'm not really a fan of films that promote a British spy, although it's true that I've made a lot of money promoting them on video."

"Yes, I've also made a lot of money from them," he said with a smile.

I couldn't help adding, though, that I really liked Connery's hairy chest in every film in which he was kind enough to display it. Perhaps that came out wrong—perhaps today I might be hauled off to the penalty box for such a comment—but he laughed and thanked me nonetheless. He had a healthy sense of humor, and I think he was well aware of his attributes.

Years later, a friend who had been at that same junket table sent me an autographed photograph of a bare-chested Connery that hangs on my wall to this day.

"HAVING FRIENDS AROUND FOR A PLEASANT EVENING IS
ONE OF LIFE'S MOST CHERISHED JOYS AS FAR AS I'M CONCERNED.
BUT WHEN THOSE WITH ME ARE FELLOW BELIEVERS, HOW MUCH
GREATER THAT JOY IS, FOR WE KNOW THAT IT'S REKINDLED,
ONE DAY IN THE ETERNITY."

Jimmy Stewart

Jimmy Stewart
writes me a letter

A problem with meeting your idols in person is they can turn out to be nothing like the roles they play. It's a constant problem for the celebrities as well, because they can see in people's faces the letdown, even fury, when fans experience that moment when fiction falls away and all that's left is reality, the very thing people try to leave behind when they go to the movies.

In 1986, our magazine wanted to do a story on Jimmy Stewart, but we couldn't get an interview with him. "What more can he say that hasn't already been said?" was the Stewart camp's reasoning for turning down interviews and limiting public appearances. Also, he sometimes forgot details, as anyone in their eighties might do. People probably thought he was losing it and wasting away, although he wound up living to a very respectable eighty-nine years old.

We resorted to something we had never done before—what they call in the business a clip job. That's where the reporter writes a profile based on already published clips from other sources. Before the internet, that kind of thing took quite a lot of work.

The reporter was Beverley Golden, already a Jimmy Stewart fan, and she did a smashing job, although she filed the story under the pseudonym Marisa Waldman. Stewart loved it so much that he sent the magazine a letter saying he thought the article was exceptional and that his wife, Gloria, thought it was "the best thing she has ever read" about him. Not just *one* of the best, *the* best. Take that, *Time* and *Newsweek*! *Videomania* beat you to the punch!

Stewart was so appreciative of the article that he later took me out to dinner and had me over to the house a few times. Gloria made meatloaf with corn in the mix, because she had heard I liked it. (For the record, I am vegetarian now and have stopped telling people I like meatloaf, so don't try to make me one, corn or no corn. A veggie loaf, perhaps?)

Some years after that, when we were going to honor Stewart with a lifetime achievement award from our other magazine, *Premiere*, he came down with an ear infection and couldn't fly. I brought the Inuit soapstone award right to his house once he was better, and in his lovely garden I explained the statue's significance.

Stewart's movie conversation was quite interesting—about how Marlene Dietrich worked her camera angles, or how Grace Kelly's natural grace on film made her perfect for her future role of Princess of Monaco. But slowly, with each encounter, I learned to love the real Jimmy Stewart a little less.

The honeymoon period was ending. We did not share the same social circles or the same values. He admired both Nancy and Ronald Reagan and was a frequent guest at their White House; like them, he was dismissive of the AIDS epidemic. He was into "family values," the catchphrase of the anti-abortion, anti-LGBTQ rights crowd. *My* crowd was everything the Reagans hated—and I had better jewelry than Nancy.

Stewart was a conservative Republican. I have many socially progressive conservative friends, but this was a bit much. He supported McCarthyism and the Hollywood blacklist. I once asked Kirk Douglas, whom we also invited one year to receive an award, about his greatest achievements and about the film *Spartacus*.

"It's just a film," he said.

But he did want to draw attention to his fighting McCarthyism and giving blacklisted screenwriter Donald Trumbo credit on that movie.

Stewart was close friends with anti-Semite and homophobic evangelist Billy Graham, who staunchly supported the Vietnam War and said it was God's will to subdue the Vietnamese; he advocated for the bombing of dikes that ended up killing more than a million people. When Stewart spoke of family values, I wanted to say, "Wait, weren't you the one who got Marlene Dietrich pregnant and made her get an abortion?" Stewart had a reputation as a dedicated womanizer back in the day—Loretta Young, Olivia de Havilland, Dinah Shore, Ginger Rogers, Eleanor Powell, and Kim Novak, to name a few.

What was odd was that this was the guy from *It's a Wonderful Life*, who sacrifices his dreams to save the good people of Bedford Falls. The U.S. senator from *Mr. Smith Goes to Washington* who fights political corruption and champions democracy. On whose behalf would he filibuster the Senate now?

He spoke of how Jane Fonda's anti-war activities had dishonored her father, his old pal Henry Fonda. Throughout our conversations, I had to bite my tongue. I love Jane Fonda! I'll bet you didn't know she is part Canadian; her mother was born in Brockville, Ontario.

Don't get me wrong—Jimmy and Gloria were genuinely warm to me. He said that the finest gift in life was the friends he had made. But we were not on the same page, and he was not the all-American hero the movies made him out to be. He was a hired actor, not the subject of a biopic.

Even Stewart knew it was all a sham. "We didn't have personal publicists then," he said. "We had a studio machine and we had no idea how they were presenting us. They promoted us as if we were not normal people. They planted stories I never knew about."

Gloria recalled how a studio-placed article referred to Jimmy as "an eligible bachelor" during the time she was dating him.

"That was my best starring role, being with you," he said.

"Co-star," she corrected him.

Jacob and I continue to watch *Vertigo, Rear Window, The Man Who Knew Too Much*, and, at Christmas, *It's a Wonderful Life*. But I can't help thinking—just how "wonderful" was life for those who were on the Hollywood blacklist? It's as if the evil moneybags Mr. Potter had triumphed after all.

"PAIN NOURISHES COURAGE.
YOU CAN'T BE BRAVE IF YOU'VE ONLY HAD
WONDERFUL THINGS HAPPEN TO YOU."

Mary Tyler Moore

Mary Tyler Moore
shoots up with me

I sent ahead a mega bouquet of flowers before I made a visit backstage to see Mary Tyler Moore on Broadway in *Whose Life Is It Anyway?* In a gender reversal, Mary played a sculptor—in the national tour, it was Brian Bedford—who becomes a quadriplegic and fights for the right to die. I met Mary again on a press junket later that year for *Ordinary People*, an unsparing family drama directed by Robert Redford that astonishingly knocked out Martin Scorsese's *Raging Bull* for the Best Picture Oscar that year. Mary received an Academy Award nomination as well. It seems 1980 was a good year for showcasing her talents as a dramatic actress.

If you're not familiar with *Ordinary People*, you might not understand how stunning it was at the time to see Mary Tyler Moore—America's sitcom sweetheart in her signature capris on *The Dick Van Dyke Show* and in one perfectly tied scarf or another on *The Mary Tyler Moore Show*—in a role like that. She played an embittered, unforgiving mother who cannot get over the drowning death of her favorite son, thus leaving her other son with crippling survivor's guilt and feelings of worthlessness. It would have been a bold role for any actress to take on—but *Mary*? Mary, who can take a nothing day and suddenly make it all seem worthwhile?

Mary spent so much of her time, energy, and fortune on raising awareness of diabetes, and also campaigning against inhumane animal-factory farming methods. In the years I knew her, I never once heard her complain. Never, "I'm having a bad day, my sugar's off." She didn't gripe about anything, despite plenty of fodder.

Her troubled only child—Richard Carleton Meeker Jr., from her first marriage—died of an accidental gunshot wound to the head at the age of twenty-four. It happened less than a month after the release of *Ordinary People*, almost as if the film had anticipated what it would be like for this particular mother to grieve the loss of her child.

Mary's sister, Elizabeth, OD'd at age twenty-one. Her brother, John, died at forty-seven from kidney cancer, three months after he convinced Mary to help him commit what would turn out to be a failed suicide attempt by having her mash his hoarded painkillers into ice cream.

At thirty-three, she suffered a miscarriage. She wrote about her long struggle with alcoholism. In 2011, she had surgery for a benign brain tumor. A few years after that, she reportedly had heart and kidney problems while diabetes left her nearly blind.

The laundry list of her challenges is almost unbearable. I wondered how someone who brought so much joy to the world could at the same time be living with so many tragedies.

A few years after the press junket for *Ordinary People*, a friend I was semi-dating—yes, that is a term—bought a table to a benefit in New York and asked if I wanted to come. My first inclination was to decline, but he knew of my passion for Mary and mentioned that she would be getting an award there and would likely be seated at our table.

"Sure, but only if I can sit beside her," I said, only half-jokingly.

I came, and I sat beside her.

At the event, I reintroduced myself to her—but I didn't do the obnoxious thing of reminding her how we'd already met. By the end of the evening, she remembered, unprompted, the flowers I had brought her backstage at *Whose Life Is It Anyway?* "They were the most beautiful flowers anyone ever sent me," she said—although she probably said that to most people who sent her flowers.

We two diabetics ordered vegetarian meals, although she also ate fish occasionally because she wasn't getting certain nutrients from her veggie diet. I've been a type 2 diabetic for over forty years, but at the time of that event, I was newly diagnosed—whereas Mary had lived with type 1 diabetes since 1969, when she was thirty-three. After the initial shock of the diagnosis—who knew you could get the "childhood" type as an adult?—she became a tireless advocate for raising funds and public awareness by being transparent about her daily struggle to control her blood glucose. She was among the first stars to humanize the disease.

We both tried to make our waiter understand what apparently was incomprehensible—that we would not be opting for the filet mignon, as good as he insisted it was, or the chocolate cake or the sorbet. In those days, the vegetarian option at events such as these was usually boiled pasta or vegetables. Just as they were starting to serve dinner, I pushed my chair back. "I need to go shoot up," I bellowed.

The others at the table looked perplexed, but Mary understood.

"Yes, me too!" she said.

Mary and I each picked up our chic little purses containing our freezer bag kits—a monitor to test a blood sample, a vial of insulin in a blue gel-pack to keep it cold, and a syringe.

She held onto me as we made our way to our respectively gendered bathrooms. Everyone at this black-tie event wanted—needed—to say hello to Mary or get an autograph, which was impeding our mission. It was like everyone "knew" her—not as a big star, but as a dear friend, the way I imagine people reacted when they met Lucille Ball. Mary was quite slender, despite her larger-than-life charisma, with a dancer's body and legs, but she gripped my arm fiercely as we made our way through the room, perhaps fearing that people would pry her away from me and interrupt her in the process of doing something that saved her life every day. It took me another "For fuck's sake, we need to shoot up" to get us through the crowd.

I waited for her unobtrusively outside the ladies' room so I could escort her back to our table. When our sad vegetarian concoction arrived, we both agreed it was *blech*.

We bonded over more than just glucose tolerance tests and sad-looking broccoli. She admired the brooch I had chosen for the evening, a starburst with a yellow diamond in the center, my go-to travel brooch. She was pleased to hear that she had helped me learn English when my family first came to this side of the world in 1965, when I picked up local expressions by flooding my senses with the popular TV programming of the day, which included *Bewitched*, *Batman*, and, of course, *The Dick Van Dyke Show*, from which I learned to do a flawless "Hey, Rob!"

Mary and I got together a few more times after that. Fans would interrupt and interfere with our meals so frequently that I had to stop and grab lunch on the street on the way back to my hotel. Our conversations were about movies we'd seen, books we'd read. Had I quit drinking? I wasn't a "drinker," but alcohol and diabetes do not mix, and I was loath to give up single malt scotch or red wine, so I always had a new answer for her. Had I gotten a dog yet? Yes, the Tibetan terrier I named Ella after you-know-who.

Mary Tyler Moore was a comic genius, but being funny wasn't the only thing on her résumé, despite the early typecasting. She was also a businesswoman, co-producing *The Mary Tyler Moore Show* (which picked up a total of 29 Emmys and produced multiple spin-off series) with then husband Grant Tinker via their MTM Productions, which in turn gave us such classic shows as *Hill Street Blues*, *St. Elsewhere*, and

Newhart. As with silent-screen legend Mary Pickford founding United Artists in 1919—along with D.W. Griffith, Charlie Chaplin, and Douglas Fairbanks—female actors in particular rarely get the credit they deserve for their business acumen. Lucy, too, with her Desilu Productions.

That's why no one should have been surprised when Mary was nominated for an Oscar for *Ordinary People.* She understood entertainment in all its forms, not just comedy. From her odd start in showbiz as "Happy Hotpoint," a little elf dancing on kitchen appliances in ads shown during *The Adventures of Ozzie and Harriet,* to playing a nun opposite Elvis Presley as a singing doctor (you read that right!) in 1969's *Change of Habit,* to winning a special Tony for *Whose Life Is It Anyway?* . . . she brought so much joy to the world and was so resilient.

On that visit backstage on Broadway in 1980, I realized that the flowers I had sent, as impressive a bouquet as it was, represented just one of numerous bouquets she had received that day alone. Love is all around!

A stage matron told me that in her thirty-five years of working in the theater, she had never seen a headliner get as many flowers, and that Mary gave them away to the staff each night and paid for their cabs home so they wouldn't have to lug the blooms around on the subway.

"She gives them all away?" I asked.

"All of them," said the matron. "Because she knows there will be more tomorrow."

Muhammad Ali

Muhammad Ali tells it like it is

I wasn't much of a boxing fan as a kid, except when it came to Muhammad Ali, but it wasn't because he was "The Greatest," or because he was to boxing what Jean Béliveau was to hockey or Willie Mays to baseball. I'd always admired him for his confidence, his defiance, and his sense of justice. His verbal sparring was as powerful as anything he did in the ring. He was more than just a boxer to me. "There are only two kinds of men—those who compromise and those who take a stand," he once said.

Muhammad Ali was my hero.

As an Arab with an Arabic name, I found a sense of pride by watching how fiercely Ali protected his after changing it. "Cassius Clay is a slave name," he said. "I didn't choose it and I don't want it. I am Muhammad Ali, a free name—it means beloved of God, and I insist people use it when people speak to me."

The anti-establishment champ converted to Islam, condemned social and racial injustice, and risked jail and his career for declaring himself a conscientious objector and refusing to fight in Vietnam. For the heavyweight champion of the world to speak out when there was still so much support for the war was an extraordinary show of sacrifice and leadership. Stripped of his belt and tossed out of the ring for four years as punishment, he made ends meet—barely—on the college speaking circuit and by doing things like making a paid appearance at a boat show in his hometown of Louisville, Kentucky.

I had met George Chuvalo and one of his kids a few times when I was younger, and I liked to think it gave me a tenuous personal connection to Ali, who always said that the Canadian heavyweight was the toughest boxer he had ever faced. Chuvalo had only sixteen days to prepare for his first fight with Ali, at Toronto's Maple Leaf Gardens in 1966, and although he ultimately lost the decision, he went all fifteen rounds and boasted that he went out dancing with his wife afterward while Ali went to a hospital bleeding. The two became good friends after that, and Chuvalo would be a pallbearer at Ali's funeral in 2016.

I turned down an early opportunity to meet Ali when his publicist invited me to do an interview touting some sort of Ali merchandise. "I'd love to, but not for that," was my response. Opportunity missed.

Not long after that, Vince McMahon, who created the World Wrestling Federation (WWF, now WWE), was getting ready to stage the inaugural WrestleMania event in New York City, which would also be the first professional wrestling pay-per-view event. McMahon was an advertiser with us and invited me along. WrestleMania? Who, me? But a friend from another magazine set me straight, so to speak, by putting it this way: a free trip to New York, a bottomless minibar at the hotel, "and a bunch of half-naked men wrestling." He did have a point. As it turned out, many of my friends in the video industry also were planning on attending, so we were a merry band of junketeers.

On March 31, 1985, at Madison Square Garden in New York City, I was there along with more than nineteen thousand attendees for the very first WrestleMania. Among the special guests for the evening were Liberace as the timekeeper, New York Yankees manager Billy Martin as ring announcer, pop star Cyndi Lauper on hand as manager for wrestler Wendi Richter—and Muhammad Ali as a guest referee for the main event.

It was a circus. There were nine matches, culminating with Hulk Hogan and Mr. T defeating "Mr. Wonderful" Paul Orndorff and Rowdy Roddy Piper. At one point, Ali broke up a four-way brawl by punching Roddy. I'm embarrassed to even mention I was there, but WrestleMania has since become the longest-running professional wrestling event in history. People refer to it as the Super Bowl of wrestling. And we did land a ton of advertising from the WWF for the magazine.

I got my interview with Ali and had a chance to drop Chuvalo's name, and his face lit up. Suddenly, I became a friend by association. He lovingly asked me about his pal and the family.

Ali was not what I had expected from the way he presented himself on TV. He was not the boisterous, blustering sports icon, the tough guy whose "float like a butterfly / sting like a bee / your hands can't hit / what your eyes can't see" taunt inspired a generation of rappers. What I got was more of a teddy bear, someone I would cuddle with in a heartbeat.

"Salah," he repeated after our introduction, assuming I was Muslim. "Are you named after the mighty Saladin?" I probably *was* named after Saladin, the first sultan of Egypt and Syria, who defeated a massive army of Crusaders in the Battle of Hattin and captured the city of Jerusalem in 1187. Christians don't usually name their kids after Muslim heroes, but my grandfather on my mother's side had named my uncle Ali because of a pact between him and his best friend in a nearby Muslim village. Their wives were pregnant at the same time, and the two men promised each other they would divvy up a Christian and a Muslim name between the two babies. My uncle's name became Ali, and the kid one village over was named John. Growing up, we didn't have the divisions that the media presents today. We loved each other's holidays, as it meant festive feasts each time. Growing up as Orthodox Christians, we sometimes got Christmas and Easter twice. Our immediate family includes Christians of several denominations, plus Jews and Muslims. Throw in an agnostic or two and a couple of atheists and you quickly realize that religious celebrations aren't about differences—they are about family and food.

Ali attended his grandson's bar mitzvah in 2012. One of his daughters, Khalilah, was raised a Muslim but was more into spirituality than organized religion. Khalilah's husband was Jewish, and their son Jacob chose to have a bar mitzvah.

It is one of religion's many dilemmas that some old men somewhere wrote the rules, and all of their carefully invented rules conflict with each other. Not surprisingly, all those old men in the desert agreed that women are inferior! According to Islam, a child's religion is passed down from the father, so from that perspective Ali's grandson can be Jewish. But in Judaism, religion is passed down through the mother's line, and that means Jacob is Muslim. I probably should not go on. I'll just say I would like all religions to buy my book.

Ali seemed fascinated by this bit of nomenclature, and from there we branched out into discussing Arab history and how I still sometimes speak Arabic despite having come to Canada as a child. It was rare back then to hear other Arabic speakers aside from my parents' friends. We would stop people in the mall or on the street if we heard them utter a word in that tongue.

Somehow, Ali and I got onto the subject of children, and how I wanted some of my own. Although I had not overtly expressed it, Ali had already picked up on my sexual orientation. Hey, if Liberace can act as the timekeeper for wrestlers and not have to explain himself . . .

"You know, you can always adopt," said Ali. "There are a lot of our children who can use a good home." By "our," I think he meant African or Arab, but I wasn't sure and didn't have time to probe further, because he immediately called over the Iron Sheik, the Iranian wrestling heel otherwise known as Hossein Khosrow Ali Vaziri. "Get this, he speaks Arabic!" said Ali, and the Sheik and I started speaking a few words in broken Arabic, with Ali having a blast watching, laughing, and joking around.

"You should take him on tour with you," he told the Sheik. Fortunately for me and wrestling fans, and perhaps for the civilized world as we know it, the Sheik declined. Not that I would ever go to another wrestling match anyway. And I wasn't too happy with Vaziri's "sheik" schtick, which felt like a racist caricature to me.

I saw Ali again during the promotion of *When We Were Kings*, the Oscar-winning 1996 documentary about the 1974 "Rumble in the Jungle" match with George Foreman. Although I had not detected any incipient Parkinson's disease when I first met Ali at WrestleMania, it was obvious now, and I felt guilty taking up even a moment of his time. I made small talk, not wanting to tax him. Even though I am not religious, I dropped a few comforting Arabic phrases, including "Allah ma'ak." It's the phrase my parents always used whenever I left for a trip: God be with you.

Ali still stirs me. We have four silkscreen prints of him hanging in our living room from Warhol's 1977 Athletes series. And there are other reminders of him everywhere, including two pairs of signed boxing gloves. One has Muhammad Ali's signature, and the other is from when he competed at the 1960 Olympics in Rome, while still called Cassius Clay.

I have some original photos of Ali by Gordon Parks. There's a stunning Flip Schulke photograph of Ali underwater, dukes up, an interplay of tension and fluidity. I also have a few of Neil Leifer's photographs— one is of Ali in his glory after knocking out Sonny Liston. Another is Leifer's personal favorite from his fifty-year career: a dramatic overhead shot of Ali's victory over Cleveland Williams at the 1966 World Heavyweight title fight.

"When the Houston Astrodome was built, it was the first of its kind. It had fifty thousand seats and the lighting fixture was eighty feet across and had to be elevated eighty feet above the ring in order to avoid blocking anyone's view in the seats high up," Leifer told *The Guardian* about that photo. "They could bring this rig right down to the floor, so it was easy to fasten a camera to it. I realized I could use a normal lens and get the full ring with the symmetry of the press rows around."

He said a photo like that could never happen again, because today boxing rings are papered over with ads. There will never again be such a clean canvas.

And I doubt there will ever be another like Ali.

"WHY DON'T I JUST STEP OUT AND SLIP INTO
SOMETHING MORE SPECTACULAR?"

Liberace

Liberace
touches me—a lot

Liberace had his hand on my knee throughout my lunch with him. It might have been a come-on, but I chose to believe it was simply a friendly gesture from someone who might not have heard of something called boundaries. Or was it all just part of his show?

Liberace was not out. He was never out. It was just one of those frustrating things, in the opinion of many a frustrated fighter for gay rights, and it sat right alongside his neglecting to reveal he had AIDS toward the end of his life. Each famous person who comes out has the opportunity to make life a little bit less hellish for confused, bullied, and ostracized kids everywhere. But Liberace took the opposite route. He even sued a British tabloid—and won—because they maligned him, his lawyers argued, by implying he was gay by calling him "fruit-flavored" and "mincing." As part of the suit, Mr. Showman himself testified in court that he was not homosexual and had never taken part in homosexual acts. I hate that tabloids slander and undermine the stars they feel they cannot control, but lies like Liberace's hurt the rest of us, too. Let's face it, though: There was no one who didn't know Liberace was gay, was there? He was hiding in plain sight, with the sequins and the sparkle, the unabashed over-the-top-ness, the candelabra atop the white grand piano, but his core audience of older ladies never seemed to mind. They ate it up. They lavished love on him, and he on them. "I don't give concerts, I put on a show," he once said. His gaudy gayness was of a piece with Las Vegas glitz, interchangeable, and for several decades he was the highest paid entertainer in the world.

I had so many questions I wanted to ask him, which is why I reached out for a possible lunch using a mutual friend, Diane Dupuy, the founder of Famous People Players (FPP), which opened for Liberace in Vegas and internationally. One of the FPP skits was "Aruba Liberace," with a life-sized, black-lit puppet playing the piano.

I had just seen Liberace at WrestleMania the night before, where he'd preened in the spotlight, squiring four Rockettes, awash in crashing waves of crowd adoration.

"Did you not *love* last night?" he asked as soon as he joined me.

He didn't wait for my response. The Italian-Polish piano prodigy plunged into how those fellas really knew how to put on a show, and he expertly flipped back through his sharp memory bank of greatest-hits moments to the time he played Madison Square Garden in 1954, accompanied by a fawning orchestra, for a single performance that earned him a record $138,000, worth well over a million in today's dollars. "One of the highlights of my career," he boasted. "The production, the costumes . . . you would have loved it!"

He must have thought I would love it because homosexuals are supposed to adore pageantry. True, we do. But I wanted to engage in a serious conversation, albeit without offending him, about why he never came out of the closet.

I chose my words carefully, contorting myself to avoid the word "gay," although I didn't have much standing to pursue this line of implicitly judgmental questioning. At the time, I was out to my friends, but not to the heads of the movie studios I regularly dealt with while running a video magazine. Also, Liberace was the product of a different era, one I hadn't lived through and therefore could never totally understand. Careers have imploded for less; who was I to question him? For all I knew, simply being onstage while looking so gay was enough in his day to inspire the unrepresented in his audience.

At any rate, it was always right there in your face—Liberace, bling-tastic, seemingly uber-gay, yet never admitting it. His sexuality swathed in sequined wraps, although he was oddly cited in pop culture as a sex symbol, as in the lyrics of the Chordettes' 1954 hit "Mr. Sandman": "Give him a lonely heart like Pagliacci / And lots of wavy hair like Liberace."

"They all know what they're seeing," he said to me, unafraid to discuss the subject in the company of someone he was confident would not betray him. His lifetime subterfuge came at a cost, though. I felt sad to hear he believed that he must be "more spectacular" with each performance, adhering to an impossible standard of his own making.

He remained a devout Catholic and said he got inspiration for some of his pageantry from the church, turning his act into a kind of Catholic Church Meets Vegas celebration. "Well, darling, you should see the pageantry of the Orthodox church," I said.

The 2013 HBO movie *Behind the Candelabra*, with an oddly cast Michael Douglas as Liberace and Matt Damon as longtime lover Scott Thorson, was wrong-headed every which way—starting with its basis in the memoir by Scott. I have a thing about viewing famous people through the lens of the odd naysayer with an axe to grind and a platform on which to grind it. They pocket their advance and their royalties while forever staining their hapless subjects in the mind of the public. Diane Dupuy described Liberace as extremely generous, and told of how people in the South had mobbed the gaudily dressed entertainer at gas station stops for autographs, not to threaten him. "Who's fooling who?" she said. But it wasn't Diane's story chosen for the screen, it was Scott's. ("Of course I knew he was gay," she told me. "Otherwise, I would have slept with him!")

I do wish Liberace had come out, for his own sake and for history at large. But would we have allowed him to be Liberace? Would the world even know who he is today? And think of the joy he brought to so many people. Paul Newman might not have cared where people put their dicks, but the rest of the world certainly does.

Times are a-changing, but they can change back just as quickly. Just ask the people in Florida, where, thanks to recent legislation, you can't mention the word "gay." Last I heard, the word "mother-er" was still okay.

> "SO WE BEAT ON, BOATS AGAINST THE CURRENT,
> BORNE BACK CEASELESSLY INTO THE PAST."
>
> *F. Scott Fitzgerald,* The Great Gatsby

☆

Mia Farrow:
a flight of grace

Say what you will about Mia Farrow—and there are many positive things I want to say—but first I feel the need to address the Woody in the room. It is disturbing to see Farrow portrayed as a ditz, just as it is to see her legitimate concerns for the safety and welfare of her children dismissed as the rantings of a woman scorned.

Ms. Farrow is more of a hero in real life than any female character ever dreamed up by Woody Allen in one of his movies. She was a huge international star and style icon way before she met him, with *Rosemary's Baby* as the anchor for what grew into a career of more than forty films, including *The Great Gatsby*. She won numerous acting awards and was the first American actress invited to join the Royal Shakespeare Company—so, none of this nonsense about riding Woody's coattails! Or those of Sinatra, for that matter, when she was married to him decades earlier.

I was a huge Woody Allen fan and never missed one of his films. But I refuse to rewatch any of them at this point, or see the later ones I neglected. It's not just about his alleged abuse of Dylan; there are still many in the court of public opinion who buy the nonsense that Mia is a monster mom who put Dylan up to saying her father abused her, even though a judge ruled that there was "no credible evidence to support Mr. Allen's contention that Ms. Farrow coached Dylan or that Ms. Farrow acted upon a desire for revenge against him for seducing Soon-Yi. Mr. Allen's resort to the stereotypical 'woman scorned' defense is an injudicious attempt to divert attention from his failure to act as a responsible parent and adult."

I will leave you with one thought among the many I have on the issue of Dylan, who was thrown under the bus by her father and the world: watch old clips of Woody descending into schtick in TV interviews at that time to "prove" he didn't molest his daughter by doing a "who, me?" riff, using the familiar shambling comic voice he uses in his movies to provoke laughs, using, in effect, the twisted logic that the accusations couldn't make sense because he could not *suddenly* have turned into a child molester overnight—could he?—after years in which he did NOT face accusations. Even the leading sycophant interviewer Barbara Walters came to his defense on *The View* and claimed that Dylan was only making a fuss because Woody was up for an award. I don't think that award was from the PTA.

And I guess we're to leave aside the codicil that maybe he simply hadn't been caught, or the ways in which his movies often have themes or jokes or scenarios in which wizened older Woody-like men help themselves to high school–age girlfriends? I'm fifteen years older than my husband, fine, but Jacob came into my life with a six-year-old daughter in tow, and as a stepfather, I find Woody's behavior particularly sickening. Think to yourself, as you watch Woody deflect questions with audience-pleasing comedy bits, *Is this the way a caring father of a traumatized little girl behaves?* To turn the child's pain into a self-aggrandizing comedy routine? I don't quite rest my case, but I'll pause here, at least about Dylan.

Things are different when it comes to Woody's well-known and undisputed seduction of his stepdaughter Soon-Yi Previn while he was still sharing her mother's bed in the "daddy" role of Mia's large family. Woody was a father figure in that household for over a decade—which was more than half of Soon-Yi's young life. I don't particularly care about the thirty-five-year age difference, but it's ridiculous to parse the morality of his actions simply by clinging to the technicality that Woody was not *legally* Soon-Yi's father. The seduction, the deception, the naked Polaroids left on his mantel in full view for his bed partner and mother of his children to find . . . what kind of disgusting, depraved man would do such a thing? Period.

Woody employed a high-powered, high-priced legal and PR team to push the theory that Mia was a hysterical witch. It was in his interests to do so, as a filmmaker whose livelihood would otherwise be in jeopardy. But note that this bludgeoning technique has been used against women from time immemorial—often, in history, with fatal consequences.

Exhale. Breathe.

Let's move beyond the smear campaign and look at Mia's care and compassion for people. She has been a passionate and determined advocate for children's and human rights for years. Appointed a UNICEF Goodwill Ambassador in 2000, her focus was the plight of children in areas of armed conflict. *Time* magazine named her one of the most influential people in the world in 2008. And all of it was later tainted by a skunk trying to protect his own image by stinking up hers.

I have had several conversations with Mia over the years on hunger and AIDS in Africa. Several of my friends have worked with her both in the entertainment field and in her humanitarian activities in Darfur, Chad, and the Central African Republic. Among her many efforts, she co-founded Olympic Dream for Darfur, which drew attention to China's support for Sudan while all the world was busy focusing on the 2008 Summer Olympics in Beijing.

My longtime friend from university days Neil Docherty traveled in 2007 with Mia through the "badlands" on the border between Chad and the Darfur region of Sudan in northeastern Africa. This is what he has to say about working with her: "I was making a documentary about the genocide. Mia, then a UNICEF ambassador, was my guide. For ten long, hard days she traveled throughout the region with me, the cameraman and soundman, and two drivers. We slept in aid agency compounds. Throughout, Mia worked day and night and her only concern was to get the word out and the world to notice. To shed light on the suffering of the people."

The Mia Farrow I have met cares deeply about people, the environment, and poverty, and wants to know what she can do to help. She is a driven, hard-working, principled human being, not some vengeful madwoman. Her Darfur campaign helped China change its tune and urged the Sudanese government to engage with the UN and the world— all of which saved millions of lives. Her campaign also persuaded Steven Spielberg to withdraw as an artistic adviser to the opening ceremony of the 2008 Olympics. During those Olympics, Farrow reported live on the internet from a Sudanese refugee camp to highlight China's involvement in the region.

What I do know is that we need more Mia Farrows in this world.

Tallulah Bankhead, dahling

I'm often asked whether there is one film personality I wish I had met or gotten to know. Well, of course! There are many. How could there not be? But Tallulah Bankhead would certainly be one.

I wanted to know more about Tallulah. She is some kind of secret code among gay critics and film people. Why did Demi Moore and Bruce Willis name one of their daughters Tallulah? "He got the Tallulah treatment," someone is always piping up.

Who was she? Was she real? Would she have lasted longer if there had been a Betty Ford Center in her day? And where can I see one of her films?

Everyone I asked who knew her, from publicists to other film stars to friends, would say she was brilliant but problematic. That's what happens in Hollywood when you're gay and speak your mind. Bette Davis and Douglas Fairbanks Jr. said Tallulah gave the best stage performances they'd ever seen. Lynn Fontanne called her the greatest natural talent of her time.

Tallulah died in 1968 after making hundreds of film, theater, and radio appearances, but might have been totally erased from history had not the drag community stepped up to keep her delicious bawdiness alive. After all, it was the same drag community that led the Stonewall riots six months after her death, thus giving the movement visibility.

The story of Tallulah quickly became a story of how you have to play by the rules to make it in Hollywood, that place where they are only as liberal as the audiences to which they pander. I bought an autographed program from 1948 of Tallulah in Noël Coward's *Private Lives* and hung it in my office next to a signed January 23, 1939, *Life* cover of Bette Davis, even before I understood the full extent of who she was and why she is important to understanding and embracing Hollywood and queer history. I knew she was a rebel whom the movies had mostly bypassed. She was out and proud way before it was popular, safe, or even decent to be so. The censorious Hays Code in the 1930s branded her as "an unsafe and unsavory person." This curtailed her film career but did not stop her from tossing off lewd asides from the stage to acknowledge her adoring audiences.

Have you ever noticed how all the best lines seem to come from Tallulah Bankhead? At a fundraising event for Best Buddies, a non-profit that helps people with disabilities, Shirley MacLaine bit into one of my pearls—I was wearing a few strands of black and white ones—to check if they were real. "Dahling, the only thing fake about me are my friends," I said with Tallulah's husky delivery. Was that one of Tallulah's lines? It might well have been. Or was it from some fabulous drag queen? The Tallulah delivery has become engrained in us all. No wonder the Disney character Cruella de Vil was partly based on her.

Tallulah was one of the giants of the stage, both in London and New York, originating many roles that went to other actresses for the film versions, once she fell victim to blacklisting because she was open about her abortions and her sexuality—she amusingly described herself as ambisextrous. She had many affairs with men and women, including Greta Garbo, Marlene Dietrich, Billie Holiday, and Gary Cooper. To "liberal" Hollywood, that was just too much scandal.

She was denied many roles on screen that she originated on stage—including in *Dark Victory* and *The Little Foxes*, which went to Bette Davis instead. Davis admitted her performance in *Foxes* was largely based on Bankhead's. The Eva Lovelace character of the stage play *Morning Glory* was based on Bankhead, and Katharine Hepburn got the part in the 1933 movie by imitating Bankhead, and that role gave her the first of four Best Actress Oscars. Dorothy Parker, a friend of Tallulah's, famously quipped about Hepburn: "She runs the gamut of emotions from A to B."

Tennessee Williams wrote the Blanche DuBois character in *A Streetcar Named Desire* specifically for Tallulah. He said he wept and bowed at her feet when she performed it; nonetheless, the film role went to Vivien Leigh. He also wrote roles in *The Glass Menagerie* and *Sweet Bird of Youth* specifically for her, and it is commonly thought that *All About Eve* was all about Tallulah. She even told Bette Davis: "I loved you in that film *All About Me*."

Many great stage actors don't have their roles preserved on film and have become invisible—such as Helen Hayes, often referred to as the First Lady of American Theater. But Hayes rarely wanted to do films and has a Broadway theater named after her. Tallulah was a star and a Big Personality, with parts specifically written for her, and she was denied those parts in movie adaptations. Bette Davis playing Tallulah in *The Little Foxes* should have gotten her a third Oscar nod, for Best Homage.

One of the only places left where you can watch a Tallulah performance, other than in Hitchcock's mediocre *Lifeboat,* is on one of Lucille Ball's TV shows, *The Lucy-Desi Comedy Hour*, searchable online. Lucille Ball, a woman who also broke down so many barriers, had the courage to cast Tallulah in a primetime episode that showcases Bankhead's comedic timing and hints of what her presence could have been on film, too.

We need to keep Tallulah's flame burning bright. Hmm, was it she or Charles Busch who said: "Good girls keep diaries. Bad girls never have the time."

Patricia Neal:
you really, *really*
would have loved her

There's a chicken-egg thing here, the question about which came first. Did I want Patricia Neal so I could give her a lifetime achievement award, and while she was there, get to know her better? Or did I want to get to know her better, and the way to do that was to initiate the process of giving her an award?

Patricia wasn't the first person about whom I asked myself that question. I only know that I became even more intrigued after discussing her over dinner one night with Paul Newman and Joanne Woodward.

Newman, of course, had starred with Neal in the Martin Ritt revisionist Western *Hud* in 1963. Of its seven Academy Award nominations, it won three, including one for Neal as Best Actress.

I mentioned how much I loved the movie, and it was Joanne who really sold me on Patricia. Joanne was full of praise for her, calling her a great beauty and actress. But she also went on about Neal's health struggles and, always of interest to me, her steely determination and grace.

In 1965, at the age of thirty-nine, Neal suffered a cerebral aneurysm while pregnant with daughter Lucy. She delivered a healthy baby, but in 1966 had a series of massive strokes that put her into a coma for three weeks. She awoke paralyzed on one side, blind in one eye, and had to relearn how to walk and talk. *Variety* ran a premature obituary, but her husband, the British children's author Roald Dahl, was instrumental in helping her through the grueling recovery process, later dramatized in the 1981 film *The Patricia Neal Story* with no less than Glenda Jackson playing her.

As Joanne was singing her praises, she mentioned what had happened to Patricia with the 1970s TV show *The Waltons*. It was quite shameful.

It seems Neal originally starred as the matriarch of the wholesome family in the 1971 made-for-TV movie *The Homecoming: A Christmas Story*, which went on to serve as the pilot for *The Waltons* and got everyone repeating "Good night, John-Boy" for years and decades to come. Neal won a Golden Globe award and an Emmy nomination for her performance.

But when it came time to cast the CBS series, producers shied away from the stroke survivor and went with what they considered a safer bet: the actress Michael Learned.

"It's a paradox," said Joanne. "Here was a series that portrayed itself as the epitome of simple, homegrown American values, and they would not even consider Pat because she was too inconvenient for them."

Today, we talk about diversity and inclusion, but is it really so different than in Patricia Neal's time? Do we include in our talk about inclusion the issues of accessibility? Must we hide away a star who has had a stroke, such as Bette Davis, or one with Parkinson's disease, like Katharine Hepburn, to both of whom Neal has been compared? We still somehow fail to include those who are disabled, instead focusing on race, gender, ethnicity, and sexual orientation.

"I don't walk divinely," Neal told an interviewer. "I walk with a limp. My right side is affected and I'll never see out of my right eye again." She lost so many roles she shouldn't have, simply for the stigma and lingering evidence of having had strokes, or for not being what Hollywood is forever after in an actress: some combination of gold-medal gymnastics skill, Barbie doll proportions, and otherworldly beauty.

I wanted to know more about Neal, particularly her survival skills. Actually, I wanted to know everything about her. Was there regret? Remorse? What kept her so strong and elegant, especially in light of all the tragedy that had befallen her? Even before the strokes, her life read like a Greek tragedy. Her marriage to serial adulterer and noted anti-Semite Dahl produced five children, but was rocky and ultimately ended in 1983 after she discovered that he had been having an eleven-year affair that even the kids knew about. Neal would later call Dahl "Roald the Rotten" and discuss his tormenting and abusive behavior.

Their infant son, Theo, narrowly escaped death in 1960 when a taxi and bus collided and struck his stroller on a New York City street. He came away from the incident with brain damage. Daughter Olivia died at seven from encephalitis after a bout of measles in 1962, one year shy of a licensed vaccine.

Neal went through all of these hardships and beat them, or at least survived them. I finally lured her to Toronto to receive an award, where we paid tribute not only to her body of work but to her strength and versatility.

Another award recipient at that gala was Douglas Fairbanks Jr. I had Fairbanks and his wife, Vera, and Patricia over for dinner a couple of times while they were in town. I was kind of smitten with Patricia in that she still looked the grande dame—always presenting herself as the big, glamorous Hollywood star, even while her conversation, in that raspy voice, was like she had just come over for coffee. Very candid and down to earth, she never complained about what might have been. She seemed to embody a profound acceptance of "this is how things are," while still taking pride in what she had accomplished in her lifetime—particularly how she had helped set up the Patricia Neal Rehabilitation Center in Knoxville, Tennessee, a world-class facility for the care of stroke victims.

When she was sitting there at my dining room table, with all the Warhols and other art on the walls and someone serving the catered lunch, she leaned over to me and said, "Why do you have to work?" But I did. I was involved in different charities and I wasn't living in my parents' basement anymore. And the Warhols were so much cheaper back when I first started collecting.

The irony in that was—why were THEY still working? Here was Douglas Fairbanks Jr., forty-six years older than I was, still at it, still making appearances. Here was Patricia Neal, still doing interviews and attending tributes and working with her pet causes, including her Knoxville rehab center. Why does anyone keep doing it? Sometimes it's just who we are. Sometimes it's habit, I suppose. In my case, it was so I could maintain the lifestyle I had built for myself, full of fine art and fine food and fine friends. Or, as I like to say, so I can afford all this shit.

But darling, it's only stuff. It's people I love.

Patricia and I kept in touch, and I would have lunch or dinner with her when I was in New York. One time, some friends and I—four gay men dressed to the nines—took her for dinner to Le Cirque. "This beats going out with anyone in my life, including Gary Cooper," she said, surveying us up and down.

That was kind of her, but an exaggeration. Cooper was stunningly gorgeous, as well as having been the love of her life. She began an affair with her married co-star while they were making *The Fountainhead* in 1949, although she had met him two years before that, when she was twenty-one and he was forty-six. The relationship was intense and star-crossed. The end of it, a few years later, led to her having a nervous breakdown and leaving Hollywood for New York and the Broadway stage for a time.

"I will always love Gary Cooper," she said to us, and then, acknowledging her gay audience, added: "Oh, you really, *really* would have loved him, too," delivered with that raspy drawl as if she were still in *Hud*.

What is it with Gary Cooper? There are four people in this book alone who had affairs with him, and he died at the age of sixty, so he must have been pretty busy. It comes out to nearly one affair per movie set, despite him being a Republican married to a devout Catholic woman, Veronica Cooper. Now, that's what I call "family values."

Patricia described her passion for Cooper, and also was very matter-of-fact in discussing him and other lovers, including Marlon Brando, with anatomical precision. Coop, apparently, was great in bed—and although he did finally leave his wife for her, the relationship disintegrated after he persuaded her to get an abortion. If it hadn't been for the death grip Hollywood held on the lives and morals of its stars, she could have had the baby, and I like to think they would have made it as a couple. And moved to Walton Mountain.

The more I got to know of Patricia's life story, the more I thought of her as a personal inspiration. Perhaps that's why I broke my steadfast rule about staying in other people's homes.

To be clear, I am awkward staying at other people's homes. It makes me tense. What should I bring? What is expected of me? I like the idea of making a mess and not worrying about it, although it's really more of a privacy thing—me having my space and not worrying about whether I'm treading on theirs. I'm fine with them coming over *chez moi*, but it's impossible for me to truly be comfortable under someone else's roof, someone else's rules. A lot of the experience becomes about not trespassing on their hours, their expectations, their space. I find being a houseguest an unnecessary chore. I'm always afraid of overstaying my welcome. My charm will wear off. I am not only first to leave the party, but also the first houseguest to pack up and leave, if I go at all.

Nevertheless, I felt honored that Patricia had invited me, and I felt so many had done her wrong that if she really wanted my company, I had no choice but to offer it. I came out for three days to her Martha's Vineyard harbor-view home in Edgartown, Massachusetts, where she spent most of the year. It was a sweet historic house, a whaling captain's home built in the 1800s for Captain Valentine Pease, rumored to be the inspiration for the obsessed Captain Ahab in Herman Melville's 1851 classic novel *Moby-Dick*. I just loved walking arm in arm through town with her, chatting away. She held to my arm fiercely, as though I were propping her up, even though I wasn't. I felt as though I were walking with my mother in the old village.

Patricia always looked dressed up and done up before she came down in the morning. As we took walks and drives around the small town, where everyone knew her, we spoke about her struggles, as well as about her marriage to Roald. She painted that union as loveless in her autobiography and described him to me as a disciplinarian. She certainly did not mention him in glowing terms.

I made her a frittata one morning. I got all the credit for the dish, even though her housekeeper prepped the ingredients I threw at her from the fridge—onions, peppers, potatoes, whatever leftover vegetables I found. I put the tomatoes on top of the eggs, and cheese on top of that, and baked it in the oven to the consistency of moussaka.

The conversation was easy, but I still wonder sometimes why I broke my rule about being a houseguest. I think with certain people you feel a connection, one that promises you will come away the richer for it. And I did. She taught me about having the strength to carry on. "A strong positive mental attitude will create more miracles than any wonder drug," she liked to say.

Patricia had turned away from religion after her daughter's death, but when I visited her, she had become a bit religious again, and in her final months, she converted to Catholicism. Although I am not religious, who am I to take someone's crutch away or argue with them about their beliefs? I figure, *Hey, whatever you need to get through life.* You never know. I reverted to my childhood bedtime ritual of making the sign of the cross sometimes during my kidney ordeal. That's when my memories of Patricia really helped me. I would think of all her struggles and pain and how she survived. It helped me push through, and I'll never forget that. Along with a couple of Tylenol 3s, bien sûr.

An unrepentant smoker for most of her life, Patricia Neal died at her Martha's Vineyard home of lung cancer on August 8, 2010, at the age of eighty-four. A reporter had once asked her how she would like to be remembered when she was gone.

"Just lovingly," she replied.

Brian Bedford
teaches me stuff

In February 1980, while I was a student in Waterloo, I ran for parliament in Perth County, Ontario, which includes Stratford. It was a significant election in that it brought Pierre Trudeau back as prime minister after his ouster from office.

Technically, I ran on the Independent ticket, but I was really running from a bastardized Marxist point of view. My poli-sci professor agreed to give me a full year's course credit for that undertaking.

My campaign staff consisted pretty much of me and my friend Larry, who was running for office in Oxford, the next county over, with one car between us. Larry would pick me up and drive me over to Stratford in the middle of winter and then go to Woodstock to campaign, dropping me off so I could canvass door to door or attend candidates' meetings. I went in armed with piles of position papers, the way I would for my poli-sci class, while the Conservative incumbent candidate didn't offer a speck of policy. He simply spent his time schmoozing the audience, all of whom he knew well. He'd call them out by name and give them leading questions, like, "Hey, Jim, when did we pave that road? Did my office help?"

Needless to say, I lost the election, receiving fewer votes than the number of people who usually attend one of our garden parties. I loved doing it, but it cured me of any desire to hold public office. When I called Bill Jarvis, the Conservative candidate, to congratulate him, he told me, "Son, we were all radical in university. I think you'll make a great lawyer someday." My debating skills were fine, although some of the ideas I represented were wonky at best.

A couple of years earlier, I'd noticed a handsome, somewhat older man—he had about twenty years on me—at a couple of cocktail parties. He kept giving me That Look.

"What do you do?" I asked, although it was a question I hated and rarely asked (that's still the case).

"I'm an actor."

"Really? Why haven't I heard of you?" Another thoughtless question.

"Well, I'm mostly on stage."

I could not take him back to my dingy place; luckily, my dad had given me his old Delta 88, which gave me more freedom than I think my father may have intended.

Brian would become one of my first loves. I'd had many flings before, but this was something more—and that's taking into account that I identify with the Chet Baker song "I Fall in Love Too Easily," by Jule Styne and Sammy Cahn.

I was determined that this relationship would not be more than it was. Even though I dressed nicer for Brian than I normally would for anyone else—Catherine Deneuve in *Belle de jour*, dolling up for her afternoon assignations—I would run late and even not show up sometimes, despite knowing that Brian was going to great lengths to make dinner. Actually, I was a little late quite a lot in those days, as I tried to attend different things on the same night without telling people I had to be somewhere else. Double- and triple-booking. I had to keep my lives separate and try to be everywhere. Brian and I finally had our most frank discussion about it, beginning with, "I love you, but I cannot love you." I couldn't let go sometimes for fear of ending up in a world I didn't want to be in, and I couldn't hurt him by disappearing. The conversation was freeing for both of us, and led to the most intense three days we'd ever spent together.

Jerk that I was, I didn't realize Brian Bedford was, in the words of the *New York Times*, "the finest English-language interpreter of classical comedy of his generation." He had already won a Tony in 1971 for *The School for Wives*, and later seemed to attract Tony nominations as a magnet does iron filings. He had seven nominations, with one win, just a hair behind the most nominated male actor—Jason Robards, with eight nominations and one win.

Although Bedford was a product of London's West End and Broadway, in this period he had settled in Stratford and become an integral part of its renowned theater festival, where he both directed and starred in mostly Shakespearean productions, with the occasional Molière thrown in.

Brian sometimes embarrassed me by coming to those dismal candidates' nights, where he always sat in the back row of folding chairs. It wasn't that he didn't want to be seen with me—he just didn't want to be seen supporting a Marxist who belonged at the time to a cult-like group that thought homosexuality was the result of degenerative capitalism. Gee, I wonder why. I would sometimes search him out in the back to see his approving smile, which made me wish I were elsewhere, maybe by the fireplace. I longed for that touch of chintz.

Neither of us was looking for an exclusive long-term relationship at the time. Hadn't heard of those, anyway. I wanted to be there with Brian, and I didn't. But there was a definite longing when I was away from him, because with him, I could be myself. No pretensions. He believed I could do anything, long before I really had done anything. It was the first relationship I'd been in where, if I said I didn't like something about my body, my partner assured me he loved it. I had a varicose vein that had developed from working out and playing sports; he would trace it with a finger and say, "How beautiful."

It was also the first time I saw how it wasn't all about how many sexual partners or trips to anonymous bath houses one could rack up. There was a danger and a beauty at play when we both knew that we could only fall so much in love, a tacit understanding that neither of us wanted to be consumed by each other's lives. To free us from the fear of commitment, we agreed to set limits going in. We may not have been in the closet to some people, but our relationship was. No meeting each other's families, no going to cocktail parties as the other's plus one. When I was with Brian, I wanted him all to myself. I wanted us to stay in. Have a drink or two and talk and take the entire experience in, whether at a country farm or in Stratford, where Brian was performing. Stratford is a small town full of the best actors and storytellers, along with world-class gossipmongers. We were both sleeping with other men as well, and had many mutual friends—including the town's first female mayor, Betty McMillan, who was the mother of my friend Eric, editor of the *Varsity* newspaper at the University of Toronto.

It was a moment in time. My first longer-than-a-couple-of-months boyfriend. Brian was part of my gay life while I also kept up with several other lives. He did not much care for sports or my interest in them, but with this arrangement, he didn't have to.

We affectionately called him the Duchess of Bedford. My friends also called him bébé, the way the French referred to Brigitte Bardot, pronouncing the letters as in the French word for "baby." A friend joked, "Well, if you become Salah Bedford, you won't have to change your monogrammed sheets"—not that I have any. But neither would a Brian Bachir have to change his.

"You will tell me if you ever need anything?" Brian asked me over lunch at a Stratford Greek diner I loved, his hand on my cheek. We couldn't exactly kiss in public. The owners had already put up with my hanging out there, ordering just a coffee, while waiting for Larry, who had my Lada, my ride back to Waterloo.

A few years later, Brian met fellow actor Tim MacDonald, who became his husband and life partner until Brian died in 2016 at age eighty.

Brian taught me about theater and culture, and I wanted to eat it all up. Maybe I taught him to relax and drop a couple of theatrical airs. He was proud of my successes, and I would go to everything he was in and send him a note, or we would acknowledge each other with sweet smiles.

There is a tender scene in Louis Malle's movie *Atlantic City*, where Susan Sarandon turns to the older, still legendary Burt Lancaster on the boardwalk while they stroll arm in arm and says: "Teach me stuff."

Brian did. Volumes.

Pierre Trudeau
has a file on me

My father always worried that I would be the one child out of five who would have trouble "making it," and not just because I was gay or a rabble-rouser at university. He thought I wore my heart on my sleeve and cared too much.

Perhaps he finally thought I would make it after all when I told him I was going to have lunch with the person he admired most, Pierre Elliott Trudeau, or "PET," as people called the prime minister. And lunch not just anywhere but at the Ritz-Carlton in Montreal.

I was going to figure out a way to make him pay for it, too. After all, our slogan at university was "Make the Rich Pay."

Long before there was Justin Trudeau, the floppy-haired twenty-third prime minister of Canada, there was his father, the charismatic fifteenth prime minister, from 1968 to 1979 and 1980 to 1984.

Canada is often cited as one of the most gay-friendly countries in the world. It ranked first in the gay travel index in 2021. It was also the fourth country in the world to adopt gay marriage. But in 1967, as the country was celebrating one hundred years of confederation, the courts convicted George Everett Klippert and locked him up indefinitely as a dangerous sex offender, merely for having gay sex. That was a tipping point. After a *Globe and Mail* investigation, the government said it would pardon men in prison for the "crime" of being gay. The *Globe* editorial on December 12, 1967, said: "The state has no right or duty to creep into the bedrooms of the nation." Trudeau took that phrase and turned it into the oft-quoted: "There is no place for the state in the bedrooms of the nation." He did thank Martin O'Malley of the *Globe* for the phrase, which might have otherwise been forgotten. How many other phrases can you remember from *Globe* editorials? Maybe I should ask former editor William Thorsell.

More important, Trudeau introduced an omnibus bill that introduced abortion under certain conditions, decriminalized the sale of contraceptives, tightened gun laws, and decriminalized homosexual acts performed in private. Although I was only twelve at the time, the discussion and debate was loud enough for everyone to notice.

Although I later demonstrated against some of Trudeau's policies, I had long admired his intelligence, vision, and quick wit. In a civil society, you discuss and debate your points of departure. In a CBC special about the greatest Canadians, as voted by twelve million people, Trudeau ranked third overall behind Tommy Douglas, who brought in universal health care, and the remarkable athlete Terry Fox.

Pierre Elliott Trudeau put Canada on the world stage. On my trips to Lebanon or China or even Albania, when I would say I was from Canada, everyone would smile and say, "Trudeau." Yes, that one. The sexy prime minister who drove people wild and inspired Trudeaumania. The one whose attempt to create a just society put him on then U.S. president Richard Nixon's bad side, a point in his favor.

Trudeau was incredibly fun to watch—like the time a photographer snapped him at Buckingham Palace at the G7 Summit in 1977 while doing an impromptu pirouette behind the queen's back. England had

Thatcher and the United States had Nixon, and the contrast could not have been more pronounced. Before we recently donated it to the Art Gallery of Hamilton, there was a large portrait of Pierre by painter Tony Scherman hanging in our dining room.

I met Pierre at the video release in 1994 of *Memoirs*, based on his book of the same title. Shane Carter, now at Polygram, arranged a private audience.

We spoke briefly. I told him I was coming to Montreal. I wasn't, but of course I would if he would meet me! I am a Montreal Canadiens fan and happily made the pilgrimage to the old Forum almost monthly during hockey season. I later followed up with a letter asking if he would meet me for lunch at the Ritz to discuss his memoir, although I mainly just wanted to tell him in person how much his famous statement about the bedrooms of the nation had meant to me as a twelve-year-old gay boy, and also the impact his decriminalization of homosexuality in the *Criminal Code* had on the world.

I reached out to a friend who had worked with Marc Lalonde, Trudeau's minister of finance, and I was also friends with the politician Marcel Prud'homme, who was friends with both Trudeau and Brian Mulroney of the Progressive Conservative Party. I came at Trudeau from all sides with three different letters. Marcel delivered them and came along to our lunch, during which Pierre was not in the mood for an interview. "Let's just have lunch," he said, and suddenly I was the one in the hot seat.

I jokingly asked whether they had a file on me, considering I had run against Trudeau for parliament as a Marxist in 1980. "Well, I'm sure they must have," he said. "There must be a few files on you and me here and there."

He had me turn off my tape recorder and wanted to know everything about that time in my life. It was almost as if I were looking for absolution when I told him I received a full year's credit in my poli-sci class for my attempt to topple him.

"Yes, those university days," he said. "Even some conservative politicians will tell you they were leftists or Marxists back then."

He also asked about my charitable work, especially in the areas of AIDS/HIV, and gay rights in Canada and the Middle East. He talked about hitchhiking through areas of Jordan to places I had not seen at the time.

We had lunch a few times. It wasn't the kind of relationship where I could phone him up and say, "Hey, Pierre, what are you doing this weekend? How about a canoe trip?" Trudeau famously had a fondness for canoe trips, including in the Arctic. "Paddling a canoe is a source of enrichment and inner renewal," he said, and he bonded with Prince Charles—now King Charles—on one of those trips, away from all the flash and protocol. He had a canoe made for Diana and Charles's wedding.

Well, no canoe trip for me. First, I don't know how to paddle one. Second, I can't swim.

At one lunch, I congratulated Trudeau on appointing Canada's first female governor general, Jeanne Sauvé. What a novel idea—an actual woman representing a female monarch! I don't think Sauvé even believed in the monarchy, but she did believe that being the first woman in that position and being from Quebec sent an important message.

"I adore her," I said. "Hey, the next time you need to appoint a gay Arab, I'm available!" My friends even came up with the idea for a mock campaign for Gay Arab Governor General, or GAGG!

"I'll make a note of it," Trudeau said dryly. "But you don't strike me as the type to get up at six in the morning and fly out to open a school or community center in northern Saskatchewan."

Great powers of observation, that one.

"Would I have to believe in the monarchy or in a higher power to be governor general?" I asked.

"Well, not believing in monarchy, I think you can get away with that. But I'm not sure I can sell the idea of an atheist governor general."

"But imagine all the art I can put on the walls at Rideau Hall!"

Years later, when Adrienne Clarkson took the position, I donated a couple of paintings by Attila Richard Lukács.

I met with Trudeau enough times that when I went back to the Ritz a few years ago with my friend Mathieu Chantelois, the editor of our magazine *Famous Quebec*, the maître d'hôtel recognized me—perhaps from my brooch, which identifies me better than a passport. Maybe I did make an impression after all, or at least on the maître d'.

"Would you like to sit at the same table where you used to sit with Monsieur Trudeau?" he asked.

I would. I did. It was a booth in the back where you can survey the whole room, but no one can truly see you.

Christopher Reeve: sometimes a kiss is just a kiss

I was taking my uncle Elias to the airport one time when we ran into my old friend Christopher Reeve, who greeted me with the classic kiss on each cheek. I introduced Elias—"This is my uncle from Lebanon"—and Reeve gave him a hug.

Uncle Elias did not give a falafel for celebrities. He barely knew who any of them were and rarely went to the movies. But he pointed at Reeve and said with awe, "Superman!"

Reeve entered every room like Superman. He generated a sexual tension. When I spoke to him, there was a palpable nervousness; I found it hard to hold his gaze as he asked questions with an engaged, earnest attitude. He wanted to know more, to understand, and all I could think in my girlish haze was, *Fuck me already and get it over with!*

I chose my words carefully around him for fear of gushing or blushing. After junkets and events, he'd jokingly ask, "Do you still have a crush on me?" I jokingly, or maybe not so jokingly, replied one time: "I found a couple of people who look like you."

"How did it go?" he asked.

"Well, one is an escort and a porn star, and it seems to be going well."

The joke (and often the truth) about actors is that they are short, but Reeve was six foot four; compare that with Tom Cruise at five foot seven. He had a powerful grace and that sexy shock of curly hair that would fall across his forehead, even before they made that curl a lasting thing in the first of his three *Superman* movies, in 1978. The action hero films gave him his career, although he feared typecasting and even turned down the leads in *American Gigolo*, *Romancing the Stone*, *Lethal Weapon*, and *Body Heat*, instead opting for *The Bostonians* with Vanessa Redgrave, and *Remains of the Day* with Emma Thompson and Anthony Hopkins.

I first met Chris at a dinner a friend had set up for him and a few gay men to discuss the 1982 black comedy mystery *Deathtrap*, which starred Reeve and Michael Caine and bore some resemblance to Caine's 1972 movie *Sleuth*. We were all immediately smitten, and that pattern would follow whenever I saw him, and in whatever company. Gay or straight, married or single, male or female—everyone just smitten. He was one of those stunning people who commands attention in any setting.

Spoiler alert: He was a bit apologetic about a scene in *Deathtrap* that immediately caused controversy, where he and Michael Caine share a kiss. There was practically no pleasing anyone, with some audience members not wanting Superman to kiss another guy, and gays wanting more than just a tepid smooch, if we were really to believe the characters were in love. Reeve said he had wanted more of a kiss, but the studio was not comfortable with a deeper kiss or deeper hints of a relationship.

What was meant to be a quick meet 'n' greet turned into a long discussion that went late into the night. Reeve captivated us all. He was passionate about life and making things better for others. We touched on civil rights, gay rights, the environment, and the arts. This was years before the ceaseless work he and his wife, Dana, would do on behalf of people with disabilities and spinal cord injury research following a fall from his horse in 1995 that left him paralyzed for the rest of his life; he died at fifty-two in 2004.

I saw Chris a number of times over the years and enjoyed long discussions about politics, art, wine, and all the charities he supported. He was interested in the work Variety Village was doing in Toronto, and we had almost crossed the *T*s on getting him there to open a state-of-the-art swimming pool when Princess Margaret accepted first. I asked if he would like to be honored with a lifetime achievement award, but like many stars still in their prime, he felt it was too early and asked if it could wait. In his place, he offered up his longtime friend Katharine Hepburn—she had chosen him in 1975 to play her grandson in *A Matter of Gravity* on Broadway.

Reeve married Dana Morosini in 1992. I never got to know her well, except on the pages of Chris's extraordinary memoir *Still Me*, but the love he and Dana shared was evident on every page and more magical than the most soaring romance. In the book, he describes the painstaking journey he made, with Dana's help, to remain a devoted husband and father and rebuild his life.

I went to see him speak after the accident a few times, including on September 4, 1996, at Toronto Western Hospital, where I later had hip surgery. He was a man of much virility—even more so in a wheelchair. I hugged Dana afterward and asked her to tell Chris that my crush on him was bigger than ever. "Mine, too," she said with a smile.

Dana also died tragically and way too early, in 2006 at age forty-four, from lung cancer. She carried on her activism until the end.

Count me among the millions who believe in these two real-life superheroes. Their courage, drive, passion, love, and generosity are exactly what the world needs, now more than ever.

Marlene Dietrich: we'll always have Paris

What would I do for love? Would I kick off my shoes and follow my beloved legionnaire on a thankless journey into the desert across the scorching sands, as Marlene Dietrich does for Gary Cooper in the 1930 film *Morocco*?

I doubt it. Then again, my husband is not a legionnaire, which makes the decision easier. Nor am I the most glamorous woman in the world, as Noël Coward described Dietrich. She has often been described as such—stylish, eternal, just this side of unknowable. Madonna and so many others took their cues from her, the way she dressed in men's clothing and embraced fluid relationships. Jacob and I have some of the most iconic photographs of her both at home and at work.

One afternoon while I was in rehab after my surgeries at Bridgepoint, my friend Suzy Okun dropped by, as she often did, to help take my mind off the pain by discussing books and movies. This particular time, she was on her way to see the play *Piaf/Dietrich*, based on a true story. I told her I was already in love with Dietrich when I saw her play the Royal York's Imperial Room in 1975 when she was seventy-three and I was twenty. Although her voice was huskier than I remembered from her movies, she was dazzling in her famous "nude dress," designed by Jean Louis—a beaded, scandalously sheer silk evening gown.

I've always been a huge fan. For her movies, such as Billy Wilder's *Witness for the Prosecution* (1957) and Orson Welles's *Touch of Evil* (1958). For the rumors of her affair with Edith Piaf, among other bisexual flings; perhaps it was Piaf she was thinking of when she sang "I've Grown Accustomed to Her Face." For her being an anti-Nazi German and possibly a spy for the Allies. For her humanitarian efforts and outspokenness during WWII, including touring with the United Service Organizations (USO) to entertain troops in Germany, the last place she was welcome. She did it, she said, "aus Anstand." Out of decency.

The least I could do was send her flowers.

I was in Paris to celebrate my friend Jim's sixty-fifth birthday in 1992. He had arranged a dinner for a group of us at the famed Maxim's restaurant in the eighth arrondissement, a chef's dinner where they had planned everything out and paired the wines for each tasting.

"I'd like a martini," Jim said to a waiter before the dinner got under way.

"Mais non, monsieur," murmured the waiter politely. "It will ruin your palate." He explained that the chef had gone to quite a bit of trouble to pair the wines with precision, and a martini just did not fit into the picture until the meal was over.

"I paid for this," said Jim, "and I would like a martini."

The waiter departed and returned with the maître d', who did not look happy. "Perhaps you should consider another restaurant, monsieur," he said.

Jim grumbled but obeyed. At the very end of the meal, the waiters delivered with a flourish two silver trays of martinis, on the house.

The moral of the story is that the French often know what's good and what's right. Which is why, when I wanted to send flowers to Marlene Dietrich—who lived at 12 Avenue Montaigne, a few doors down the street from the Hôtel Plaza Athénée, where I was staying—I followed the instructions I received from the concierge and asked to speak with the florist who provided the arrangements for Maxim's. That florist had a flower shop right next to the restaurant.

I could not just send Marlene any old flowers. They had to be good. They had to be right.

"Give them your credit card, tell them how much you want to spend, and they will know what to do," the concierge told me.

I did as he told me, and wrote out a card to be hand delivered to Madame along with the flowers. I knew she'd be there to receive them; Dietrich spent the last thirteen years of her life mostly bedridden at that address, seeing only a few close friends and family.

Upon my return to the office in Canada on Monday, my editor, Cathy Prowse, asked about my trip.

"All good. I brought you a tin of cookies from Maxim's," I said, deliberately burying the lede, before exclaiming: "I sent flowers to Marlene Dietrich!" A line, I guess, I had been waiting most of my life to deliver.

I am happy to know Madame received them, and I like to believe they brought her some pleasure. She died two days later, on May 6, 1992, at age ninety, which I heard about only when I came into the office and Cathy jokingly accosted me with: "You killed Marlene Dietrich!"

At least she died with roses and peonies.

Douglas Fairbanks Jr.: a class act

If the 1928 silent film *A Woman of Affairs* had been made a year or two later, during the more rakish pre–Hays Code years when just about anything went on screen, perhaps it would have kept more scandalous details from its source material, the 1924 novel *The Green Hat*. Nevertheless, you can read between the lines—syphilis, heroin use, homosexuality. Among others, it starred Greta Garbo and Douglas Fairbanks Jr., playing, respectively, a woman of—yes—affairs, and the brother who disowns her. The movie still holds up today.

I was fortunate to get to know the legendary Fairbanks and his third wife, Vera, late in his life. He hadn't lost a bit of what made him a star of Old Hollywood—everything about him was magical. He was engaging, approachable, and gracious. I just hate to admit that the first time I met him, it was under circumstances in which I feared I was doing him a serious dishonor.

One year, the magazine's Premiere Awards Gala at the annual

Focus on Video trade show was all set to pay tribute to Jimmy Stewart. We had the sponsors lined up and the tables sold. We had painstakingly produced a clip reel of Stewart's film highlights, which was not so easy to do in those days before you could google and download everything. Not all the clips we wanted were readily available on video, either.

Two weeks before the event, Universal Studios, which had secured Stewart for us, called with bad news: the star had an inner ear infection and wouldn't be able to fly from his home in Beverly Hills to accept his award. We were in a tough spot, but Stewart wasn't about to leave us in the lurch—he suggested we honor instead his friend Douglas Fairbanks Jr., who was living in New York at the time. "You'll love Doug," he said. "He has done everything and knows everyone."

I was hesitant to go to Fairbanks, as it seemed quite insulting to ask an actor of his stature to fill in at the last minute. It would be like saying, "Hey, we weren't going to honor you, but we're stuck, so we'll whip something up and slap it together."

It was clear that the tribute had to go ahead, even without the guest of honor. Those who had bought tickets expected it. I asked Stewart if he could record an acceptance video for us to play, but he had already talked to Fairbanks and lined him up, making it all a double diss, in a way: "So glad you're on standby, but we don't need you after all." I preferred to give him his own tribute with all the bells and whistles, but we already had an honoree lined up for the following year, Patricia Neal.

Then it occurred to me that we could have two honorees the next year. Why not? Lots of honor to spread around, and it would give us time to prepare properly to honor the star of *The Prisoner of Zenda* and *Gunga Din*.

I telephoned Fairbanks with this new arrangement. He immediately told me he'd been expecting my call. After my song and dance, still trying to avoid having him feel like a second banana, I mentioned I would be in New York in a few weeks and would love to take him to lunch. Fairbanks lived on Park Avenue and suggested a lovely restaurant nearby.

To be fair, I didn't really know that much about Fairbanks except for what everyone knew—that his father was the even more legendary Douglas Fairbanks Sr., the swashbuckler of the family, who had married along the way the legendary-to-the-max Mary Pickford, Canadian-born America's Sweetheart. But after I spoke with him, my older showbiz colleagues bombarded me with tales of how exceptional Fairbanks the Younger was—"a gentleman's gentleman" and a true Hollywood legend, known everywhere and to everyone.

"Did you know that his first wife was Joan Crawford?" gushed one. He was nineteen when he married the slightly older Crawford in 1929, leading his father to call her a cradle snatcher and an opportunist who wanted only to glom onto Douglas's famous name. They divorced after four years and mutually admitted infidelities, but Fairbanks was always supportive of her, including when Joan's daughter savaged her mom in the tell-all *Mommie Dearest*.

"Are you aware he tried to date Katharine Hepburn and she wouldn't bite, even though everyone compared him to Valentino? Did you know he has three stars on the Walk of Fame, one apiece for radio, television, and motion pictures? Have you seen him in this? Have you seen him in that?"

My friends kept hammering at me to watch old Fairbanks movies, which I did. Another filled me in on the star's three-year, very public affair with Marlene Dietrich, who had been in an open relationship with her husband, Rudolf Sieber.

By the time I had my meeting with Fairbanks in New York, I was much more up to speed on his career than when I'd first telephoned. But it didn't matter to me what movies he had made or who he had slept with—the man was every inch the gentleman. He embodied every aspect of it. He was open, caring, and charming. No topic was off the table—from WWII to the royal family (his friends, as it happened) to homosexuality and censorship in Hollywood. And even though I was a little shy asking him questions, he encouraged me. He never said an unkind word about people in his life; it was as if there were an unwritten agreement that friends don't embarrass friends.

He and his wife, Vera Shelton, came to Toronto the next year, and we paid tribute to him and to Patricia Neal, as promised.

"I feel like a mosquito at a nudist colony. I don't know where to start," he said as he accepted his award. I later realized it was his signature opening line at events to get the crowd relaxed and laughing.

Fairbanks ended up staying in town for a while after the ceremony, and he returned on occasion to help support various charities. During those times, I got to know him better. After every meal we shared, he would follow up with the loveliest personal note, handwritten with an old-fashioned fountain pen on the finest paper.

In New York we would hit the town, see a play, and go for dinner at the best restaurants. Everywhere we went, people recognized him and came over with eyes shining to say hello.

I just adored the man and his wife, who took time off from being an executive at QVC to care for him lovingly. Vera would order the same drink after every meal: hot water with lemon. I wasn't trying to show off my friendship with the couple, but among my circle I couldn't help it. After every meal, we all started saying, among ourselves: "I'll have the Vera."

A few years after we first became friends, there was a fundraiser for the Canadian Film Centre, where I was on the board. The event was celebrating *The Gold Rush*, the silent movie that Charlie Chaplin called upon its release in 1925 "the picture that I want to be remembered by." It contains the famous scene of the Little Tramp so hungry that he tries to eat his shoe.

As part of the fundraiser, the film would screen at a local concert hall, with full orchestral accompaniment by the Toronto Symphony Orchestra.

I was trying to think of a hook that could turn the upcoming gala into something bigger, when I remembered that Fairbanks had actually known Chaplin quite well. Fairbanks Sr. and Mary Pickford had been close friends with him—not to mention that Fairbanks Sr. partnered with Pickford, D.W. Griffith, and Chaplin in 1919 to create their own film studio, United Artists Corporation, a bold move toward giving artists more leverage.

I called Douglas, who naturally said he'd be delighted to come and regale the audience with a few stories from the Golden Years.

Well, he kept that audience in stitches, especially with the tale of how his father offered to host a screening of *The Gold Rush* at Pickfair, his home with Mary, before the movie's official release. As a prank, the elder Fairbanks hired actors to sit in the audience and paid them *not* to laugh at the film. If they laughed, they wouldn't get paid.

As the movie unspooled and the secretly paid audience sat there in silence, Chaplin grew ever more anxious. His new comedy, of which he was so proud, wasn't getting a single smile! Finally, Fairbanks Sr. took pity on his suffering friend and told the audience they could go ahead and applaud all they wanted. The eruption of laughs and cheers reassured Chaplin of the film's eventual place in history.

Fairbanks always knew his audience. With people clamoring to meet him during that visit to the CFC, he immediately turned the spotlight back on Norman Jewison. "I came up for *The Gold Rush*, but I'm really here to meet you," he said to Norman. Turns out his stepmother, the Canadian-born Pickford, had festooned her celebrated house with Canadian flags on Canada Day; Fairbanks called it "festoonment." "When Norman made *In the Heat of the Night* and *The Russians are Coming, the Russians are Coming*, she would exclaim: 'That's a Canadian director!'"

Fairbanks was incredibly generous with his time. He did several charity events I was involved in and would never say no or take a penny. There was a fundraiser I was working on for Casey House, with Nancy Moyen and David Arathoon, that we called "Message in a Bottle." I asked Fairbanks if he would write a message that would go inside a bottle we would auction off. He said he would and that he would also ask a few of his friends. Well, his close friends included Jimmy Stewart, Laurence Olivier, Rex Harrison, and the Queen Mother. Not shabby. He also donated a sketch given to him by his old friend Chaplin, which went at auction for a record amount. I still regret not buying it.

A few years after I bought my weekend country house in Paris, Ontario, Fairbanks finally took me up on my standing offer for him to visit. It could easily have been the other Paris, because Fairbanks was fluent in French and had starred in some French films.

He asked what I had going on, what I was working on, and I told him I was doing a few things for my small town on the fiftieth anniversary of the end of WWII. "I can come that weekend and say a few words," he suggested.

Who better than Douglas Fairbanks Jr.? He was a decorated war hero who had been a reserve officer in the United States Navy and assigned to the United Kingdom's commando unit under Lord Mountbatten, the uncle of Prince Philip and like a father to Prince Charles. A line he used to drop that cracks me up to this day is: "I was only saying to the queen the other day how I hate name dropping." Except, in his case, he really *was* friends with the royal family.

Fairbanks wrote about all that and more in a memoir, *Hell of a War*. He was decorated at the highest levels in both the United Kingdom and the United States.

This was way beyond movie stardom. The more stories Douglas shared, the more I wondered . . . is this just one person?

When he and Vera arrived at the house, they got out of the limo and Fairbanks asked whether this was the town's city hall.

"No, this is my actual house," I said. "It was built in 1842."

"Look, Vera, they have houses older than me on this side of the Atlantic!"

I couldn't imagine why he would want to spend an important military anniversary making remarks at the war memorial cenotaph in the heart of a town with a few thousand residents, but that is exactly what he did, with verve and grace. The *Paris Star* newspaper had mentioned Fairbanks would be attending, and the center of town was packed.

After he told the crowd a few stories about the war, someone approached and told me that his mother wanted to meet Fairbanks. Just as I was about to tell him that we had time pressures, that we had to go, the man explained that his mother hadn't been out of her nursing home in more than a year, but had insisted on coming when she heard her idol would be there. Fairbanks went right over to the woman and before I knew it, he was kneeling by her wheelchair for a five-minute conversation. I gave the son my business card so he could contact me, and Fairbanks later sent a framed, autographed photo, and a lovely handwritten letter. He told her she had made his day. He also sent me a long letter and photos, all of which we framed and gave to the local veterans hall. When we got back to the house, I thought he might plop on the couch in utter exhaustion. Instead, he turned to me and smiled.

"This has been one of the loveliest days I can remember," he said.

For me as well.

John Huston dashes my Ireland fantasy

Ah, the days of university. What could possibly have been more thrilling back then than sex, wine, and dancing the night away?

For me, the thrill came from reading James Joyce (well, maybe after the sex-and-wine part). It was a passion of mine to decipher his lines and let my imagination run free. Joyce gave me the freedom to interpret and dream. English is my third language, and I did not feel constrained to interpret a word or passage any particular way. It was literature by which to daydream.

When I was not studying or raising hell, I was staying up late with a glass or two of something neither Lebanese nor Irish and reading and rereading Joyce. I have always thought that the Lebanese and Irish are kindred spirits. I felt it was like interactive literature, but when friends complained that *Ulysses* and *Finnegans Wake* were unreadable, I recommended *Dubliners*, his more accessible collection of short stories. Every Feast of the Epiphany, my friends and I gathered and recreated the feast from "The Dead," one of the stories from *Dubliners*—with special attention paid to the goose and the pudding. Joyce described the meal in such detail that we could recreate most of it, down to the port and sherry.

When I read that the incomparable John Huston, of *The African Queen* and *Chinatown* fame, was going to direct an adaptation of "The Dead" with his daughter Angelica starring and his son Tony adapting the screenplay, I did everything I could to get myself onto that set. I knew that as a lover of Ireland, John would call on the talents of many Irish theater legends, and that, given his advanced age and poor health, it would most likely be his final film.

I pestered Susan Senk with the big curly red hair at the newly created studio Vestron, which owned the theatrical and video rights. Dinners, gifts, phone calls. Pleading, cajoling, demanding.

"We'll give you the cover," I said, promising to splash the movie on the front of our video trade magazine.

"Salah, it's not going to be that big a film," she said.

"I don't care!"

I prepped feverishly for the invitation I knew would come. I checked the weather in Ireland so I'd know what to pack. I figured out my flights. I dreamed of what it would be like—*I'm going to be in Dublin with John Huston!*

I finally got the go-ahead to be on the set. And then it turned out that he was filming the end of *The Dead* in a warehouse in Los Angeles. Los Fucking Angeles!

Huston, a heavy smoker, was quite ill with emphysema by then. He shot the movie from a wheelchair, hooked to an oxygen tank. He died in 1987 at eighty-one, nearly four months before the movie's release.

It remains one of my favorite films. Every nuance and gesture, captured with precision. On the Feast of the Epiphany, whatever that means, we still have the goose or veggie option, and the pudding and the port and the sherry, and then we sit back to watch Huston's masterpiece. And sink into a dream amidst one of the finest pieces of prose ever written.

"Yes, the newspapers were right: snow was general all over Ireland. It was falling softly upon the Bog of Allen and, further westwards, softly falling into the dark mutinous Shannon waves. It was falling too upon every part of the lonely churchyard where Michael Furey lay buried. It lay thickly drifted on the crooked crosses and head-stones, on the spears of the little gate, on the barren thorns. His soul swooned slowly as he heard the snow falling faintly through the universe and faintly falling, like the descent of their last end, upon all the living and the dead."

Christopher Plummer
is eager to leave

I was lucky enough to get to know the simpler, kinder Christopher Plummer—but only after I had to fight my way through meeting the *other* Christopher Plummer.

To be fair, Plummer was in rehearsals at the time, and in a rush to get onstage and accept our bloody video industry award, which he was only doing as a favor to director Norman Jewison, who in 1995 had suggested his fellow Canadian as a recipient.

"Why would you want to pay tribute to me in the video industry other than for S&M?" Plummer asked me over lunch, using one of his many pejorative references to *The Sound of Music*. He hated that movie from the top of the mountain where the hills were alive to the bottom of those grinning Von Trapp Family singers, even though film lovers revere him for his dashing role of Captain von Trapp. He described it as "so awful and sentimental and gooey." He praised his co-star, but said that working with Julie Andrews "is like getting hit over the head with a Valentine."

Nevertheless, he agreed to attend our gala and accept his accolade in 1996 while he was in the middle of rehearsals for *Barrymore,* a virtually one-man show about the elder statesman actor John Barrymore that would be opening at the Stratford Festival in Ontario. I felt anxious about the timing, but we had a limo pick him up in Stratford and bring him to the Constellation Hotel in Toronto, where a sold-out crowd awaited, and we would return him to Stratford within a decent window of time.

But, hey, you know galas! Actually, *I* know galas, and this one admittedly went a bit over time. A lot over time. Some of that time was taken by showing film clips that Chris did not feel represented his proudest moments. His best performances at that point were really on stage, and not in "The Sound of Mucus," as he also liked to call it.

Upon arrival, the limo driver informed me that Mr. Plummer had drunk liberally from the vehicle's provided libations, particularly a rare single malt I hardly ever serve myself.

The event quickly began falling behind schedule. Turns out it's hard to serve four courses to six hundred people! I only learned to time these things better after doing many more galas over the years.

Plummer grew increasingly agitated about the hour, and it took Norman's constant pleading to keep him in his seat. Irritated and inebriated, he lashed out at Norman—"Why have you never put me in one of *your* movies?"

Norman laughed it off. "Schedules, probably. I would love to work with you, and there will be other films," he reassured Plummer— although, in the end, the two never did work together.

On stage to accept his award, he was the "good" Plummer, warm and gracious while speaking of the importance of both the American Film Institute and the Canadian Film Centre, and encouraging young filmmakers to tell different stories in different voices.

When the awards finally wrapped, I walked Chris out to his limo and told him how much money the event had raised for charity and thanked him for his time and generosity—and that was when I met the *other* Christopher Plummer. He turned on me. Rehearsals were important, he declared. He didn't appreciate staying longer than agreed. He still had a two-hour commute back to Stratford ahead of him.

I took a deep breath and wished there was something in that limo minibar left for me.

Plummer called a few days later and apologized. I thought, *This is insane, I should be apologizing to him!* We had promised he'd be back by a certain hour and had not kept our end of the bargain. It had been a full eight hours from when we picked him up in Stratford to when we got him back. But I thought it was refreshing that he was so normal— no handlers, no pretension. "I would have left myself if I weren't hosting," I told him, to set him at ease.

I continued meeting him for lunches throughout the run of *Barrymore*. I even brought along former lifetime achievement award winners Douglas Fairbanks Jr. and Patricia Neal to the play's opening night in New York. "You, sir, did a finer Barrymore than Barrymore himself would have done," said Fairbanks, who had known Barrymore. He sketched Plummer in the role right onto the cover of his *Playbill* as a gift.

At the afterparty, I sat next to Zoe Caldwell, and promptly shoved my foot in my mouth by saying, "I loved you in *Piaf*," a Royal Shakespeare Company production with Jane Lapotaire that had wowed Broadway. "Thank you, darling, but that was Zoë Wanamaker," she corrected me, to which Patricia Neal added: "I know there's not a lot of Zoes out there, but the best thing to say to someone when you see them is, 'I loved you in . . . everything!'"

Chris would thereafter remember my birthday and I would remember his wedding anniversary, as they were a day apart, and I continued to catch his various stage performances—*King Lear, Inherit the Wind*— and meet him for the occasional meal. He came out to the house in Paris, Ontario, a few times when he was in Stratford, a half-hour drive. The caterers had no idea who he was but treated him (and everyone) like royalty anyway.

The Academy of Motion Picture Arts and Sciences finally recognized Plummer in 2012 when he became the oldest actor, at eighty-two, ever to win an Oscar, for his supporting role in *Beginners*. It was way overdue. (Anthony Hopkins beat the record in 2021 when he won at eighty-three for *The Father*.) In *Beginners*, Plummer plays a father who, late in life, comes out to his son, inspired by the real-life story of the director, Mike Mills.

I don't believe in a ranking system like the Oscars to judge who is "best" or "runner-up." Peter O'Toole received eight nominations and never won! And it's all arbitrary; no one gets the same conditions or environment, education, or money. We should just celebrate great roles. But it does seem an injustice that Plummer had to wait so long for that damned Oscar.

> "SOMETIMES IT'S NECESSARY TO GO A LONG
> DISTANCE OUT OF THE WAY IN ORDER TO COME
> BACK A SHORT DISTANCE CORRECTLY."
>
> *Edward Albee*

Edward Albee: no topic off the table

Not long after I began writing on entertainment, I ran into my former literature professor—I was a history and English lit major at university—at a farmer's market in Waterloo with my friends Wayne and Nancy Carter. I had just published an article on how home video would change the entertainment industry. The professor reached into her bag and pulled out the largest rolling pin I've ever seen, some wooden Mennonite job they were selling at the market. "Salah Bachir, you have sold out!" she chided me in her English-German accent, wagging her rolling pin at me. "You're writing fluff now. You had such promise!"

"Yes, but fluff pays," I told her.

What would that professor say if she knew that I subsequently befriended Edward Albee? Perhaps she would say, "I told you so," because the esteemed playwright likewise thought I wasn't living up to my potential. Although I never showed him my poetry, I did show him some of my creative writing, knowing he wouldn't bullshit me about it. He knew that I was politically inclined, although I wrote mostly about film and video, and he thought I should do more, go deeper. Stop writing about things I was not passionate about. "Your radicalism needs a voice," he told me. "Stop trying to take care of people and just write." He didn't even need a rolling pin to make his point.

I had wanted to meet Albee because he was essential for my generation, particularly as a gay man. I was young and not-quite-out, a writer who had not yet found my footing, and Albee was everything I was looking for—as a mentor, role model, someone to talk with about things that mattered. Bold. Handsome. Funny. Unapologetic. Powerful. His plays are entertaining and engaging, brilliantly written and mildly provocative. I spent hours after performances passionately discussing them with friends. Themes, images, ideas. Entire scenes from *The Zoo Story*, *A Delicate Balance*, and *Who's Afraid of Virginia Woolf?* stayed with me long after I'd seen them. In later years, I added *Three Tall Women* and *The Goat, or Who Is Sylvia?* to the mix.

My love of his work led me to go see Albee speak at an event. I was entranced. He railed fearlessly against conservative politics and an uneducated electorate. How can people deny other people freedom in the name of freedom?

It was electric.

I introduced myself. Slowly, we developed a friendship. I have to admit, I felt an immediate attraction to him. An intellectual attraction, sure—anyone would feel that—but there was more. He was only three years younger than my dad, which brought up a dazzling bouquet of transgressive issues, ones Edward was totally open to discussing. He loved nothing more than a passionate discussion of politics, relationships, and sex. No topic was off the table. He enjoyed pushing the boundaries. Our conversations were more like the ones you have in all-night college dorm sessions and never encounter again after university.

Albee was everything the 1980s was not—with the supremely superficial at one end and Albee ("I write to find out what I'm talking about") at the other. I can't even fathom it today. I was young, that time of life when you think you can do anything, so I didn't think it was the least bit out of my league to befriend Albee. I'm astonished I wasn't more nervous or didn't try to choose my words more carefully while in the company of one of the most notable American playwrights. Language, after all, was his thing, for better or worse. I say worse, because although he was proud that he never sold out or practiced self-censorship, he did get in trouble for speaking his mind in unfiltered language.

For example, despite the many awards it won, *Who's Afraid of Virginia Woolf?* lost out on the 1963 Pulitzer for drama only because the award's advisory board mopped their brows over the language and sexual themes. Albee always claimed he had "three and a half" Pulitzers, having felt cheated of one for *Virginia Woolf* when several voters refused even to see or read the play.

I never tried to sound literary or change the way I spoke around Edward. Yet we often talked about language and its role in society. He thought of language as a flowing river that should bend and go where it goes. It ain't a matter of who versus whom! This is a way society restricts people, he said. Anyway, it's in the quiet times you get to know someone, maybe from the words unsaid. The quiver of the lips when they speak. The anger they still carry and the passion they choose to unload. I always felt restricted because I never paid attention to grammar and had sleep-walked through spelling classes. English was, after all, my third language.

We shared a dislike of the chiding William Safire language column in the *New York Times* and discussed how language is often the thing that holds back immigrants and those from lower economic classes who haven't had the time, luxury, entrée, or inclination to get a private tutor in Greek or know just where to put a comma. There are neighborhoods where the guiding principle is to invent words. It frees you from the shackles.

I visited Edward in New York and sometimes in Montauk, where he lived with his husband of 34 years, artist and sculptor Jonathan Thomas (who was born in Hamilton, Ontario, near our country place). Jonathan helped him give up alcohol, after which he became more focused and less, possibly, like the squabbling, passive-aggressive George in *Virginia Woolf.*

Albee carried a certain regret that Warner Bros. did not go with Bette Davis, his personal choice, when it came to casting the film. "That would have been different," said a friend on our way home from that discussion. "Bette Davis opposite James Mason," which is what the studio had first suggested.

Albee had written the award-winning play—first staged in 1962— with Bette in mind. Think of her—the "fasten your seatbelts, it's going to be a bumpy night" Bette, the "old age isn't for sissies" Bette—having at Albee's biting dialogue as half of a middle-aged university faculty couple plumbing the depths of their complicated, deteriorating, fantasy- unraveling relationship. Albee has said that his play was about the fear "of living life without false illusions."

Still, the Taylor-Burton double-bill was quite a casting coup at the time of the movie's release in 1966, with Elizabeth Taylor hurling vit- riol against real-life sparring partner and on-again-off-again husband Richard Burton. Albee thought it was Taylor's best work, and did not at all mind that those royalties became his cash cow—royalties equaling freedom. Yet, he still had quibbles, including the emotionally-leading score that he detested.

I had always wondered, what was he thinking while writing a play as important as this? But he said he usually didn't go into a play knowing where it would lead, or where it would go after it's done. What would a sequel look like? Would George and Martha get their act together and have kids? Move to the Hamptons, maybe? Edward always said that men see themselves as lacking in his plays, while women get it.

Albee is another of the very few people whose place I stayed at over- night. Well, I was a bit more than a houseguest. I knew there would be no boundaries and I actually looked forward to that.

Funny I should be his houseguest, though, in light of *A Delicate Balance*, where various houseguests descend upon an upper-middle-class couple in the wake of an unnamed terror. It challenged the nature of friendship, or the boundaries we maintain, and won him the first of his three Pulitzers—the other two were for *Seascape* and *Three Tall Women*—and the 1973 film adaptation starred Katharine Hepburn, Paul Scofield, Lee Remick, Joseph Cotten, and my old friend Kate Reid. Albee called it his social comedy. I saw the Lincoln Center production, with Rosemary Harris and Elaine Stritch, a few times. Albee came along twice, but was aware that everyone might know he was there—so I bought tickets for seats in the back to help him go incognito.

The play very neatly presages the COVID-19 pandemic; at least, that's how it seems at the pandemic time of this writing. I wonder what that couple in *A Delicate Balance* would do today? Would they take people in and have them stay a while if they were in need? We certainly have done that many times in cases where friends of friends or even total strangers were fleeing conflict.

In truth, I felt lost sometimes, not knowing what I had to offer a man like Albee. But I also saw his invitations to Montauk as ones of camaraderie, thought and reflection, with more added benefits than just a sensational view. I first needed to exhaust myself in the art scene and hot asphalt of New York for a few days beforehand so as not to seem overeager or have him think I came just to see him. I readied myself for that gorgeous spot overlooking the Atlantic. As freeing as it could be, I could also feel trapped in another man's house, with another man's desires—a man whose voracious appetites helped fuel his art.

I had no doubt that Jonathan was the love of his life. No illusions. But they had an open relationship, and Edward and I had discussed our mutual dislike of sleeping alone in our country houses. So, it just happened. What stays in my mind is how someone who was three years younger than my father would want to cuddle with me, or put his head in my lap and talk about family and the sins of our fathers, and the sins of our mothers as well. Sometimes I'd stroke his hair and kiss his forehead, and say, Let it go. Can we? Should we?

For a time, we did.

By cuddling and comforting him, I had the sensation of comforting my father when *his* father left him at age nine. Staring out into the calm waters with this brilliant, gorgeous man, I wondered: When does the child become the parent? What kind of father would I be someday?

In return, just his hand on my cheek was, in a way, something a parent does to a child. The approving touch. An appreciative smile. An intimate gesture that could mean so much more. It was also a reflection on how those in the AIDS generation were losing that connection with families who rejected them, especially mothers. Mothers are supposed to forgive everything, but Edward did not get that from his adoptive mother.

The hand on the face, as if leaning in for a kiss if the time or situation had been different. I got it from my parents, and from former married lovers who knew they could not come out, and wished that the situation had been different. The erotic, gentle power of a hand on the face.

Those visits turned out to be as much therapy for me as for Edward. When do we get past the hurts of childhood and recognize who we have hurt in return? What grief and disappointments do we carry and freely pass along to others?

A friend who noticed photos of my Toronto apartment listed for sale online commented on the round Biedermeier-type table and the rock crystal chandelier. I was shocked to realize it was pure Albee. I hadn't made the connection until the friend mentioned it, that I had surrounded myself, in some ways, with items that emulated the look of Edward's place in Montauk. We internalize the comfort and love we receive from others, and we unconsciously decorate our lives with reminders of those we treasure.

When I think of Edward, which I often do, I think of our walks around Montauk and on the beach, tender moments, and also conversations where I really had to keep up—but the image that most comes to mind of our friendship is the silence between the words. The reflecting upon the words of a man whose plays have haunted me. The white space between some of his most brilliant lines, but what a view.

"PEOPLE SAY THAT MONEY IS NOT THE WAY
TO HAPPINESS, BUT I ALWAYS FIGURED IF YOU
HAVE ENOUGH MONEY, YOU CAN HAVE A KEY MADE."

Joan Rivers

Joan Rivers:
Can we really talk?

After I met Joan Rivers a few times through different events and awards shows, she asked why I never had her as a guest entertainer, so we hired her for one of our fundraisers for The 519. A natural fit, I thought, given her popularity with the gay community. I, too, had fallen under her spell and laughed at the put-downs, rationalizing that the jokes were not about me. She had not specifically mentioned me by name, so they didn't apply.

After we booked her, she wanted us to change the date to coincide with her appearances on The Home Shopping Network, where she was promoting her jewelry and clothing line. We were already paying for her flight and hotel, and had advertised her appearance, so it was an inconvenience, but she continued to think of us as the side dish to her HSN entrée, the wilted spinach to the main course. We duly moved the date of our gala at the last minute to accommodate her selling schedule.

Joan was high maintenance from the get-go—always wound up and tense, like someone trying to get a task done at record speed so she could move on to the next thing.

"High maintenance" is actually a kind term for her bad behavior. We had jazz icon Jackie Richardson, a talent powerhouse, open the show, and Joan didn't like that. Anyone who sees or hears Jackie sing winds up open-mouthed in awe, but Joan summoned me backstage to say: "Get that bitch offstage, she's stealing my thunder." We had to cut Jackie's three numbers down to two.

When it was Joan's turn in the spotlight, I laughed politely at some of her jokes, which I felt I had to since I was in the front row. We all laughed nervously.

But I felt queasy about it and later reassessed. She had not bothered to update any of her material for the occasion, even telling a joke about Amy Carter some twenty years after Amy was a kid in the White House. Cringeworthy, recycled jokes about the tragically departed Karen Carpenter's eating habits, or non-eating habits.

"Madonna has just lost 30 pounds—she shaved her legs!" Huh?

Worse, I thought, were her fat jokes about Elizabeth Taylor and Orson Welles. A new generation was starting to know of Orson only through Joan's put-downs of him and her jabs at his wine commercials. "We will sell no wine before its time; that obviously doesn't apply to meals," she'd joke at Orson's expense. I wasn't the only one cringing at her assaults on body image, especially when Jackie Richardson and I failed to meet Joan's weight-based beauty standards. With her huge success and $26 million Manhattan apartment and countless plastic surgery procedures, Joan increasingly made a living off of savaging other celebrities for how they looked and what they wore, endlessly recycling the punchlines, dialing it in. It was lazy and disingenuous, and never acknowledged the pain she inflicted on real people.

Although she was a friend to gays, she also insulted them and palled around with the Reagans and Barbara Walters—who dated the notorious Roy Cohn—at the height of the AIDS epidemic. I think it became a knee-jerk thing with her, a treadmill she fell onto that she mistook for a comedy routine. She was so wound up for success and unable to get any distance from it, wanting desperately to be the Lucille Ball of her time. This was the contrast I found between her and Phyllis Diller: Phyllis was also not comfortable in her skin, but she made fun of her facelifts and Botox injections. She owned it, as well as owning her imperfections, and thereby rose above them—whereas Joan remained trapped in an old-school pulverizing of every perceived threat, of anyone who presented to her as competition.

I told her backstage after the show that I was not happy to have felt compelled to lead the obligatory standing ovation at the same venue where Tina Turner, Ella Fitzgerald, and Eartha Kitt had performed. "I'm not sure what's going on in your life, but that wasn't cool," I said.

She would have none of it. She left behind the flowers we had given her in her dressing room, so we gave them to one of the women cleaning up after her.

Sometime later, I was at a Four Seasons brunch with her and some others at a big table in the back. She insisted on sitting where she could survey the room and make comments about who was wearing what. "Who are your earrings by?" she asked me. I wore big white diamonds with a square yellow diamond in the center, but I said I didn't want to be part of that "who are you wearing" game. I hated that whole schtick and the red-carpet criticizing.

"Oh, Salah is angry because I didn't tell his favorite jokes at one of his fundraisers," she griped to the table at large.

"You don't want to piss off Salah, because he knows everybody," piped up one person, who added dismissively: "The good news is he has a fundraiser every month. You'll get another shot."

"Oh, there won't be a next time," I said pointedly.

Joan didn't eat her lunch. She never seemed to eat anything. She took a little taste and then pushed the food around her plate like a landscape architect hard at work. I excused myself and left early, blaming it on my blood sugar.

After that, when she saw me at events and awards shows, she did not bark at me: "What are you wearing?" At least she had learned that lesson: I wear whatever I want.

I saw her one more time before her death at 81 in 2014. Her invitation demoted me from lunch to a mere tea, but I still kept in touch, looking for something deeper or more personal beyond the act. She hardly ate the food. She said the smoked salmon tea sandwich would give her fish breath, so she nibbled only on the cucumber and cream cheese one.

She was at least slightly apologetic. Said she felt pulled in every direction all the time, didn't know how to slow down. And I do recognize and respect all the barriers she had to break through.

She gave me a little gift of monogrammed handkerchiefs along with a hug, and even seemed to shed a tear. With that, she was off to sell jewelry on the air to women, many of whom were plus-size, just the sort she ridiculed in her act. She left me alone with a three-layer tea tray full of untouched food. I was up to the task.

Later, I had to chuck the handkerchiefs, a combination of silk and linen that needed dry cleaning after every use. Too high maintenance for me.

MY PATRON SAINT: Andy Warhol. *Photo by Greg Gorman, 1986*

THE MOST DIVINE: Fearless. One of the first photographs in our collection. *Photo by Greg Gorman, 1987*

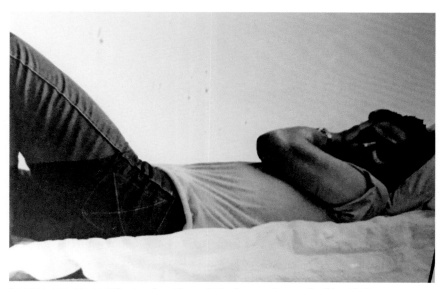

SALLLLAHHHHH: That's what I heard Marlon say instead of "Stella" in *A Streetcar Named Desire* when I was seventeen, first year of university. *Photo courtesy of the author*

A LITTLE PIECE OF HEAVEN: My two grandmothers, best friends Anissa and Sadie, in front of our house in Lebanon. I was born in the room right behind them. *Photo courtesy of the author*

WE ARE FAMILY: My mom, Najla, and my grandmother Anissa with the five of us in this 1963 photo taken among the oak trees of the backyard of our house in Lebanon. From left: my brother George, sisters Anissa and Inaam—which means "gift" in Arabic, although she later changed it to Grace when some locals could not pronounce it. Front row: I'm waving while holding my younger brother Ziad's hand. *Photo courtesy of the author*

BEYOND *THE CHIFFON TRENCHES*: The most fabulous André Leon Talley. *Photo by Kate Daniels*

THE LOOK OF LOVE: Hollywood Icon Ruby Keeler, born in Nova Scotia, in one of her last public appearances. *Photo by Nancy Carter*

THE WINDSOR DECISION: With Edith Windsor, whose landmark case led to gay marriage in the United States and overturning the Defence of Marriage Act. *Photo by Kevin Beaulieu*

ALLY. HERO: Celebrating author John Irving with the Ally Award. "I try to tell well-plotted stories that broaden readers' empathy for characters who are overlooked and prosecuted, especially queer and trans characters." *Photo by George Pimentel*

FANG!!! Leave 'em laughing as you go. Phyllis Diller at the Premiere Video gala, 1999. *Photo by Nancy Carter*

SUNRISE BOULEVARD: I am ready for my close-up, Mr. Gorman. *Photo by Greg Gorman*

CONSTANT CRAVING: k.d. lang singing at our wedding, October 17, 2017—a fundraiser, of course. We raised enough money for a community garden, something we would have put on a wedding registry if we'd had one. *Photo by John Narvali*

NOT SO GINGERLY: Belting out "They Can't Take That Away from Me" to Ginger Rogers. *Photo by Keith Houghton*

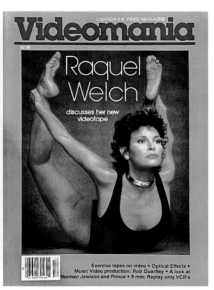

BEYOND CLEAVAGE: That's what Raquel Welch called her autobiography. You would not think that one of the most beautiful women would be dismissed because of body image! Here she is on the cover of *Videomania* in 1984 to promote her yoga tape. *Cover design by Kim-Lee Koh*

THE STAR RUBY: No matter how many rubies I wear, nothing can outshine the spectacular Kim Cattrall at the 2017 Canadian Fashion Awards. *Photo by Kate Daniels*

C'EST SI BON: The great Eartha Kitt in 2004 as she kicks off The 519 capital campaign at the Imperial Room. *Photo by Keith Houghton*

TRUDEAU-MANIA: My nephew John Salah Bachir in 2017 with current prime minister Justin Trudeau. And me with Justin's father, the great prime minister Pierre Elliott Trudeau, who decriminalized homosexuality fifty-six years earlier. *Photo courtesy of the author*

VIEW WITH A VIEW: My nephew John Beale at my grandparents' old house—with my uncle Elias, who was my grade three teacher, and my uncle Chawki, who was Lebanon's ambassador to the UN. *Photo by Eli Khalife*

ROSE VIDEO: Eugene Levy, long before *Schitt's Creek*, hosting a tribute to MGM's Golden Boy Van Johnson. Van was in a touching mood that night. Maybe grabbing mood is more accurate. *Photo by Shane Carter*

THE CANDY MAN CAN: With the mesmerizing Ben Vereen at The 519 gala. Ben would call me in the hospital to sing to me on the phone. *Photo by George Pimentel*

TAKE ME TO YOUR LEADER: Margaret Atwood comes to visit, bearing gifts: a limited-edition copy of *The Testaments* for Jacob's birthday, in addition to celebrating my touch-and-go but ultimately successful kidney transplant. *Photo courtesy of the author*

TIARA FOR TWO: David Furnish at my 60th birthday celebration in Paris. David and his husband Elton John have raised an astonishing six hundred million dollars for HIV/AIDS prevention and education. *Photo by Mathieu Chantelois*

CORONATION STREET: Toronto Pride Parade 2016, my second time as Grand Marshal. *Photo courtesy of the author*

ALL OF ME: Feeling comfortable enough with my body to allow the great Greg Gorman to snap me in the nude in our garden in Paris. *Photo by Greg Gorman, 1999*

"THEY PUT ME IN SO MANY WAR PICTURES
BACK THEN, AS IF BEING A WAR HERO MEANT
YOU COULD NOT BE A HOMOSEXUAL."

Van Johnson

Van Johnson learns to fly

When *SCTV* debuted in the late 1970s, I raved about it to anyone who would listen. John Candy came to quite a few Variety Club events and I interviewed him for our magazines whenever he had a film out; we had a routine where I'd be the adopted Lebanese brother of his delightfully smarmy Johnny LaRue character. After lunch one time, when we'd both had a couple of drinks, I took him to Kings Sport, which specialized in oversized clothing. We both bought shirts. I even passed up an interview with Richard Pryor to put John on the cover for *Brewster's Millions*, but we were a Canadian magazine, after all, and tried to cover homegrown talent whenever possible. One of our video galas raised funds for a heart centre in John's name at a local hospital after he died of a heart attack at age fifty-two.

Also from *SCTV*, Andrea Martin headlined a couple of galas for us—one for The 519 and one for Saint Joseph's Health Centre in Toronto. I got to know her through her sister Marcia, a well-known television producer, and she bonded with Jacob's dad, asking after

Patrick by name from the stage when she couldn't spot him in the audience.

We've had so many memorable times at our galas that it's hard to pick favorites: Halle Berry attending when she was first starting out, Ali MacGraw promoting her yoga tape and talking turkey with Norman Jewison about her one-time husband Steve McQueen. Donald O'Connor asking the lead singer of the band if he could sing "Fly Me to the Moon," and the band, if not the whole room, in awe. Yes, please! Janet Leigh getting stuck in the bathroom when the power went out; seeing the concerned look on my face when she finally returned to the table, she put her hand on my cheek and reassured me: "I did more than twenty takes with Alfred Hitchcock for the shower scene in *Psycho* and I was married to Tony Curtis. Don't worry about me."

Eugene Levy, also from *SCTV*, was a total sport and hosted a couple of the early galas. One that stands out was a tribute to MGM musicals— "more stars than are in the heavens"—with several of those very stars on hand, including Van Johnson and June Allyson. The gala seemed straight out of a Marx brothers movie, slapstick at its best, with one of the guests at the head table falling off the raised dais—he wasn't hurt— and the Czech Canadian opera singer Jan Rubeš, best known for playing the Amish patriarch in *Witness*, deciding to serenade "June Allysonova" with an original song about how much her movies meant to him as a young man in Czechoslovakia.

But the evening started to feel a bit sad. Van Johnson kept grabbing Eugene's ass at the podium, not to mention the rears of a few other people nearby. I got a dose of both ass and crotch grab—and this was a few years before crotch-grabbing became an acceptable thing in music videos. Even then, you grab your *own* crotch, not someone else's. It was only the comic genius of Eugene Levy that kept the evening on topic and moving along.

Van was MGM's all-American golden boy. The studio helped us put together the clip reel for that night, including a suspicious amount of Van's war-movie footage, considering that it was an evening to honor musicals.

I see no problem with an all-American hero being gay, but that night with the ass-grabbing was the first time I realized that Van Johnson was gay. But how do we retain our memories of a movie icon, and not of a lecherous older guy trying to make up for lost opportunities?

We took the still boyish matinee idol for drinks in the lounge of the "glamorous airport Marriott," where everyone was staying. It was partly to pay tribute to a guest who had co-starred with Garland, Gable, Bogart, and Hepburn and Tracy, among others, but it was also to make sure he didn't get into any further shit that night. After the lounge closed, I invited him and a few friends back to my suite, which was on the same floor as Van's. He seemed quite taken with my good-looking friend Lance. We wanted to talk movies and what it was like not being out, but he would not have any of it. "Everybody in Hollywood knew about me," he insisted. "I just would not have a job or be here at all if the rest of the world knew as well. Would Cary Grant have had a career?"

It was only in 1999, five years before her death, that his ex-wife publicly admitted that the studio put pressure on her to marry Van "to quell rumors about his sexual preferences," dubbing MGM honcho Louis B. Mayer "someone with the ethics and morals of a cockroach."

After some banter and anecdotes—he credited Lucille Ball for saving his career by making sure an MGM casting director was sitting at the next table when she took him to dinner—the evening turned reflective about the actor's life and career. He said his co-stars had played along, and even tried to set him up, "but I knew falling in love would be bad for my career."

As the night went on, he began to regret the ass-grabbing, fearing he might have embarrassed me, but I was exhausted from working on the gala all day and didn't want to sit there as everything turned maudlin. We walked him down the hall to his suite, where he asked if my friend Lance would stay with him. Lance demurred.

Van wrote me a lovely note afterward to thank me, and we met for lunch a couple of times close to his Fifty-Fourth Street penthouse. Was there regret? Remorse? No, he said. He was just grateful. "We all have lots of baggage and if we say we don't, we're just being the mediocre actor reading someone's lines," he said. "Being in the closet does not mean you don't have a great love life. It was never a case of me being repressed, as you call it."

He even described those days as possibly an easier time for him than it would be today, with paparazzi lying in wait for every hand held or every mouth kissed. Back then, you ran the scoop the studio sanctioned, or there would be no more scoops.

"When I did *The Music Man* in London, I felt so free," he said.

But it was only when he appeared in *La Cage Aux Folles* on Broadway, playing a gay man comfortable in his own skin, that, as he put it, "I thought I could fly."

Celeste Holm joins us for an Uncle Vanya

A friend of mine had brought Celeste Holm to the famed Russian Tea Room in New York for lunch and a few rounds of Uncle Vanyas—vodka, lemon juice, and blackberry liqueur. She quickly realized it was a party comprising her and three well-dressed and rather good-looking and adoring men. She still looked much the same as we remembered her from the silver screen—elegant, if a bit grayer. Celeste and I both wore a navy suit (mine was midnight blue, actually), and we both accessorized with a brooch. There was an instant connection.

But Celeste seemed distant. Someone brought up *All About Eve* and I bragged about my dinner with Bette Davis—not realizing that Celeste and Bette famously did not get along, even though they had played besties in the multi-Oscar-winning 1950 drama. The two actresses got off on the wrong foot when Celeste's morning-person cheeriness set Bette's teeth on edge, and things between them didn't improve after that. When I mentioned my adoration for her nemesis, and blurted like a know-it-all that Bette's performance has been called "syllable-perfect" by writer/director Joseph L. Mankiewicz, Celeste was completely professional and merely murmured a tight-lipped "Mm-hmmm."

We soon found the way to Celeste's heart, though—by turning the conversation back to her.

"Salah just bought this stunningly beautiful house in Paris," one of my friends enthused, purposely leaving off "Ontario" to give the location more cachet. "It was built in 1842 and has acres of gardens and antiques and art," he said, exaggerating just a bit. "It's absolutely stunning."

"Oh, well, that's amazing," said Celeste.

"We all go there to recuperate after a breakup or when we need pampering. In fact, we call it the Celeste Home for Wayward Fags!"

The actress burst out laughing in a way we never saw her do in 1948's *The Snake Pit*, or 1947's *Gentleman's Agreement*, for which she won an Oscar, and loudly enough that everyone in the restaurant noticed and must have wished they were at our fun table.

Maybe she should have come over one day. Take Celeste and mix with three adoring men, bottomless Uncle Vanyas, and the Russian Tea Room. A recipe right out of *All About Eve*.

Margaret Atwood is for the birds, literally

Just as you can run into famous actors on the streets of Manhattan, you can also run into the most renowned literary minds at a Canadian book prize event or even the grocery store—if I ever did the groceries, that is.

At the annual gala for the Giller Prize—an award created by our friend Jack Rabinovitch in memory of his wife, Doris Giller, at one time the book editor of the *Toronto Star*—I would see three powerhouse authors sitting all in a row at a center-front table: Margaret Atwood; her husband, Graeme Gibson; and Nobel-winner Alice Munro. "For the price of a dinner in this town you can buy all the nominated books. So, eat at home and buy the books," was Jack's favorite saying. But of course, we always attended the Giller awards in person. I would walk by that center-front table and bow—not because they were literary royalty, which they were, but to acknowledge the spirit of creativity and perseverance they personify. I certainly would not bow before any pope or king and queen.

Margaret—Peggy to her friends, although I have always been too abashed to call her that—is probably the only person around whom

I choose my words carefully, or at least make the attempt. How can I not? I certainly realize the enormity of Atwood's output—more than fifty books of fiction, poetry, critical essays, and graphic novels, published in more than forty-five countries. She has probably come out with a new book in the time it has taken me to compile this list.

When it was released in 1985, *The Handmaid's Tale* vividly anticipated the perils women today face at the hands of a totalitarian, white-supremacist-leaning patriarchy; this prescience has made the Hulu series adaptation a huge streaming hit. Staffers at my office would stand with nervous attention when Atwood visited; Zandra even wore the red *Handmaid's Tale* outfit in her honor.

"May I?" asked Margaret. She approached Zandra and adjusted the headpiece as if she were directing an episode.

That is why, when I call or send Atwood an email, I edit myself. I'm surprised I'm able to get any words out at all.

I had met her many times in passing, but I got to know her better while helping to organize a gala for Margaret's beloved Pelee Island Bird Observatory (PIBO), a welcoming rest stop for migrating birds as well as an observational lab for studying migration patterns. She and her husband helped found it in 2003. Sometimes people go directly to Gala Salah for help raising money for good causes, and sometimes Gala Salah simply barges in and offers to make himself useful, which is how I came to emcee and co-chair the PIBO event.

After I introduced Atwood from the stage, she thanked the sponsors and attendees. "I never dreamed this could be done on such a scale," she enthused. "It's hard to raise money for a cause like migratory birds. It's not like we're raising money for some medical issue like kidney disease, after all!"

This met with polite applause from the audience. Back at the podium, I thanked her, adding: "Gee, Margaret, I rescheduled my dialysis so I could be here!"

This got a bigger response from the audience, many members of which had donated millions toward kidney research and the Bachir/Yerex clinics, named after me and Jacob, at St. Joseph's Health Centre. "No worries," I assured the crowd. "If Ms. Atwood has not yet, she will be solicited later tonight." And, of course, she came through.

Our lead sponsors that night were a bank and a beer company. Atwood had written newspaper op-ed pieces, one of which had dropped that same week and another a few weeks earlier, criticizing both entities. "Forget it, we've already cashed the check," I joked when a bank representative came over to greet me at the event.

What I learned that night was that Margaret never forgets. You do something nice for her just once, even the smallest gesture, and she repays it many times over. She becomes a part of your community. We all fell under her protective cloak. There she is on a video tribute for my sixty-fifth birthday, singing "Happy Birthday."

With her boundless energy, she seems to have found the fountain of youth. Here she is at a demonstration. There she is helping to organize a fundraiser, or writing a column defending the environment or transgender rights. She is always up on the latest events, and on language, politics, and history.

"There's a difference between belief and fact," she has explained about transgender rights. "And you should not confuse the two. You can believe all you like that trans people aren't people, but it happens not to be a fact. It is not true that there are only two boxes. So, the two questions to ask about anything are: Is it true? And is it fair? So, if it's not true that there are only two gender boxes and gender is fixed and immutable, then is it fair to treat trans people as if they're not who they say they are?"

She has more than two million avid Twitter followers. ("Rejoice in Nature's infinite variety!" is one of her tweets.) She always tells interviewers she "goofs off too much," but I'm exhausted just hearing her schedule. You have to do your research to keep up with her.

When she visited our apartment in Toronto, the concierge called up. "Mr. B, you've had some interesting people over, but this is really the Great One." In hockey circles, that would be Wayne Gretzky, but in overall star power, it's Margaret Atwood.

She had arrived at the apartment that time to bring Jacob a birthday gift—a rare collectors' edition of *The Testaments*, her 2019 sequel to *The Handmaid's Tale*.

"You're one of the most significant futurists of our time," Jacob told her—not to flatter her, just a statement of fact. It was a fact, and it was fair.

She spent the next several minutes rejecting the label of "futurist." By the time she wrapped up her thoughts on it, after summing up a few of her story narratives, she conceded: "Oh, well, maybe I *am* a futurist."

Later, to welcome me home from the hospital after my kidney transplant and subsequent series of medical traumas, she sent the most gorgeous bouquet of flowers and regularly checked in on me from her world tours. Not only will she lend a hand if asked, she will suggest other people to approach, or will approach them on your behalf.

Sadly, her husband fell prey to dementia and died in 2019 while accompanying her on tour to promote *The Testaments*. Margaret had decided to take him along so that they could stay close and share her success. When the two were at my Toronto apartment for dinner one time—a Lebanese feast prepared by renowned chef Simon Kattar— what impressed me most was how the two interacted, with intelligence and low-key humor, despite the progression of his disease. She allowed Graeme to be Graeme in a way we never really see in a society that shields age and impairment from the collective gaze. It was such a tender way to see them.

It's still crazy to me to think that I was reading Margaret Atwood in high school—she is only sixteen years older than I am—and that I'd wind up being friends with her all these decades later. When I marched in demonstrations when I was younger and had no money, and had only my dad's broken-down Delta 88, I kept a list of three people I could call in case of emergency—to pay for a tow or for bail. If I had such a list today, Margaret would be on it. Not only am I certain I can count on her if I'm ever in need, but no one will do more research and argue a case more passionately and persuasively—and all because I helped out with something I felt passionate about anyway: birds and the environment.

"SHE HAD A VOICE, AND SHE USED HER VOICE NOT ONLY
IN THE MUSIC WORLD, BUT IN THE POLITICAL WORLD.
SHE WAS SUPREME. SHE WAS AND IS SUPREME, ALWAYS.
SUPREME IN ALL THAT SHE DID, SUPREME IN
ALL THAT SHE WORKED FOR."

Smokey Robinson

Mary Wilson, always supreme

There should be another Supremes song: "B-E-T-R-A-Y-A-L." I would love to hear Mary Wilson sing it.

Marvelous Mary. But what a tough life.

Mary was born into poverty in Detroit, and her earthy voice was never allowed to soar at full volume; she was negated every step of the way as Berry Gordy and Motown squeezed her out of her rightful place in the Supremes. It was almost the classic immigrant story—always on the outside looking in.

I was in New York when my friends Randy Erickson and Walter McClenton mentioned that Mary had a new apartment and would we like to go for drinks and check it out. Walter had gotten to know Mary through his old friend Allen Poe, who had a beautiful bond with Mary— he was her assistant, her stylist, her jack-of-all-trades. He designed some of her "most fabulous" gowns.

Drinks at the apartment led to dinner at a nearby restaurant, which led to after-dinner drinks back at the apartment and laughs and conversation until early the next morning. None of us left the party. None of us noticed the time pass.

"What could be better than having dinner with four gorgeous gay men?" she said to us.

As I developed a friendship with Mary, I also developed a huge feeling of brotherly protection for her. I felt personally offended by every sling and arrow of outrageous fortune that came her way.

As most people know, the bigger the Supremes got, the more of the limelight Diana Ross wanted—limelight that also rightfully belonged to the other Supremes. If you look at photos from the earlier days, you'll see Mary smack in the center of the group. She and Florence Ballard had the strongest voices.

Motown executive Berry Gordy groomed Diane—as Mary always called her—to be the star (and his lover), and soon she was making decisions for herself, not for the group as a whole. She made other people smaller so she might look bigger. When reporters visited backstage to do interviews, Diana's dressing room overflowed with flowers—but she'd had many of them sent to herself so she would look even more beloved.

B-E-T-R-A-Y-A-L.

While taping the 1983 TV special *Motown 25: Yesterday, Today, Forever*, the highly anticipated "reunion" of the Supremes became anything but. Ironically, it was while performing their hit "Someday We'll Be Together" that Diana turned on Mary with such a vengeance—in front of a live audience, no less—that the altercation was cut for the broadcast but was widely publicized anyway.

"Diane turned and forcefully shoved me aside," explained Mary in her memoir *Dreamgirl: My Life as a Supreme*. "The audience gasped, appalled. Diane's eyes widened in shock at the realization that I wasn't about to back down, and that all these people had just witnessed her little tantrum. She got so flustered she lost her place in the song . . ."

Mary was a huge talent—and beauty—in her own right. The bitterness that marked her relationship with Diana was because Mary always got the short end of the stick. Never paid fairly. Never sharing equally in the billing, the profits, the legacy. "I love Diane, but we are into different things right now and sometimes you need space," Mary said one time over dinner—she loved to cook, and even when we offered to take her out, she'd already have something in the oven. "If another opportunity for a reunion comes up, I would be right there."

She was more than just Diana's castoff, of course. Author, activist for musicians' and civil rights, motivational speaker on overcoming adversity. She was a businesswoman, as well as the inspiration for the Lorrell Robinson character in *Dreamgirls*. She was wife, mother, glamorous grandmother. When I asked why she worked so hard, she said, "That is what I do. I love to sing and work."

For me, it has never been about meeting a celebrity for the sake of celebrity. I have always said that the only autograph I want is on a check. It's really about seeing the connection between how they do their job and how they use that celebrity to promote good in the world.

What I remember most vividly about Mary is the passion with which she spoke about social justice and humanitarian issues. She used that powerful voice of hers not just to sing but to help change the world. She was active in missions all over the world to eradicate hunger, and she addressed social, political, and cultural issues, including civil and gay rights. Colin Powell appointed her as a cultural ambassador in the United States.

Mary Wilson made herself heard, both as a Supreme and post-Supremes. She used that powerful voice to give a voice to others.

Finding Omar Sharif
after a sandstorm

Everyone knew Omar Sharif, or so it seemed. Ask film people in the Middle East, and they knew him or knew someone who knew him, or they played bridge with him or went to the track with him. Maybe they knew his wife's family. It was almost a joke, albeit a sweet one, that everyone claimed to know Sharif. But it made it hard to tell who, if anyone, could actually help me sit down with the Egyptian actor for an interview to celebrate the thirty-fifth anniversary of *Lawrence of Arabia*.

The first time I saw the 1962 David Lean epic, it blew me away—nearly four hours of beautiful men in gorgeous flowing robes, beautifully shot in spectacular Panavision! Noël Coward said that if Peter O'Toole in the lead had been any prettier, "it would have been Florence of Arabia."

Although the movie, about the WWI British officer who led the Arab revolt against the Turks, was not entirely true to history—biopics seldom are—I had already heard that Lawrence was as "gay" as anyone could outwardly be in that day and age. With the addition of Omar Sharif, stunningly handsome and mysterious as the guerrilla fighter

Sherif Ali, it was as gay a movie as I'd ever seen. It certainly sparked my imagination. I mean, what really happens in those lonely tents in the middle of the Jordanian desert? Midnight at the oasis, indeed.

David Lean said as much in an interview with the *Washington Post* in 1989, when asked whether the movie was as "pervasively homo-erotic" as it appeared. "Yes. Of course it is. Throughout," he said. "I'll never forget standing there in the desert once, with some of these tough Arab buggers, some of the toughest we had, and I suddenly thought, 'He's making eyes at me!' And he was! So, it does pervade it, the whole story, and certainly Lawrence was very if not entirely homosexual. We thought we were being very daring at the time: Lawrence and Omar, Lawrence and the Arab boys."

It was also the first time I had seen an Arab play an Arab in a Hollywood movie without being a terrorist or a thief. British Alec Guinness and Mexican Anthony Quinn played other notable Arab characters in the film—and Sharif was not even first choice for the role of Ali. He got it only after others had turned it down, but he certainly made it his, and the role reportedly expanded to keep up with him.

Sharif was the most famous Arab actor in the world. It was unthink-able to me that we would not commemorate his achievements in our magazine, especially when a video rerelease would help new genera-tions find him. My editor at the time warned that our readers didn't know him, but that was exactly the reason for putting him back in the spotlight. They *needed* to know him. Even though I was the publisher, I reluctantly agreed.

Shortly after that discussion with my editor, I was in Lebanon and decided to add a few days in Cairo to the end of my trip, on the off-chance I could meet Omar. I checked into my room at the Sheraton on the morning of May 2, 1997, and even before unpacking, I heard sirens. An orange-y red fog quickly began to block the view. "Please do not open your windows. Please do not go on the balcony," came the warn-ings, alternately repeated in English and Arabic. It was the worst sandstorm to hit Cairo in thirty years, killing twelve and blinding drivers. Falling trees and debris kept the airport closed. I followed every moment of it on CNN from my hotel room. The concierge said he had never seen anything like it. Because of all the flight cancellations I could not even have dinner with the friend of a friend—let alone find and meet Sharif.

There were so many willing, unsolicited advances during those few days spent surrounded by Omar lookalikes in Cairo, where it is illegal to be gay. It must have been my cologne, Eau Sauvage. Upon leaving Cairo and flying to London, I bought a new bottle of it at the duty-free.

My parents had asked me to connect with a family friend from the village who had moved to England after the civil war in Lebanon. The man, Hanna Ghosn, had been my dad's next-door neighbor as a child, and his sister Violet had become my aunt when she married my uncle Jamal. Hanna invited me to a well-known Lebanese restaurant, and when he heard my sandstorm tale of woe, he called over Farid, the maître d', who laughed along with him when he heard my story. This made me a bit angry. I had just been through hell, and for nothing—or was I being too melodramatic about it? I mean, not a single handsome Arab with smoldering eyes had ridden a camel through that sandstorm for me.

"Oh, we have dinners all the time with Michel," said Farid, using Omar's original name. "We play cards upstairs or go to the casino. He likes the track nearly as much as your father, or even the queen!"

I wasn't sure whether to believe him. After all, every Arab knows Omar Sharif, whether they do or don't.

Hanna went on about my grandmother Anissa, and how she was renowned for her kibbe aras and sambousek, and for helping people prepare for weddings and baptisms, and for bringing food to families that needed it. He said that of course he would introduce me. "We are family, after all. Did you know Michel's mother is Lebanese?"

I had already interviewed Peter O'Toole at various film junkets. His pal and drinking buddy Richard Burton would say about O'Toole that "his voice had a crack like a whip . . . most important of all you couldn't take your eyes off him." I can report that this was true.

Technically, I was not supposed to ask about any film other than the one currently under promotion on these junkets, but O'Toole easily talked about Beirut and Omar once he discerned that I was Lebanese. He and Omar had been great drinkers, smokers, and womanizers while making *Lawrence*. The stories.

"Everything was available at any time," he said of hanging out in Beirut with Omar, whom he called "Freddy" when they needed a little privacy, the way I had called Marlon Brando "my cousin George."

"He was already a star there. We would deny it was him and say Freddy just looks like Omar Sharif."

I finally did meet Omar, for dinner in 1998, and I can report that he was even more handsome than that speck of dust coming through the desert at the beginning of *Lawrence of Arabia*.

"I heard you went through a sandstorm to see me," he said with a grin.

His best roles after *Lawrence*, playing non-Arabs, were as Yuri Zhivago in *Dr. Zhivago*—again directed by David Lean—and as the romantic cad Nicky Arnstein opposite Barbra Streisand in 1968's *Funny Girl*, which sent the Egyptian government into a lather. They banned the film because Streisand was Jewish and had spoken out in favor of Israel. "You think Cairo was upset?" she quipped. "You should've seen the letter I got from my Aunt Rose!" It didn't help that the two stars were married to others at the time and had an affair while filming.

But Sharif agreed about readers at that time not knowing him. "I don't want to tell you how to run your magazine, but shouldn't you try to interview someone from *Star Wars*? I haven't made a movie in years."

He insisted that there was no need to interview him. Everything that needed saying about *Lawrence* had already been said, was his attitude, although he admitted that he wouldn't have had a career at all without that early role, his first English-speaking one. And without David Lean, who remained a close friend.

I dined with Omar a few times that year and ran into him on several later occasions. He seemed a little lost, often longing to return to an Egypt that no longer existed. He made me think of my romanticized version of Lebanon. I was heading to Beirut after our last dinner in Paris, and I suddenly realized I could never live there again. It was the songs of Fairuz that I would play at home and hear in the streets and hotels of London and Paris, praising a romanticized Lebanon, that kept my longing alive—but they would also be songs of freedom and resistance. If we can't dance in Beirut, then we dance in Damascus. If only.

One night at my hotel, Omar noticed the waiter paying special attention to me.

"You know hotel policy," he said to me gently. "He can't go to your room, and don't *you* go to the working-class side of Paris. Not at night. Not dressed like that."

In 2003, Sharif finally had a worthy role—"I went twenty-five years without making a good movie," he had said—with *Monsieur Ibrahim*, where he plays a Muslim Turkish merchant who takes a Jewish boy under his wing. "It has nice big chunks of dialogue, which is what I like to do, rather than riding horses or camels."

After years of turning down "rubbish," he read the script and phoned the producers. "I said, 'Hang on, I'm coming, wait for me.'"

"WHAT GOOD IS SITTING ALONE IN YOUR ROOM?
COME HEAR THE MUSIC PLAY."

"Cabaret," music by John Kander, lyrics by Fred Ebb

Liza Minnelli comes through

I was obsessed for years with *Cabaret* after the Bob Fosse movie opened in 1972. At seventeen, I'd never seen a musical or movie like it before: Berlin. Fascism. War. Concentration camps for homosexuals. Why had I not known about this? Why didn't anyone ever talk about it?

"Yes, the pink triangles were how Nazis branded homosexuals," my history teacher confirmed.

Michael York, so young and preppy—I knew right away he was playing a gay character, the one that represents the young Christopher Isherwood, on whose semi-autobiographical novel the musical is based. Joel Grey was the teasing, insinuating Master of Ceremonies.

And then there was Liza Minnelli with a performance so original, so risqué, so . . . gay! Leather. Cross-dressing. In encounters with her later in my life, the story unwound for me bit by bit and grew in stature.

Was Liza gay? No, I don't think so, although at least two of her four husbands were.

Was Joel Grey gay? "No, darling, he has a daughter," Liza said, referring to Jennifer Grey of *Dirty Dancing*—but of course Joel would later come out.

Christopher Isherwood? Gay. We all knew it, and that's why we were excited to see the movie, but others would have to read between the lines, or at least know that he later said that the movie *Cabaret* was not gay enough for him.

Bob Fosse? A prolific womanizer, although he admitted in his autobiography that he had an attraction to men, and there were rumors that he acted on it. Considering his era, was it cooler to admit the act or the attraction?

But in the Berlin of *Cabaret*, only the Nazis cared who was gay.

Liza's whole life had prepared her for the role of Sally Bowles, and she adopted it like a favorite pair of leather hot pants. She said she modeled Sally at least in part on silent-film star Louise Brooks at the suggestion of her father, Vincente Minnelli (gay!), director of the musical *Gigi*—although I wonder what kind of reception its song "Thank Heaven for Little Girls" would get today.

I was lucky enough to hang out with Liza at a few events. I got to know her better after bonding with her backstage at the opening night party for *Kiss of the Spider Woman*, with the music by composers Kander and Ebb, starring the tender, beautiful Brent Carver, and Liza's pal Chita Rivera. I had known Carver for years and would go anywhere to hear him perform. He won a Tony and wowed New York, as he had previously wowed Toronto. But in some ways, maybe the adoration for the sensitive Brent was too stifling and the applause too loud.

I was standing around with Brent when Liza admired my blue and gold velvet Liberty of London scarf. I took it off my neck and gave it to her. She laughed and said, "I should have said I liked your pearl earrings instead!"

She gave me a gift, too, in a roundabout way. Liza puts on this act where you think she's totally distracted, but she remembered my love of *Cabaret* and introduced me to Patrick Quinn—a founding member of Equity Fights AIDS (later called Broadway Cares) who was hand-in-glove with the powerhouse Canadian-American actress Colleen Dewhurst, he as vice president and she as president of Actors' Equity. With Patrick, we began to hatch a tie-in scheme. Liza got Kander and Ebb to write out and sign some of the lyrics to *Cabaret* on parchment. The limited series would go to those who donated to Broadway Cares. A perfect gift for a *Cabaret* lover like me, better than all the pearl earrings in the world.

We all fell in love with Liza—adored her, rooted for her—and not simply because of her mother. We had a real affection for her. Her voice, her spirit, her stage presence. She gave it everything she had, and was thoroughly spent after every performance, if not every song. Hey, Liza, don't let those bastards do to you what they did to your mom! We stood by her during her many struggles: hip replacements, addictions, rehab. Repeat. "She's been in and out of Betty Ford more than Gerald Ford," Joan Rivers said of her.

One night, she changed some of the famous "Cabaret" lyrics around, just for us. After singing about "a girlfriend known as Elsie" who died "from too much pills and liquor," Liza belted out:

And as for me,
I made my mind up back in Chelsea,
When I go, I'm NOT going like Elsie!

With tears of pride, we stood and cheered. Thank you, Betty Ford!

> "DRAWING IS STILL BASICALLY THE SAME AS IT HAS BEEN
> SINCE PREHISTORIC TIMES. IT BRINGS TOGETHER MAN AND
> THE WORLD. IT LIVES THROUGH MAGIC."
>
> *Keith Haring*

Keith Haring
does New York

I was out and I was not out. I never totally "came out," even in the mid-1980s, instead trying to keep my lives and friends separate. It's not that I was necessarily *in* the closet or *out* of it, just that I presented myself as different things to different people and carried a free-floating anxiety about someone catching me between my two lives, the implicit lie of it. I didn't exactly want a tattoo that said GAY, either. Or to fit into a box like those on *Hollywood Squares*.

For someone coming out, or thinking of doing it, the late seventies and early eighties was a time of unique opportunity and experimentation. All the boundaries were gray and blurred. Everything was available. "Straight" men wanted to try it, even if only for a blowjob. Maybe it had always been so and I was just new to noticing.

The hottest place, presumably, was the iconic disco palace Studio 54. It was notoriously hard to get into, but a friend hauled me along on his press pass and we were ushered into the VIP area. I felt so uncomfortable there. I feel the place has been wrongly glamorized; it was really all about excess and class and who you were and what purpose you served. How impressive you seemed. What jewelry you wore. To get past the velvet rope, you were judged by how you looked, and merely gaining entry became your badge of honor, an endless loop of self-regard. It was a reactionary response to everything the sixties stood for and to everything people like me had fought for in terms of diversity and inclusion. Studio's claim to fame was its policy of *exclusion*. You had millionaires who dressed down in expensive ripped jeans next to billionaires in $50,000 designer gowns. Ripped fucking jeans! I have volunteered in community centers where those were the only pants people had, and where they came by the rips honestly.

At Studio, you were nothing more or less than your net worth. Inherited or stolen or laundered; they didn't care how you made it. I would have befriended a lot of plastic people, if only I had played the game, but my instincts said it was all headed for disaster.

In the original lyrics of the hit song "Le Freak" by Chic, "Freak out!" was "Fuck off!"—written after the band was denied entrance to Studio on New Year's Eve, as 1977 turned to 1978, even though they had arrived at the invitation of no less than Grace Jones. Fuck off, indeed.

In those days, I combined trips to Lebanon with wild weekends— dance-and-sex layovers in Paris or London. I escaped most often to New York and Los Angeles on film junkets where the queers among us would plan our own escapades. I didn't care who saw me at clubs and events. I was anonymous there. It was still a time of arrests at bathhouses and parks, but if anything went wrong, no one back home was likely to hear about it.

Often, the worse the movie, the more freebies they showered on us, since home video was the salvation of a bad theatrical run. Wine, dine, and sixty-nine. One studio that shall remain nameless sent a well-known porn star to my hotel room; porn videos were a big, if separate, part of the industry. I invited her in and told her the situation. I don't think she wanted to be there any more than I wanted her to be. I told her I was a fan and had seen the film she was promoting, *Easy*.

"I can recommend someone else, a guy, if you want," she said. "It's already paid for."

"I'm good," I said, and ordered room service, with the best bottle of wine on the menu. All on the studio's bill, of course.

We had a nice lunch.

You could always partake of more than just seconds at the video buffet. In some ways, having sex back then was much like having lunch, especially since we had sex on lunch breaks anyway. That was the only time married men on the down-low could get away with no questions asked.

It was not a time of monogamy. A lot of gay relationships were open and a lot of activists even opposed the idea of marriage—a straight institution that required sanction by a homophobic church and a homophobic god. Marriage was for straight people, and why would we want something they clung to so tightly, the way children do when they grab for a toy? To have them parcel out our "rights" only if we behaved by their arbitrary rules? It has been playing out this way in waves across different communities: minorities, women. The elitist, country club set make a big deal out of letting you into their club, and then they turn around and ban you again. What kind of "rights" can be pulled back at any time? Lucy holding a football for the reliably gullible Charlie Brown.

Where were our relationship role models, anyway? It wasn't as if the *New York Times* was celebrating gay unions in the "Vows" column back then. Same-sex marriage wasn't legal. We wondered if it ever would be, although I went on to fight for it quite publicly, despite death threats. What we had instead was an intoxicating, risqué, risky element of fun on the edge. There were all these incredible orgies of pleasure: bath houses, dance clubs. There was an overall vibe, a sparkle to that life, but there was also a lot of running and hiding. The dalliances were discreet, with a hair-trigger of danger. It was also a culture that took shaming to a new level, with only a towel for modesty in the baths.

It was interesting that so many of our trysts unfurled in the shadows of grand art museums, because a lot of the best art of the time came from the gay subculture and infused our lives. New York was exploding with vibrant art and homoerotic photography. Warhol. Mapplethorpe. Haring. These artists were not off-limits or cloistered away in an atelier somewhere. New York was the one place in the world where I could meet almost anyone I wanted to.

And so it was when I first met Keith Haring at an art opening in 1981. After seeing him a few more times at other shows, I became interested in buying one of his pieces. That turned into occasionally hooking up and hanging out when I was in town.

We were opposites, at least physically. He was scrawny and I was beefy. He was cut and he was attracted to me because I was not. "But you're Lebanese!" he said, astounded and, frankly, more interested than at first. The games people can play with a foreskin is for another time, another place.

"Yes, but not Jewish or Muslim," I replied.

I adored Keith. He was so sensitive, so funny, so eager to please. I could barely keep up with all that he was doing. I loved that he was painting graffiti in subways and murals in playgrounds and children's hospitals. But how could anyone make a living doing that?

Like other artists I know, Keith found it exhausting to be continuously judged and reviewed. We had no agenda—just no art talk. A chance to unwind. It seemed so natural. I always brought the wine. Which got better over time as I started doing better financially; Keith began to get decent prices only after he died.

In public, everything was on display. His art. His activism, both politically and in the art world. That openness was his calling card. He was photographed naked on a few occasions, and even had one portrait done by Annie Leibovitz showing his endowment, of which he was very proud. That photo hung on my wall over the years. I have sold it at auction and bought it back a couple of times. Sometimes you want to remember and sometimes you want to remember even more.

Keith opened wide the doors to the art world and beyond for me. It started my interest in collecting, which became an obsession.

He dragged me along everywhere. He had joy in finding a new coffee bar or a new collector. The Village was his backyard. We all thought the Stonewall uprising was just the start and we were well on our way to full civil rights for all. Men were dressing differently; people were more open. Warhol's Factory, Elton, Bowie, Boy George, none of this had ever happened before, or so we thought.

I developed a huge crush on the American art curator and collector Sam Wagstaff, who was mentor and lover to the photographer Robert Mapplethorpe. He was deliciously handsome and so articulate. I could hardly breathe in his presence, let alone speak, but I got better at it. In a moment when I was both nervous and cheeky, I exclaimed: "But anyone can take a photograph. It's not like it's a painting or a sculpture." I thought of a good portrait photo as the result of how good the model was.

This, despite my father and his best friend, Soheil Garzouzi, often dragging me along to meet one of the greatest portrait artists of the twentieth century—the Canadian Armenian photographer Yousuf Karsh. Karsh, who spoke perfect Arabic, had survived the Armenian genocide and come to Canada as a refugee from Syria on a boat via Beirut. He frequented Soheil's café, and they would often gather over pastries and what they refused to call Turkish coffee and cigars. Yousuf was only three years older than my dad. There would be a backgammon game at some point, or the promise of one. Sometimes we would deliver homemade pastries and jams to Karsh at the Chateau Laurier hotel, where he kept his studio and surrounded himself with his most famous portraits. We now have his portraits of Mandela, Georgia O'Keeffe, John and Jacqueline Kennedy, and Martin Luther King Jr.—all bought after Karsh died.

I took Sam to lunch at Lutèce, where he addressed the topic of photography as art for an hour and began what I imagine must have been an arduous process to move the needle on my appreciation.

"There's power in photography," he often said. "Photographers have changed everything. They've changed the world." But you could still develop twenty-five prints of the same photograph, when there is ever only one oil.

This was, of course, all while Warhol was changing the rules. I remember having a long discussion with my art collector friends Nancy Lockhart and Murray Frum, who donated a Bernini to the Art Gallery of Ontario. Murray took me aside and told me he had just bought his first photograph. "Your secret is safe with me," I said. "We just bought our first piece of video art."

Sam didn't only change my way of thinking. He and Susan Sontag changed the perception of photography for museums and galleries and art collectors. I recently mentioned this to the portrait photographer Greg Gorman, who had worked with Warhol on *Interview* magazine. I met Greg through Canadian bad-boy artist Attila Richard Lukács, and we now have more than a hundred of his original photos on our walls and on those of friends.

"Anyone with a cellphone with automatic exposure and automatic everything is a photographer," said Greg, trying to make me feel better about my age-old gaffe by saying it has all come to pass anyway. "You have so many self-appraised artists—and some of them *are* artists—but many of them would be hard-pressed to reproduce an image they got on their iPhone. If you said, 'I want a portrait that looks like that,' they wouldn't know what to do, because today it's such an automated process."

It's obvious to me now that good technology is nothing compared to the ineffable qualities that a good portraitist brings to the shoot. "The one exception I have always made for having my portrait taken is Greg Gorman," Elton John has said. "His magical lens is able to peer deep into the soul of his subjects and reveal their inner beauty, their struggles, their happiness. Greg's photographic wizardry captures the sitter with penetrating clarity and perfect focus to communicate something beyond the subject itself."

I'm with Elton on that. Greg is the only one I would sit for, too—nude, as it turns out, for a portrait he did of me in my garden. I got a few mosquito bites during that shoot in places where you don't want to get mosquito bites, but I toughed it out, remembering what John Waters had said: "Greg Gorman is the only person I'd let photograph my corpse."

As the eighties progressed, I was more cautious around the New York and L.A. scene. I didn't want the whole thing to swallow me up, and I saw how easily that could happen to anyone with an appetite for anything. And you could get anything, from coke to AIDS. I worried that I would not be able to say no, and that I would fall prey to dancing as fast as I could, trying to fit in. There were no half-measures with me, in this realm of my life and in fundraising and fighting for a cause. I don't have an off switch.

Also, in the eighties, the rise of AIDS changed everything—from attitudes and risk tolerance to how we mobilized. We moved into protest mode and are still, to this day, the envy of other "causes" in terms of how we brought about change. Even though we all disagreed with one another, we came together for one purpose. A common front.

But it also brought on fear and caution. A main motivator in coming out to my parents then was so that they would understand that I could get AIDS. I didn't want them to be the last to know.

We didn't know much about AIDS except that gay men got it and therefore became seen as the enemy. We were afraid to kiss or hug or drink from the same glass. All that fear. Your friends were dying and you couldn't see them in the hospital because you weren't "family." Or you could see them, but only in a hazmat suit. No touching. Parents whisked their dead kids away to burials in unmarked graves. I kept a dark jacket in my car because there were funerals every week, with eulogies that never mentioned the deceased's grieving partner.

My doctor, an old friend, dismissed my fears—after all, it was "a gay man's disease," and he assumed that ruled me out.

I changed doctors.

Because of AIDS and the toll that it was taking, I found that by the late eighties I could no longer cry. I was hoarse from shouting my distress in the street and running to yet another home decimated by loss. From showering and getting ready for some gala where everyone was dolled up in the latest fashions, and people only mentioned AIDS in passing, like passing around canapés and cocktails. We would go to those galas in hopes of finding an ally, a benefactor whose money and connections might pry open a hospital door that had been slammed in our faces. To find someone whose clout could make a difference in the face of this avalanche of grief.

I wanted to cry. But I couldn't. Somehow, I just became stoic, even though I didn't want to be like that. I made sure everything that needed to be done got done. But I could not simply let go of my emotions and allow them—or my tears—to flow.

I saw several therapists over the span of a decade with the hope of finding some mental cure. Some psychobabble that would break the logjam, some new pill I could take. At funerals, I stood there as stolidly as possible. Sometimes it was the funeral of someone who had been an occasional fuck, or someone I had signed up to tend on an overnight shift at the hospital in the final days, when we all divvied up care duties according to complex schedules that looked more like battle plans. Determined not to be defeated, I grew depressed and angry at the smallest details. Frozen in fear and anger.

It was only when my dad died that I was finally able to cry, out loud and in public.

The crisis drove me from my old haunts and into flirtations with food and alcohol. From there, it was into the arms—sometimes literally—of psychologists. I finally went to a female psychologist who sat me down and told me that I was like "a beautiful urn with a crack in it." And after that Henry Jamesian spiel, and admitting that she didn't know how to help me, she advised me to try a gay psychiatrist—but this time one who would respect professional boundaries.

I stepped up my activism during those early days of AIDS. The movement borrowed heavily from the civil rights movement. I would get to know all kinds of people, and it was almost like a VIP club of connections. I got to know Larry Kramer, the playwright and founder of ACT UP, the most effective organization in the fight against AIDS. It moved the disease from hushed tones in dingy hospitals to the national stage. Most people thought he was too angry all the time, though he had every right to be. But there were many other facets to Larry as well. The man was incredibly funny and thoughtful. He found out about my activism at university and how I'd been arrested a couple of times, and he lit a fire under me to keep going. We had to be in the streets, just like the civil rights and the anti–Vietnam War demonstrators.

And so, we marched. And marched. At times it felt like a scene from *They Shoot Horses, Don't They?*

My activism led to an unintended career boost. On an Orion film junket, I met Arthur Krim, the chair of the studio, who introduced me to his wife, Mathilde Krim, a medical researcher and the founding chair of amfAR, the Foundation for AIDS Research. Through him, I had access to almost anyone I wanted in Hollywood. I didn't do it for the connections—I did not have any way of knowing how many doors would open—but it was certainly a happy by-product.

I felt guilty about not seeing Keith more often later, although we did manage to stay in touch until a few months before his death in 1990 from complications of AIDS.

In the end, I wound up HIV-positive after all. Not from Keith or any particular person or moment that I can put a finger on. I only disclosed it to family and a few friends, as I didn't want to be known by my HIV status any more than I wanted to be known by my net worth or romantic partners or by any other gratuitous factoid.

But look how far we've come. We have cured several AIDS cases. We raised enough funds to help turn it into a treatable disease, one with which you can live a full life. In that sense, and against the odds, we beat it—at least for those with access and who can afford the drugs. But it is still illegal to be gay in sixty-nine countries.

Today, we also need to switch gears and support our trans kids. We need more transgender and gender non-binary doctors. There is still severe stigma, discrimination, and systematic inequality facing the trans community specifically. This is not just a question of coming out—it's a lifelong journey.

"IF YOU WANT TO KNOW ALL ABOUT ANDY WARHOL,
JUST LOOK AT THE SURFACE OF MY PAINTINGS AND FILMS
AND ME, AND THERE I AM. THERE'S NOTHING BEHIND IT."

Andy Warhol

Andy Warhol:
your signature is just
as good as mine

In 2006, I gave a dinner party celebrating the birthday of Oakville Galleries curator Marnie Fleming, whose insights into the art world I valued. Marnie gazed around at the walls of my apartment and said in astonishment, "There must be fourteen Warhols I can see right from where I'm sitting! How many do you have in here?"

"Oh, I don't know," I said. "Maybe fifty or sixty?"

"How many in your entire collection?"

I tried to do the math in my head. "Some are in the office, some are in our country house," I said. "Maybe seventy or eighty?"

That Marnie discovered the Warhols that evening was fortuitous. A show had just canceled on her and she was looking for something with which to replace it.

Until then, I'd been rather quiet about my collection of Warhols, but now I really believe Andy would have loved the show we put together.

The Oakville Gallery is in a beautiful old Tudor estate with bountiful gardens in a parklike setting on Lake Ontario. Hidden from the road, it could be anywhere. It could even be on Andy's sprawling old Montauk estate—a spot to which I was too shy to accept invitations. In my twenties then, torn between brash defiance and a touch of bashfulness, I didn't think I had enough to offer.

I knew Marnie would understand and appreciate my collection and point of view, unlike many in the art world. I cannot tell you how many people have looked at my walls and exclaimed, "I have a friend who paints naked men, I think you'd like his work!" All they see is the nudity, not the art. We also have Haring, Mapplethorpe, Herb Ritts, Greg Gorman, and renowned Canadian artists General Idea, Michael Morris, Attila Richard Lukács, Stephen Andrews, Andy Fabo, Gordon Shadrach, and Kent Monkman—all brilliant, daring gay male artists who have produced some of the most powerful works, yet all some people can see is the occasional penis.

Don't get me wrong, we also have other artists on the walls, such as Betty Goodwin and Jamelie Hassan, Annie Leibovitz and Sheila Gregory, who speak through their work about the human struggle to survive and overcome tragedy and persecution. But many try to pigeonhole me as being all about collecting pictures of naked guys. I once told the great Canadian artist Betty Goodwin that I feel that the art on the wall talks, piece to piece. Before I could finish my thought, she said that of course it is about "struggle and existence and the need to be seen."

A light turned on for me when I started to buy Warhols, when I saw how his work told me to be free and daring. It's all over the place—from Hollywood icons and political statements to sex drawings, endangered species, and trans heroes. A license to be seen, to do whatever we want in a society that lives behind drawn curtains and rigid boundaries. Warhol is all about accessibility. The art speaks for itself. I can hang Warhols on my wall, but having other people see them has always stirred up a host of intrusive questions no one should have to answer.

A 2002 article in the *Globe and Mail* compared me to a Medici in terms of my arts patronage and support of up-and-coming creative people, before going out of its way to reassure readers that I had not slept with any of the artists I collected. Hey, I also collect the work of female artists and computer-generated video, but don't let that stop them from speculating!

It was a shockingly insulting question that the *Globe* interviewer asked. I do not believe a heterosexual arts patron or collector would have been asked about their sexual relationships. Would they have asked a Getty or a Saatchi? Only queer folk get this kind of dismissive treatment. It was doubly insulting that the writer's editors thought it necessary to include such a disclaimer, thus taking an otherwise lauda-tory piece into a sordid sphere that had nothing to do with art.

Keith Haring first introduced me to Andy during the days when we would run into him at gallery openings, both for Warhol's own shows and those of other young artists he supported, including Keith, Jean-Michel Basquiat, and Robert Mapplethorpe. It was really that simple at one point.

The first practical lesson I learned from Andy was something I incorporated into the design of my magazines. He explained the impor-tance of maintaining eye contact with the face in the painting, so that your eyes lock on the subject's and both of you sort of follow each other around the room. It was about positioning the image of a celebrity so that the eyes made the most impact. Andy had won numerous awards as an illustrator and graphic designer, and this was a key point I would drive home with my staff of editors and art directors.

Despite so many claims that he was self-centered, Warhol was quite generous with the people he knew. He gave oil paintings of Liz to Liz, of Liza to Liza. The ballet legend Karen Kain tells me she was too shy back then to accept his oil painting of her.

I, too, was a bit shy in this regard, loath to accept the many freebies Keith—and, to a lesser extent, Andy—offered me. Partly it was because I was still a free spirit, moving about quite often, and didn't want to carry that kind of baggage. Whenever I moved apartments, I left most things behind. It was too cumbersome and expensive to move everything, so I often left the furniture and took only my clothing. Who knew that these works would be worth what they are today?

But after one Warhol show, where I admired several paintings of flowers, I mentioned how I always identified my mother with her love of gardening, and Keith told Andy that I called my mom twice a day. Andy also was close to his mother and loved to garden at his Montauk estate. After that, Andy gave Keith ten prints to pass along to me. I kept them rolled up in brown cardboard poster tubes, the ones that came to me containing movie posters for the latest video releases, and I'd put a bow on them and give them out as wedding gifts. I also gave one to my mother. Several recipients subsequently threw them out, "like the base Indian threw a pearl away / Richer than all his tribe," per *Othello*. Each print was probably worth $1,500 then, $50,000 today.

It seems that only my mother, who adored everything her children gave her, kept hers.

The more I knew about Andy, the more I realized how out and proud he was, and how much his influence permeated me and everyone else and created an entire school of up-and-coming artists. I like to say that we are all the children of Andy Warhol. There is art before Warhol and there is art after Warhol. He defied the rules, the homophobia, and the intense glare under the microscope.

With all of his works, he blew closets wide open, including the gilded cages of the art world. All you have to do is to look at the graphic sex drawings, or the ten-part *Ladies and Gentlemen* series of trans people that Warhol did in 1975, which features, among others, Marsha P. Johnson of the Stonewall riots. Who else was championing trans people back then? It was a more radical act than the soup cans.

Some of my more "intellectual" friends never took Warhol seriously and resented what they thought of as his removed attitude, or the hedonism of the Factory, sometimes forgetting how Andy put so many aspects of our culture center stage, way before it was fashionable or even "a thing." This is typical of the way gay artists are treated, with a pervasive undercurrent of homophobia. People are more obsessed over whether Andy's claims to be a "virgin" and "asexual" were true than with his work, his genius, and his legacy. People fetishize the gossip, weigh in on the platinum wig and soft voice, and forget that Warhol democratized the art world and turned it on its head.

Just one example of democratizing and the accessibility of art is the *Sunday B. Morning* series of prints, which are reproductions, including Warhol's original Marilyns, soup cans, and flowers. Some have a stamp on the back marked: *fill in your own signature.* He was saying that anyone's signature is as important as his. You own it now. He also signed some: *This is not by me. Andy Warhol.* Classic cat-and-mouse with the art world. I discussed this with Jed Johnson, whom I got to know a bit after Andy died. Jed, a successful designer, had been Andy's partner for twelve years, only to hear Andy claim in the press to be a virgin. I imagine that must have stung, but in any case, Jed had moved on by then. I forgot to thank Jacob one time at the podium when I was getting an award and it still bugs me.

To some, Warhol was, and remains, an enigma. Maybe, as he said, just look at his art to know him. But Jed just smiled at my theory that Andy's book *The Andy Warhol Diaries* was another cat-and-mouse game, more of a gift to Andy's friend Pat Hackett, to whom he dictated the episodic memoir—all 807 pages of it—and who profited from its posthumous publication. Why else would a man who was so prolific and pretended to be so shy, and who was known for his creative embellishments, seriously dictate a diary to someone if not mostly to share the wealth?

In many ways, Warhol played the game perfectly. What could be more American than Campbell's soup? He said it tasted the same, whether to prince or pauper, and claimed he got the idea from eating Campbell's tomato soup every day for twenty years—but he didn't, of course. He and Jed were both fine chefs.

Jed was aboard TWA Flight 800 when it crashed on July 17, 1996, twelve minutes after takeoff. I had been toying with the idea of going to Paris on that same flight, and have been a nervous flier ever since.

I continued to collect Warhol for his influence and for what he stood for. He believed that at some point, everyone could have a Warhol. He was against the manipulation of the art market and the way billionaires hid their money-laundering operations behind it. I think he'd have been horrified by the Christie's auction in May 2022 where one of his Marilyn silkscreens went for a record-shattering $195 million. Why do you think he named his workspace the Factory? It echoed the conveyor belt of American goods. I doubt he'd be up for a bidding frenzy over one single piece. No surprise that it amused him to know that my dad had worked at the Ford Oakville factory, which in my father's time put out a car every two or three days.

In a 2006 interview with Deirdre Kelly for the *Globe and Mail* about the Oakville show, Tom Sokolowski, director of the Andy Warhol Museum in Pittsburgh, credited me with having "a marvelous range" of screen prints, oils on canvas, drawings, printed photographs, and Polaroids, and said that I "represent one of about fifty people in the world with such a sizable Warhol collection." But I never planned my collection with a future accolade like that in mind. I never wanted to be known as a Warhol expert or have the art take a back seat to whatever relationship I did or did not have with him. I collected what I wanted to collect because I liked looking at the pieces on my wall.

And I don't collect just to collect. We rotate our Warhols. We sell them and then miss them and buy them back. We donate some and sell others for the odd charity—which I believe Andy would have loved.

Sometimes I feel our art works from numerous artists and backgrounds complement each other and are like different words that together make a paragraph coherent. Our collection is wall-to-wall and on doors and from ceiling to floor. Some dub it "salon style." The artist Stephen Andrews dubbed it Salah style.

And so it's somewhat fitting that from that birthday dinner for Marnie emerged the idea for the show *Wall to Wall Warhol*, with fifty or so Warhols exhibited in floor-to-ceiling Salah style. We had loaned our pieces to different galleries and museums—including the National Gallery of Canada—but had never put on a show of this size in one venue. If I had reservations, it was because a show like this would put a lot of me out there for others to judge and pick apart. There are snobs in the art world who define you solely by what you collect, and I was tired of all the self-proclaimed "experts" out there dismissing artists and making galleries increasingly exclusive, including by raising entrance fees beyond what's reasonable, which effectively dictates who can—and can't—get in.

The Warhol show was a grand success, although the homophobic daggers came out right away. "I heard men were having sex in the bathroom at the opening," claimed one attendee. I dare not ask which bathroom she was in.

While I was eager to discuss the artist and how he turned the art world on its head and democratized art—I called Warhol the poet laureate of Western culture—most of the press questions I received were along the lines of whether I had slept with Andy, and if I could please describe the drug-and-sex parties at the Factory. Or even to account for why Andy made an appearance on the TV series *The Love Boat*. People sought me out as a Warhol "expert," but I was not willing to pontificate or dip into the gossip at the expense of the artist's work and legacy. Too many forget that it is on Andy's shoulders that many of our artists stand today.

Despite what others have said about him, I knew Warhol only as a generous man and a revolutionary who would change the perception of art the way Monet and the Impressionists did in the 1870s and 1880s. He presented himself to others, mainly the press, as a kind of simpleton—but he was astute, opinionated, and, despite his paintings of soup cans, had elevated tastes in everything from food to literature. I would hear from his friends about his deep knowledge of world events, and in a discussion of Lebanon one time he told me things even I did not know. He feigned ignorance only when people tried to capture him on record, guessing correctly that his words, once snagged by the vast media machine, would be twisted and turned against him or used to serve other people's agendas.

And, face it, he loved to fuck with the tabloid press. He gave them what they wanted, and they trafficked and wallowed in it.

He knew exactly what he was doing. In his first statement about the Pop Art movement he created, he discussed "the symbols of the harsh, impersonal products and brash materialist objects on which America is built today."

But his soup-can era was only one small part of his enormous and multifaceted output. Among other firsts, he understood art as a collaborative process, with his Factory foreshadowing the kind of collaborative workspaces we take for granted today. If you study his work, you can see he was a political artist.

"There's more to him than his trademark blankness," says the artist Jeremy Deller, who, as a naive twenty-year-old, hung with Andy and learned to see things anew. "The working environment he created at the Factory is a norm now for creative people. There's a flow of people from whom you get ideas that feed into the art."

In any event, Andy's generosity and legacy will live on forever. He left his entire estate to his charitable foundation, which he dedicated "to the advancement of the visual arts" and is among the largest of its kind. To date, the Andy Warhol Foundation for the Visual Arts says it has "given more than $250 million in cash grants to more than 1000 arts organizations . . . and more than 52,786 works of art to 322 institutions worldwide."

So, what is this whole fixation with sex about? Even the birds and bees do it, according to the song. Did I sleep with Warhol? Did I sleep with every single one of the artists I collect? Other than my husband, who is an artist? Well, yes, of course, darling. And I still do! Because when I go to bed at night, there they are on my walls, leaning against walls from the floors, everywhere—the last things I see before I descend into my psychedelic dreams.

k.d. lang sings
at our wedding

I started to change my mind about marriage around my thirtieth birthday, although I did not actually get married until after my fiftieth. Old habits die hard.

An old married lover from New York had come back into my life and wanted to take me on the Concorde to Paris to celebrate. Nothing had ever entirely ended between us except that we still lived in different cities and he was still married. He loved me, and he also loved his wife. Anyway, long-distance relationships worked best for me. It was like being on vacation.

I couldn't go with him to France on the actual date of my birthday, October 3, 1985, because I was living part-time in my parents' basement and Mom was making my favorite dishes for my birthday dinner. Mom's dinner ranked higher than any three-star Michelin restaurant.

For a time, my parents' basement in Rexdale was my sanctuary. I had moved back in because it was closer to my office and also helped me resist temptation—my downtown place had become a revolving door of it. I still kept an apartment with a friend but hardly ever went there.

Paris was different this time than on other trips. I was in someone else's snack bracket, which afforded a different, more refined experience. But there was a black cloud overhead. Rock Hudson had died a few days earlier, on October 2, of AIDS-related causes. Talk of his sickness and death made it into almost every conversation. The grande dame of French cinema, Simone Signoret, had also recently died, on September 30, and France was still in shock and mourning. Her comments about husband Yves Montand's affair with Marilyn Monroe—"Marilyn must have good taste if she was interested in my husband," and "Chains do not hold a marriage together"—assured me that it was okay to have a mistress. Or, in my case, a mister.

At dinner one night in Paris, Mark and I ran into Yves Saint Laurent and Pierre Bergé—a loud, loving, laughing couple, unashamed to display it. The world was changing, I thought. More male couples were open about being together. And if those two could be a couple, why shouldn't I think about it for myself?

Yves spoke to me in French and Arabic and suddenly I didn't feel like a hanger-on. I had never met him before, but it was one of those cases where, hey, if you're at this person's party then you must be worth talking to. He seemed genuinely interested, despite his reputation of being notoriously shy. He had the most beautiful skin and soft silky hair—you know, that Nice 'n Easy shampoo commercial type. His fabrics were what I bought my mother to make her dresses. Her seamstress friend took the black-banded hem from inside the fabric of one of the dresses to add bands to both sleeves. Mom went along with it. In Lebanon, which was a French protectorate at one time, it was Dior and Saint Laurent who held sway.

I knew Yves suffered from depression, and a friend who was also bipolar said that he could not imagine how such a couple functioned day to day. Clearly, it was about support—having someone who supports you, whatever you are going through.

All these strands wove together and preyed on my mind, including a dinner with Mark and another friend at one of Paris's many three-star restaurants. This Parisian friend, like Mark, was married—although I was sure he was simply gay when he was in New York and L.A. He mentioned that he had waited too long to have kids. "I should have had them when I could still lift them," he joked. He was forty-five and athletic, but the point was not lost on me.

Which is why, on the flight home from my thirtieth birthday celebration in Paris, I decided that from then on, I needed to get serious and make it on my own. I would pay for my own trips, throw my own birthday parties, and have my own kids before my back gave out.

A few years later, I got engaged. To a woman.

She was someone I knew—and that our families knew—from neighboring villages in Lebanon, and I really did love her. Her name was Daad, the same name as my favorite aunt. We had glorious times together and got along famously, but for me it was all about wanting to have children. I had a four-carat diamond ring made from one of my designs and I stopped in Paris along the way to pick up some Saint Laurent and Chanel jewelry and accessories.

We got engaged during Christmas and set the date of our wedding for July 14, Bastille Day—which, in retrospect, was ominous.

Almost everyone in my orbit encouraged me to go ahead and get married. Maybe it was because it was the eighties, the time of AIDS, and there were still very few options for gay men who wanted to raise a family. The only person who told me to get out, the way audiences yell at the screen during horror movies, was a closeted doctor friend. "End it right now. It's like surgery," he said. "It hurts at first, but it will heal day by day."

I ignored him and went ahead with the plans.

The custom in Lebanon is for the groom to pay for the bride's dress, and I had a dress made for Daad that I'd be proud to wear myself! It was Belgian tulle with Swarovski crystals and hundreds of freshwater pearls individually sewn in. It was from the same designers who would do my Fashion Cares wedding dress.

The nuptials—with eight hundred guests, including sixty-five who would fly in from overseas—were to take place in Lebanon.

The parties continued. A huge bachelor blow-out. The carousel kept going round and round, and I, though dizzy, clung to it.

It was only when I set foot back in Lebanon after a weekend of wild abandon in New York that I knew it was all impossible. I couldn't see it through, partly because it wouldn't be fair to Daad. I had just come from partying in one of the epicenters of AIDS. It wasn't right to assume that I was safe.

Many friends told me it was possible to do this and still enjoy my flings. Sure; I knew the scenario, but I decided I didn't want to be that person. I didn't want to sneak around and have dangerous sex in parks or with a serial killer, as had happened to a friend. I also did not want to take the chance of bringing HIV home. I genuinely loved the woman but needed to stop this charade.

My fiancée was disappointed, certainly, and even said that she was still willing to go through with it, after learning I was gay. But I didn't want to continue to lie or go have sex in some park. I have met too many men doing exactly that.

Word quickly spread between our two villages that the wedding was off. One of the bride's male cousins from Atlanta and a female cousin from Australia stopped by my place the same night. They told me they admired my courage and asked if they could take me out for the night. Gazing at the male cousin with his dark black eyes during a slow dance, I thought I had definitely made the right choice. It was also the only fair thing to do for Daad, and for me.

Predictably, Daad's family and village took her side, and my family and village took mine. Everyone had an opinion. Naturally, the story about my sexual leanings was circulating. I sometimes think that all the projects I did and still do there, like building a community center and a park, are a form of penance—or at least my way of apologizing.

It hasn't always gone well, though. An archbishop asked my family for help building a medical facility, and I helped them out on the condition that it accept and treat individuals with HIV. Later, it and the American University of Beirut were the only facilities to deny me dialysis because I had become HIV-positive.

When we prepared to return to Canada, my mother insisted that we bring the dress home with us. It still hangs in the closet. Well, something's got to be in the closet! And it eventually got worn: Canadian artist Attila Richard Lukács wore it for one of Greg Gorman's photo portraits.

In time, my mother was satisfied that someday, I would have my own children. Although I never did, and realized along the way that children aren't necessarily for everyone, I do have a stepdaughter, and many nieces and nephews and grandnieces and grandnephews. I even have a nephew and a grandnephew with the middle name Salah. Fifteen different people call me godfather, and I never had to change a single diaper!

In the ensuing years, I fought for the right to gay marriage, even at the expense of the occasional death threat—most notably in 2005 after placing ads for marriage equality on the movie screens leased by Famous Players, a division of Viacom. I was a partner in the media division and ran day-to-day operations, and we decided to place the ads in February, the month of Valentine's Day. It was so perfect! One of the slides in our ad said: "'I do' means the same thing, whether you're straight or gay. Let your member of parliament know you support our Charter of Rights and Freedoms." Another said: "Marriage is a fundamental human right, whether you're straight or gay."

Lovely sentiments. Followed by death threats and harassing calls. Sabre-rattling from organizations that had the words *family* and *civil rights* in their titles, although I'm not sure whose family or civil rights they felt they were protecting.

Yet, as I recently told a reporter from the *Globe and Mail*, I would do it again. It only strengthened my resolve. For every call for a boycott—including from Alabama and Florida, where we didn't even have theaters—we had five times more people saying they intended to see a movie that weekend and thanking us for standing up to hate.

People pitched in to make sure I didn't walk my dog alone. They offered places to stay if I felt unsafe in my home. My colleagues and friends Cathy Prowse, Mathieu Chantelois, and Sheila Gregory would not let me answer my calls directly anymore. Publicity gurus Pat Marshall and Nuria Bronfman coached me on how to deal with the press. But, yes, I would do it again in a heartbeat.

I declared to friends that if I ever did get married, I'd want k.d. lang to sing at the wedding—although marriage, for me, was still just an idea, a concept worth fighting for. And then I met Jacob Yerex.

From the start, I knew that Jacob was different. An artist and an avid reader, he was loving, passionate, reassuring, engaging. He loved all that I hated about myself. It was as if my entire life's journey had led me to him.

Although he was fifteen years younger, there was no real gap in our conversations. No lack of shared social, cultural, and political touchstones, and it was the first time someone walked into my apartment and knew every piece of art on the way to the bedroom—although he assumed they were posters, not originals, or that I was part of some art rental program.

Jacob had been married and shared custody of a daughter with his ex-wife. A couple of months in, he hedged by claiming he was bisexual.

Bisexual? I told him I couldn't go back there. No pressure, but he was much younger. I would be the one who ended up hurt. I told him we should move on.

We didn't.

We both decided we really needed to take this more seriously. I gave him some books to read, including *Becoming a Man* and *Borrowed Time*, by Paul Monette, an old friend. There is a beautiful line of his that has always stuck with me—when the writer turns to his lover and says, "We're the same person, aren't we. When did that happen?"

When Jacob finally went home to come out to his parents, I packed him a care package that included literature from PFLAG (then called by its full name, Parents, Families, and Friends of Lesbians and Gays), along with French chocolates for his mom, Elaine, who very much reminded me of my own mom.

How did it go, coming out to his parents? Great! His father proclaimed all would be fine "as long as there are no public displays of affection," and as long as Jacob promised not to go to "that parade." His brother nudged him and Jacob had to admit to his parents that I had been the grand marshal of "that parade" the previous year.

Jacob took care of his daughter, Ivy—she changed her name from Isis for obvious reasons—half the time at the beginning of our relationship. Ivy moved in with us a few years later, but back then, Jacob would get up at six every morning to get her ready and take her to school so he could get to work on time. He was a scenic artist on the popular Canadian teen drama franchise *Degrassi*, with home-grown rapper Drake in the cast.

One time, when I was frustrated with Jacob's frustration, he said, "*You* try doing this, juggling all these things!"

I encouraged him to quit his job. I would take care of him, and he would take care of me. Actually, he helped take care of all of us—we set up a little "village" in our apartment building, buying up units and parceling them out among family, friends, and even recent immigrants who needed a place to stay. After my father died, I moved my mom into an apartment above ours; she insisted on giving me back all the money I had given her over the years—$80,000—to help pay for it. In another unit was more family, along with our two younger nephews, all of us on the same floor.

When my older sister, Grace, received a diagnosis of progressive supranuclear palsy (PSP), a horrible degenerative disease that affected cognition, we installed her and a caregiver in the apartment next door. Grace had been a caterer and chef, renowned for her rum and

Christmas cakes. She made them when I first started in business and could not afford to give my new clients Christmas gifts. Even later, when I could afford to send the latest Hermès scarves, everyone still asked me for Grace's cakes.

We also took a year and, with the help of a major architectural firm, cut through one floor to make a duplex, giving us nearly seven thousand square feet overlooking Lake Ontario. We turned it into an art gallery and a place to entertain.

When Jacob's mom, Elaine, died, we moved his dad, Patrick, into his own apartment in the building. And when my mom developed dementia, we gave her and her caregivers a new space. Jacob ran around and made sure everyone had what they needed, from food to medicines. People said I was generous, but it was also selfish. It would have been impossible to see to everyone if they weren't all together in this arrangement a friend called a Lebanese Knots Landing. It was how I remember growing up in Lebanon before the civil war; we always took in sick relatives and pitched in to care for them. I could afford it, and the stars seemed to align.

Jacob also had another job, and that was taking care of me. He became my nurse after my kidneys began to fail. He learned how to administer dialysis at home so that we didn't have to spend our days in the hospital. He learned to cook a kidney-friendly diet. He also bakes. Does he juggle plates? I'm sure he can. We would joke, "Why go out when the food is so good and good *for* you at Chez Jacob?" He claims I am easy to cook for, as I love everything.

When I had my kidney transplant, Jacob organized all the doctors and made sure everyone coordinated in my care. Through kidney failure, diabetes, sepsis, a stoma bag, Hoyer lifts, everything, Jacob was on top of it, calling meetings and taking notes. I'd have to insist he go home and get some rest. And when he did, in my drugged stupor and hallucinations, I would ask the nurses, "Where is my Jacob?" (They found this quite charming.) Even now, with many medical issues still unresolved, he is on top of it. All my specialists end their calls with, "Give my love to Jacob."

My Jacob. Sometimes, even when he is just in another room, I miss him.

The first time I worked with k.d. lang was when I hosted the WorldPride Awards Gala in 2014, a fundraiser in support of Camp fYrefly, a leadership retreat for queer and trans youth. "Let our diverse freak flags fly," lang proclaimed in advance of the June event.

I first heard her perform live in 2000 at a Fashion Cares fundraiser put on by MAC cosmetics, and I desperately wanted her for the WorldPride event. I contacted everyone I knew who could help— including Tony Bennett, who had done the album *A Wonderful World* with her in 2002. I had met Tony a few times through Variety Club, and he performed at one of our galas. We made the mistake of putting him on late, after some guests had already left. I was so embarrassed. I apologized profusely the next day at breakfast.

He put his hand on my shoulder. "I feel terrible for you," he said. "You put so much effort into it and it wasn't a success."

He was apologizing to *me*?

I assured him it was our biggest fundraiser yet, in spite of the scheduling mishap.

Tony believed k.d. lang was the best singer performing today, and credited her with reviving his career. He helped us line her up for the gala, where we honored Gilbert Baker, creator of the rainbow flag, and Jóhanna Sigurðardóttir, the first female prime minister of Iceland and the first openly gay or lesbian prime minister anywhere. Introducing her was Kathleen Wynne, the first openly gay premier in Canada.

We also honored gay rights activist Edith Windsor, who was the lead plaintiff in the landmark 2013 lawsuit *United States v. Windsor*, which paved the way for same-sex marriage and equal benefits for same-sex couples in the United States. She had previously flown up to Toronto in 2007 to marry her ailing partner, in a service performed by

Canada's first openly gay judge, Harvey Brownstone. Edie and I had bonded a few years earlier—over her brooch, naturally. Thea Spyer had given her a simple circle with diamonds instead of an engagement ring so as not to out Edie at work or to friends who didn't know. She often kidded me that my own brooches seemed to get bigger every time she saw me. Jacob was running around that night, attentive to details, including my sugar levels and making sure I had eaten, and Edie kept nudging me: "Look at the way he looks at you. Why have you not married him yet?"

A year later, on October 17, 2015, Jacob and I got married. We'd been together nine years by then, which was enough of a test run.

The lead-up to the event was a seventeen-day whirlwind, mostly in Paris—not our country house in Ontario, but the Paris in France. Along with twenty-two friends, we celebrated my sixtieth birthday and also that of Cathy Prowse, my friend and colleague of thirty-five years. There was an exquisite lunch at Le Taillevent. There was a dinner at our favorite restaurant, Arpège, with chef Alain Passard preparing a spectacular twenty-four-course vegetarian meal, mostly from his garden, with a number of courses featuring beets. Plus, his gift of fresh turbot as the main course. "What? Are you out of beets?" our friend Pat said when dessert finally came.

Another night, we dined at the Georges restaurant with its lavish view of the city on the rooftop of the Pompidou Centre.

On the final night of the trip, our friends at the Georges V wanted to put on a show and not be outdone by any other restaurant in Paris. I asked David Furnish, Elton John's husband, if he would join us. We had hosted a reception for Camp fYrefly at our place when he was Pride grand marshal. I was much inspired by his and Elton's relationship and how they operated together as a family and as a business, with David as Elton's manager and chair of the Elton John AIDS Foundation. I think Elton has the better art collection and I have the better jewelry, but we both scored big-time in having great husbands. I have also been inspired over the years by Jane Wagner and Lily Tomlin, who have been together some fifty-two years. Jane has written some of Tomlin's best material.

Then Jacob and I went to Lebanon for ten days, where we worked on the house and the family foundation and finished organizing our upcoming nuptials. I had piggybacked our wedding onto the same weekend as a gala for The 519, so that both nights would serve as fundraisers. The wedding raised funds to create a community garden in honor of our families at St. Joseph's Health Centre. Then, on Sunday night, we repurposed the same flowers and equipment to put on the gala for The 519. A lot of friends and supporters were at both events.

It was a perfect night. A fundraiser, instead of gifts, for St. Joseph's to establish a Bachir/Yerex community garden, with two hundred of the best family and friends anyone can imagine, not to mention all of our nurses. It was only fitting to be married by our good friend Brent Hawkes, who had performed the first same-sex marriage in the world.

Ivy did the toast. Samantha Young was Jacob's best man; my younger brother Ziad was mine. Additional toasts came from Nancy Lockhart, Cathy Prowse, Kate Alexander Daniels, and Nada Ristich.

Jann Coppen made sure everything ran smoothly. Jamie Kennedy and Simon Kattar did the food, a touch of Canadian and Lebanese. George Sawa played the oud during dinner.

We had five singers, including Molly Johnson, John Alcorn, Billy Newton-Davis, Louise Petrie singing a bit of Sondheim and Sinatra's "All My Tomorrows"—and k.d. lang, just as I'd always hoped. She performed both nights, but she actually wound up singing longer on our wedding night. Friends still talk about her rendition of Leonard Cohen's "Hallelujah" and, my special request, Joni Mitchell's "A Case of You." Pure magic.

The next night, Sunday, was the actual 519 gala. Two friends from the University of Alberta who had founded Camp fYrefly, Fern Snart and Kristopher Wells, flew out to see k.d. and to tell me I was being awarded an honorary doctorate from the University of Alberta. For the first time in my life, I was too exhausted to have sex. And on my wedding night! Maybe this time, I was secure in knowing there would be many other days and nights to come.

And on Monday I had dialysis at home with My Jacob as my nurse, of course. It was as if I had been rehearsing all my life for that weekend.

Letters & Messages

WE'VE GOT MAIL! Over the years, I have received many thank-you notes—some handwritten, some typed, some inscribed on a publicity photo. Some were clacked out on an old-fashioned typewriter, and some were even faxed. Always send a thank-you note. (An email works too.)

Here are a few:

September 19, 1992

Mr. Salah Bachir
President
Premiere Video Magazine Inc.
1314 Britannia Road East
Mississauga, Ontario
L4W 108

Dear Mr. Bachir:

Congratulations on receiving Paramount's Humanitarian Award!

I wanted to personally thank you for the strong commitment you have made to the "Time Out" project. I can only hope that as more people are made aware of the staggering statistics regarding the increasing rate of HIV infection in the world, we will gain many partners in this fight against a blind killer.

You are setting a wonderful example for others in your industry, as well as business people in general. Together, I know we can make a difference.

Keep up the great work. I'm with you all the way.

...busy,

Arsenio Hall

AH:cs

CABARET

What good is sitting a-lone in your room? Come hear the music play.

John Kander & Fred Ebb

June 13, 2004

Salah Bachir
#3901
2045 Lakeshore Blvd. W
Toronto ON
M8V 2Z6

Dear Salah:

You are a jewel of a man. You go
around rescuing flounding campaigns
(like 519) and many other individuals
and organizations. You are <u>very</u> busy
but you turn up at the Casey House
party, which was a gift enough,
and then you send a CASE of the best
olive oil I have ever tasted.

It was a grand scale, glorious gift.
The man who delivered it guessed that
the box contained bricks, and I said
"I hope they are gold bricks."

And they were.

How very very kind of you. I am
very touched and delighted.

affectionately

june

June 4, 2005

Salah Bachir
3901
2045 Lakeshore Blvd. West
Toronto ON
M8V 2Z6

Dear Salah:

You are the most generous man
on the planet, and your florist
must drive a Rolls. The bouquet
you sent me on my birthday is
almost too big to get through
the door, and contains wonderful
huge, <u>huge</u>, roses and peonies
and lilacs and spikes of white
flowers I don't recognize, but love.

I am touched by your kind and
your note. Please take very
good care of yourself. Look both
ways when crossing the street.
You are a very valuable man.

Love and thanks

june

KIRK DOUGLAS

May 26, 1999

Dear Salah Bachir:

Thank you so much for inviting me to be your guest of honor at the gala awards banquet in Toronto. Unfortunately, I will be in Europe. I want you to know quickly so you can make your plans, but I thank you sincerely for thinking of me.

Warmest regards,

Kirk Douglas

When I love
myself, then I
can love you —
Zareta Gief Osho

June 7, 1995

My dear Salah,

We — that is Vera and I —
are still woozy with pleasure and
gratitude for the truly splendid
time we had in Toronto, thanks to
you. Every moment of every event
has been reported to family and
friends in happy detail. The warmth
with which we were greeted by
everyone will remain indelibly
lodged in our memory. Once
more, my dear Salah, thank you.

Very sincerely indeed,

Douglas

575 PARK AVENUE
NEW YORK, N.Y. 10021

19 Sept. 1995

Dear Salah,

It should be easy
to write a "thank you" letter —
at least I had always found
it so in the past. But your
great, warm hospitality is quite
unique, quite special — and
therefore to write an even adequate
expression of gratitude is a
challenge beyond my ability to
meet. We did have such a fine
time! I did appreciate your every
thought and gesture. What's more,
Vera was — and remains — as touched
and grateful as I.

A warm, firm, happy
clasp of your hand, and a hope
we may meet again soon — those
are my "better than words" sentiments.

Yours aye,

Douglas

 **Ginger Rogers**

September 22, 1993

Mr. Salah Bachir
Premiere Magazine
1314 Britannia Road East
Mississauga, Ontario L4W 1C8

Dear Salah,

    My grateful thanks to you and all your staff at
Premiere Magazine for a wonderful weekend. It was a
wonderful honor for me to accept your Continuous
Outstanding Achievement Award.

    I hope the Focus on Video trade show and the dinner
on Saturday night met your expectations for the Canadian
Film Center. It was a most enjoyable night.

    The dinner on Sunday evening was absolutely
delicious and you are a most gracious host. Thank you
for a memorable dining experience. (And thank Chef
Jamie, too).

    I look forward to hearing from you in the near
future. Again, thank Toronto for me.

                              Blessings,

                              Ginger Rogers

GR/rjo

To: Mr. Salah Bachir/PREMIERE
        905/564-3398

From: Mr. Gregory Peck
        310/274-8855

Date: April 15, 1998

Dear Salah Bachir

Thank you for your kind invitation. Sorry I will be in France, and cannot accept.

Perhaps we can arrange something another day, with proceeds to go to the Gregory Peck scholarship in Film Studies at University College, Dublin.

Yours sincerely,

Gregory Peck

Gregory Peck

III - 17 - 1994

Salah Bachir, Publisher,
Premiere Magazine
1314 Britannia Road East
Mississauga, Ontario
Canada   L4W 1C8

Dear Salah Bachir:

I'm grateful to you for telling me that I
have won an Award. At the same time I have to say
to you that I don't go to these celebrations. I
think you should give it to someone who would love
to the attend because I am unwilling to pay that
price of fame. Thank you anyway.

JAMES STEWART

October 16, 1990

Salah Bachir
c/o Premiere Magazine
1314 Britannia Road, East
Mississauga, Ontario L4W 1CH
CANADA

Dear Salah Bachir:

I want you to know I'm very grateful
for the beautiful stone bird sculpture you presented to me. It's something very special and I regret very
much that I was unable to get to
Toronto because of illness.

I send you my sincere thanks and
best wishes,

JS:vl

JAMES STEWART

April 24, 1986

Ms. Marisa Waldman
VIDEOMANIA
1314 Britannia Road East
Mississauga, Ontario L4W 1C8

Dear Marisa Waldman:

I want you to know that I'm very grateful to you
for the story you wrote about me in VIDEOMANIA.

I found it very interesting because it was different from many other things that have appeared
over the years about me -- and my wife, Gloria,
thinks it's the best thing she's ever read.

I send you my thanks and my best wishes.

James Stewart

Janet Leigh Brandt
1625 Summitridge Drive
Beverly Hills, California 90210

Friday, November 10th

Dear Saloh,

I enjoyed your photos -- memories of a happy evening. I must tell you -- my husband, who very seldom makes any comments about awards, thought the one I received from Premiere is the most beautiful he has seen. So much so, it is sitting on top of our gate-legged table in the living room. I was thrilled by your honor.

Thank you, too, for allowing me a tape of the film clips. I did have fun with that!

I sent off messages today for the Casey House Benefit. Bless you and the entire organization for helping those who are in need.

Happy Holidays!

Warm regards,
Janet

JESSICA TANDY CRONYN

Wyndham Hotel
42 W 58th St
New York 10019
7·24·90

Dear Mr Bachir
        I'm afraid I cannot
accept your invitation to
be with you in Toronto on
Sept 17 as I am starting to shoot
a movie in Los Angeles on
the 19th.

            Regretfully

            Jessica Tandy

NORMAN JEWISON

Dearest Sabah,

What a generous, loving friend you are!! The champagne you sent to my 90th. Birthday party was perfect for all the toasts that were given.

Lynne & I really missed you both, but somehow you both were present with every sip.

Have a safe and happy visit in Lebanon.

When you come back we will show you the video of the event.

Thanks again for your wonderful gift.

We love you,

Norman + Lynne

KATHY BATES

Sept. 1991

Dear Mr. Boehm,

Thank you very much for a lovely evening at Focus-on-Video. I was deeply touched by the honour shown me by Premiere magazine and by the Canadian Video industry.

I was sorry to leave my beautiful Inuit sculpture behind, even for a short while. It is quite the most beautiful award I've ever received. I shall treasure it and your kindness to me.

Sincerely,
Kathy Bates

September 23, 1990

Salah Bachir
PREMIERE
1314 Britannia Road East
Mississauga, Ontario, Canada L4W 1C8

Dear Salah:

Thank you so much for the most beautiful arrangement of
flowers last week. They still, in fact, grace the
dining room table in my suite and are, in fact, still
quite beautiful.

I do appreciate your kind invitation and I am terribly
sorry I was unable to attend the Gala. I trust the
evening was a wonderful success.

Thank you, again, for your thoughtfulness.

Sincerely,

LIZA MINNELLI

LM/rga

PATRICIA NEAL

28th September 1994

Salah Bachir
Publisher
PREMIERE
1314 Britannia Road East
Mississaugo, Ontario,
Canada L4W 1C8

My Dear Salah,

I am so very grateful to **you** for making my recent trip to Toronto so much fun! You are a very generous man indeed, and I thoroughly appreciated every minute.

I am deeply honored to have received *"Premiere's" 1994 Continuous Outstanding Achievement Award.* I consider myself in very good company to have been recognized alongside the illustrious Douglas Fairbanks, Jr.; and of course it was a special treat to have had the good fortune of being introduced by the beautiful Ali MacGraw.

I have cleared off a space on my "trophy shelf" in anticipation of that gorgeous award I long to see. May I thank you also for the generous gift you have given to "my" hospital (The Patricia Neal Rehabilitation Center), they will be so impressed!

Please keep us posted as to whether you will be joining us on the Theatre Guild trip to the Amazon. I certainly hope so.

Until we meet again,

[signature]

MESSAGE IN A BOTTLE. For five years in the 1990s, Nancy Moyen, David Arathoon, and I—along with June Callwood—hosted an annual fundraiser for people suffering with AIDS at Casey House and Trinity Home hospices. Nancy donated a different stunning bottle each year to act as the vessel for handwritten messages from stars of the entertainment and sports worlds. Some of them drew caricatures of themselves—including Loretta Lynn and David Crosby. Sting wrote out the lyrics to his song "Message in a Bottle." There were literally thousands of celebrity participants over the five years and very few ever turned us down.

HOW THE HECK CAN I FIT
IN A BOTTLE?

Jason Alexander

Mario Andretti

Not much is taken, much abides; and tho'
we are not now that strength which in old days
moved earth and heaven; that which we are, we are;
one equal temper of heroic hearts
made weak by time and fate, but strong in will
To strive, to seek, to find, and not to yeild.

— Tennyson, "Ulysses"

Best wishes from

Margaret Atwood

Margaret Atwood

It aint over til its over
Yogi Berra

Yogi Berra

If you stand for Nothing
you will Fall for Anything

Cher

David Crosby

𝔑ever go to bed mad. Stay up and fight. *Phyllis Diller*

Phyllis Diller

Stay Strong...
I'm With you...
Love.

Céline Dion...

Céline Dion

Go ahead — make my day!

Clint Eastwood

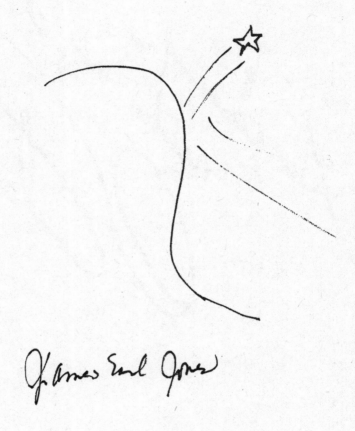

James Earl Jones

this.
like all things
past and present,
remains.
a simple
interval
in which all
potential
thrives.

k.d. lang

k.d. lang

Janet Leigh

me singin' a message of love!

Loretta Lynn

There is a world elsewhere . . .

Ian McKellen

Ian McKellen

Bette Midler

Alanis Morissette

Live Long & Prosper!

Leonard Nimoy

Leonard Nimoy

I love you with all
my Heart! I wish you Love,
Energy and Heaven!
RuPaul

RuPaul

"MAKE IT SO!"

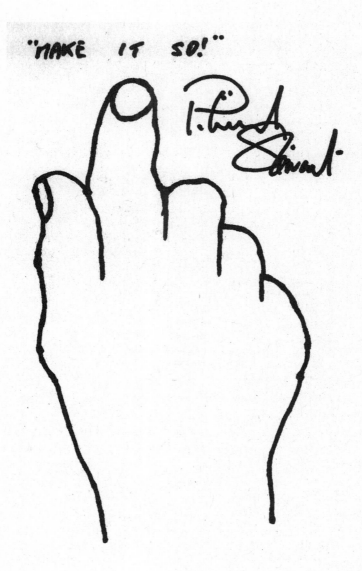

Patrick Stewart

Message in a bottle

Just a castaway, an island lost at sea
Another lonely day, no one here but me
More loneliness than any man could bare
Rescue me before I fall into despair
    I'll send an S.O.S to the world
I hope that someone gets my message in a bottle

A year has passed since I wrote my note
I should have known this right from the start
Only hope can keep me together
Love can mend your life but love can break your heart
    I'll send an S.O.S to the world
I hope that someone gets my message in a bottle

I walked out this morning
I don't believe what I saw
A hundred billion bottles
washed up on the shore
It seems I'm not alone in being alone
A hundred billion castaways looking for a home
    I'll send an S.O.S to the world
I hope that someone gets my message in a
                                    bottle

Sting

Elizabeth Taylor

TRUe Desire FOR ANYTHING
(Good)

IS God's Proof sent TO you
beforehand.

that is it yours already.

Denzel Washington

Thank you . . .

. . . to the many who believed in and nurtured this book. And to all who love me, have loved me, and still love me after reading it.

About the Author

SALAH BACHIR (He/Him) is a successful entrepreneur, executive, magazine publisher, producer, and patron of the arts. He has published several of the best-read magazines in Canada and set up some of the most creative and innovative programs in the media and sponsorship worlds, including co-creating the Scene loyalty program. He is widely known to be one of Canada's most outstanding fundraisers and philanthropists, helping to raise hundreds of millions of dollars for public health and humanitarian causes, the arts, diversity and inclusion, the 2SLGBTQ+ community, social justice, and more. Bachir has received many awards for humanitarianism, volunteerism, and entrepreneurship, and has received several Icon and lifetime achievement awards. He is the recipient of both the Order of Canada and the Order of Ontario and was inducted into the Canadian Film and Television Hall of Fame. He has also been awarded several honorary doctorates. Salah Bachir lives with his husband, the artist Jacob Yerex.